Embracing a Western Identity

Embracing a Western Identity
Jewish Oregonians, 1849–1950

ELLEN EISENBERG

Oregon State University Press   Corvallis

The paper in this book meets the guidelines for permanence and durability of the Committee on Production Guidelines for Book Longevity of the Council on Library Resources and the minimum requirements of the American National Standard for Permanence of Paper for Printed Library Materials Z39.48-1984.

An earlier version of Chapter 5, "A Western Exception: Zionism and Anti-Zionism," was published as "Beyond San Francisco: The Failure of Anti-Zionism in Portland, Oregon," *American Jewish History* 86, no. 3 (1998): 309–21.

Library of Congress Cataloging-in-Publication Data

Cataloging-in-Publication data is available from the Library of Congress.

Oregon State University Press
121 The Valley Library
Corvallis OR 97331-4501
541-737-3166 • fax 541-737-3170
www.osupress.oregonstate.edu

Contents

Acknowledgments

This book was born through my connection with the Oregon Jewish Museum (OJM). In late 2007, I was invited to serve on an advisory committee for a planned "core exhibit" on the Oregon Jewish experience. In the course of several meetings over the next two years, the committee worked to define the themes that would anchor such an exhibit. For me, the timing was particularly fortuitous. By 2009, I had just finished my collaboration with Ava Kahn and Bill Toll on *Jews of the Pacific Coast: Reinventing Community on America's Edge*. Several years of discussing western regional history with my wonderful co-authors provided an excellent frame for approaching the particularities of an exhibit focusing on the experience in Oregon.

With the co-authored project complete, I realized I was excited about zeroing in on the Oregon experience. When I approached OJM Executive Director Judy Margles with an idea for a book project that could serve as companion to the core exhibit, she responded with enthusiasm. The idea of a book comprised of thematic chapters that spanned Oregon Jewish history was also well received by Mary Braun of Oregon State University Press. Although both the exhibit and this book took on lives of their own (each with paths somewhat longer than originally anticipated), at the time of this writing it appears that they may be coming back in sync, with the exhibit to follow the book sometime in 2016.

In early 2013, as I was starting work on what were to be the final chapters of this volume, focusing on the post-World War II period, the course of my work was again shifted by an OJM project. Rabbi Joshua Stampfer and a group of dedicated volunteers had determined the need for a follow-up book to Steven Lowenstein's *The Jews of Oregon, 1850–1950*, which had been published in 1987 by the Jewish Historical Society of Oregon (an earlier incarnation of the OJM). This group invited me to submit a proposal. Enthusiastic about my current project, I realized that this would be an opportunity to extend my work on the post-World War II period, and proposed a book that would, like this one, use a series of thematic essays to examine this more recent period in Oregon history.

This volume, which I soon began calling Oregon I, is the first of a two-volume project for me, while Oregon II, sponsored by the OJM group centered around Rabbi Stampfer and also slated to be published by Oregon State University Press, became both a sequel to this book and to Lowenstein's. The convergence between the two projects has invigorated each, and I am delighted that, as I finish out this volume, I will have the opportunity to continue to work with many of the same supportive and enthusiastic people as I proceed with Oregon II in the coming years.

Particularly critical are the folks at the Oregon Jewish Museum—especially Judy Margles and Curator Anne LeVant Prahl—who have been absolutely indispensable, not only to this project, but to much of my research for the last two decades. Anne has gone the extra mile to keep me informed about new acquisitions, direct me to potential sources, assist with images, and generally make the collections as accessible as possible. Both she and Judy have been excellent sounding boards and resources as I explore Oregon Jewish history. Judy has provided unfailing encouragement and has been my guide to the contemporary Portland Jewish community. She has read proposal and chapter drafts, and provided thoughtful suggestions and unflagging enthusiasm.

Many others behind the scenes at the OJM have also been critical to the success of this project. I offer particular thanks to all the interviewers and transcribers, past and present, who have been involved since the 1970s in the museum's Oral History Project. Without the many, many interviews detailing the Oregon Jewish experience going back to the late-nineteenth century and without the transcriptions that make them so accessible, this project would not have been possible. In addition, many volunteers have joined Anne in the process of making many other collections at the museum available and accessible. Of particular note are the Beth Israel and Neighborhood House collections, which have been recently added to the archives and which were essential to this book.

Another source of archival help was Kylie Pine of the Willamette Heritage Center. Kylie is a former student who first assisted my early forays into Oregon Jewish history as a research assistant. Over the years that I have been working on this project, she has been quick to help by providing documents that have fleshed out the stories of Jews in the mid-Willamette Valley and making the archives available to me and my students.

Thanks also go to the archivists and librarians at the Oregon Historical Society, the Oregon State Archives, the Portland City Archives, the University of Oregon, and Willamette University for their assistance in tracking down all sorts of obscure publications and documents over the course of my research. Mary McRobinson, Willamette's University Archivist, and Sara Amato of the Hatfield Library provided much needed help in working with images.

A number of current and former Willamette students have made valuable contributions to this project. With the support of a grant from Willamette's Center for Religion, Law and Democracy, I hired Jenna Sjulin as a research assistant, reading newspapers and oral histories. I have learned much about Oregon history over the years from student papers. Of particular note are the work of Alyssa Romane, whose project on Civil Rights in Portland for my local history class led me to oral histories documenting Jewish involvement; Kelsey Ledford and David Reid, whose (separate) papers on prohibition helped me to understand the connections between suffrage and prohibition campaigns in Oregon; and Felix Jones, whose paper on the house in which he lived in 2007 led me to the Adolph family. Finally, Alison Ezard has served as copy editor extraordinaire as I prepare the final manuscript.

Friends, family, and colleagues have read drafts of individual chapters (or, in a few cases, the full manuscript), and offered excellent suggestions and thoughtful critiques. They include: Jennifer Jopp, who read the full manuscript and provided a detailed and very helpful review; Alex Korsunsky; Meyer and Carolyn Eisenberg; and Judy Margles. Very early in the process, Kristi Negri read a sample chapter and the proposal, and shared excellent editing advice.

After several previous long distance relationships with editors, I was very attracted to the idea of working with someone local, so that I could have more than a virtual relationship. From our first meeting in my office, Mary Braun of Oregon State University Press, has been available, enthusiastic, efficient, and helpful. I have enjoyed getting to know her and the others at the press through the process of working on this book, and, over the last year, as a member of the press's editorial board. I look forward to my continued work with them on the board and on the next book.

By the time this book appears in print, Willamette University and the History Department will have been my very happy academic home for twenty-five years. I have been honored to hold the Dwight & Margaret Lear Chair in American History since 2003. It has provided the financial support for my research, as well as enabling me to attend conferences and bring in guest speakers who have informed my work and inspired me. I have been blessed with a department in which everyone not only gets along, but actually really likes each other. This—along with our engaged and exceptionally nice students and the broader community of faculty and staff—has made Willamette a place where I have been able to thrive as a scholar and teacher.

Finally, thanks go to my family, my husband, Ami Korsunsky, for his unfailing support and love, my sons Ben and Alex, and my parents Meyer and Carolyn Eisenberg.

Introduction

Like many western Jews, I am a transplant from the East. After a childhood in suburban Washington, DC, college in Minnesota, and graduate school in Philadelphia, I moved to Salem, Oregon in 1990. At the time, I had no intention of doing research on Oregon Jews—my dissertation focused on Jewish agricultural communities in New Jersey, and I was interested in comparative research on similar settlements in Argentina. Yet within a few years, I found myself increasingly intrigued by the Jewish history of my newly adopted state and region.

To be sure, shifting my research westward had practical benefits. Moving to Oregon with an infant in arms and having another child four years later provided a strong incentive to find projects that could be supported without prolonged trips away from home. Yet along with such pragmatic concerns, I was intrigued by a Jewish community that, while certainly not completely foreign, was noticeably different from those I had known back east. Part of this difference was simply a reflection of social differences between regions. I quickly learned that some Oregonians wear jeans and Birkenstocks (with socks) to synagogue services, just as they wear them to restaurants, meetings, and the theater.

Yet some differences seemed deeper. At a temple board retreat a few years after I arrived, all participants were asked to present a brief "Jewish autobiography." I was surprised to learn that, of about a dozen participants, the rabbi and I were the only two in the room who were born Jewish and married to partners who were also born Jewish. I had grown up in a Conservative congregation where it seemed virtually all my peers shared a background roughly similar to mine—two Jewish parents from New York or some other eastern city and grandparents (possibly great-grandparents) who had immigrated to the United States from Eastern Europe. In Salem, the stories were far more diverse—converts, children of converts, children and grandchildren of immigrants who had settled in Colorado or Idaho or California rather than New York—as well as descendants of families who had been in America longer and come from a variety of places other than Eastern Europe.

Teaching immigration history at Willamette University and participating in the American Ethnic Studies program, I learned that the kinds of East/West differences I was observing were not confined to Jewish ethnic identity. European American ethnicities in general seemed blurrier in the West. Growing up in the East in the 1960s and 1970s, "ethnicity" had included many categories of European Americans; as kids, we were aware of one another's ethnic past. It was not a major issue—there were no ethnic gangs in my suburban neighborhood—but there was an awareness of roots. Many families identified as Jewish or Italian or Irish or German American, and, although there were exceptions, most seemed to identify with just one of these identities. There was a set of ideas associated with each of these labels that included how many children the family was likely to have and what kinds of foods they were likely to eat. By the time we were in grade school we could easily sort surnames into the most common ethnic categories. The Goldsteins? Obviously, Jewish. The O'Shaughnessys? Clearly Irish. The D'Ambrosios? Italian. There were a few more recent Asian and Latino immigrant families, but in such small numbers that they didn't seem to constitute a group, so conversations about ethnicity were far more likely to focus on European categories. And in suburban Washington, DC, in the 1960s and 1970s, the language of race tended to employ only two categories: black and white.

In contrast, I found that my (mostly) West Coast students have trouble thinking about ethnicity as a category they can apply to European Americans. When I talk with them about immigration, they think of Asians and Latinos, not Europeans. When I ask them about their family histories, the majority of those of European American origin are unable to point to one ethnic identity and instead present a laundry list—"my mom's family is Norwegian, Swedish, Dutch, and French; my dad's mom is Irish and his dad's family is Scottish, German, and Russian." Students in Willamette's Jewish Student Union present "Jewish autobiographies" not unlike those I encountered at the board retreat—few were born to two Jewish parents and raised Jewishly. Far more come from families with diverse ancestry and a mix of traditions.

Not only do my western students of European descent not identify with a particular ethnic group, they also have little ability to recognize European ethnicity. When I talk in my American Jewish history class about a film or television character who, to me, seems obviously Jewish, I learn that a number of my students completely miss the identifiers. And, because they don't speak the "language" of European ethnic identity, they frequently mistake non-Jewish New Yorkers for Jews. For years, my friend and colleague, Bill Smaldone—whose name is obviously identifiable to most easterners of my generation as Italian American—often has been misidentified by many of our students (and more than a few colleagues) as Jewish, based on his New York accent. They make the same mistake with the character George Costanza from *Seinfeld* (and Kramer and even Elaine, despite the *shiksappeal* episode).

In this, of course, students are reflecting not only a lack of familiarity with European American markers of ethnicity, but also a popular culture that has strongly identified Jews with New York—so much so that, for many of my students, to be a New Yorker is to be Jewish (at least if one is white). As Hasia Diner explains in her essay "American West, New York Jewish," New York has been depicted as "the essence of what it means to be Jewish in America." And New York is often juxtaposed in American culture with the West, identified as "that which has long been essentially America."[1] Diner argues that films such as *Blazing Saddles* (1974) and *The Frisco Kid* (1979) play on the contrast between that which is Jewish and "not quite America" and the "real" America that is the West.[2] Thus, Jews—especially East European ones—are, quite literally (and often comedically) "out of place" in the American West, particularly the stereotypical, historic frontier West.

These patterns of ethnic understanding in popular culture mirror scholarship on ethnicity and the West. Over the last several decades, there has been a proliferation of work on western ethnicity and diversity in the wake of the New Western History.[3] Yet in this scholarship, "ethnicity" and "diversity" nearly always denote non-European identities, and European immigrants have generally been neglected in western history.[4] With the exception of Los Angeles, where a scholarship focusing on the interplay among a wide variety of groups including Latinos, Asian Americans, Jews, and other European Americans has emerged in the past several decades, much of the literature on ethnicity in the West focuses on non-Europeans, with Jews and other European immigrants simply categorized as "white."

Such thinking is reinforced by scholarship on American Jewish history, which has focused heavily on New York as the mother lode of all that is Jewish in America. Reflecting the dominant place of New York Jewry in terms of community demographics, historians have often equated New York with American Jewry. Even locally produced western histories portray communities as a pale shadow of the "true" New York Jewish experience. Thus, community histories frequently compare "Jewish" neighborhoods such as Boyle Heights in Los Angeles, the Fillmore in San Francisco, South Portland, and Seattle's Central District to the iconic Lower East Side. In *The Jews of Oregon*, Steven Lowenstein describes South Portland's community as "largely self-contained," "a separate community," and explicitly links it to the Lower East Side of New York.[5] Oral histories focusing on South Portland in the 1920s and 1930s describe a strong Jewish atmosphere, with frequent comparisons to the Lower East Side, and even some, however metaphorical, to a shtetl.

Despite the explicit or implicit connections in these descriptions to the landscape of the Lower East Side, Jewish communities in the region were profoundly shaped by the western experience, beginning with the distinctive migration pattern that brought Jews to the West. Whereas millions of Jews migrated directly from Europe to eastern ports, including New York, Boston, Baltimore, and Philadelphia; or immediately transmigrated to inland industrial centers such as Chicago, those who settled in the West arrived gradually and in far smaller numbers. This meant that, particularly before the turn of the century, even the largest western Jewish communities remained quite modest. As late as 1915, the Hebrew Sheltering and Immigrant Aid Society of America reported that over 80 percent of immigrant Jews were bound for northern and central Atlantic states, and less than 1 percent for the West. Of those, only a fraction came to the Northwest.[6] Those who came to Oregon were making a conscious choice to move outside the normal paths of Jewish life and into the American hinterland. They were attracted by opportunities that were shaped, in turn, by the distinctive environment, commercial prospects, and racial landscape of the region. The process of self-selection among migrants, combined with the particular opportunities and challenges of the region that they chose, shaped their experiences. They neither recreated the Lower East Side nor seamlessly blended into the local white landscape. Rather, they reflected both the Jewish and western forces that shaped them.

What began as curiosity about my new community and my students' perceptions has led, over the last two decades, to a deep appreciation of the complex factors that have shaped Jewish history in the West, and, specifically, in Oregon. Along with my fellow historians of the Jewish experience in the American West, I have worked to break free of generalizations based on the eastern metropolitan experience that have ruled American Jewish history. Critical studies of Jewish life in the western states have delineated important points of contrast with eastern Jewry, such as the continued dominance of Jews of German descent into the twentieth century; the relative mildness of anti-Semitism; the declining Jewish percentage of the total western population at a time when the Jewish population share in the East was increasing rapidly; and the small numbers of East European migrants to the West and their correspondingly more modest impact on political and cultural developments. These contrasts have led historians to argue that concepts as basic as the customary periodization of American Jewish history do not apply to the American West.[7] The challenges of the frontier, the particular mix of people who settled here, and the ethos they developed, along with the selective migration of Jews to this remote state have all contributed to the distinctive characteristics of Oregon Jewry. Yet Jewish Oregonians were also strongly shaped by the broader western and American Jewish communities of which they were a part.

In discussing regional history, American Jewish historians have asked whether, for example, southern Jews have historically been more similar to other southerners or to non-southern Jews. In recent years, historians Mark Bauman and Marc Lee Raphael have come down on the side of the latter, arguing that, whatever regionalisms were embraced by southern Jews, "to a remarkable degree . . .their experiences were far more similar to those of Jews in similar environments elsewhere in America than they were to those of white Protestants in the South."[8] Part of this was due to the fact that, however well accepted and acculturated they were, there were some aspects of southern life that seemed incompatible with Jewish culture—indeed, "Southern Jewry" has been seen by some as a term that is "oxymoronic."[9] Yet, as Ava F. Kahn, William Toll, and I have argued in *Jews of the Pacific Coast: Reinventing Community on America's Edge*, Jews found western civic culture and identity far more compatible with their Jewish identity than appears to have been the case in the South.[10]

This book enters this discussion of regional identity by focusing closely on the Jewish community of Oregon. The aim is to place Oregon Jewish history in the larger contexts of western and American Jewish histories through a series of essays, each focused on a particular theme, institution, or issue, to explore both the echoes of and the departures from the broader experience of Jews in the West, and in the United States.

The first chapter, "Pioneers and Native Sons," sets the scene by exploring the role of nineteenth-century Jewish Oregonians as community founders. In many communities in Oregon and throughout the West, Jewish merchants constructed the first brick buildings on Main Street, and their services were essential to founding and growing towns. In small towns and in Portland, Jews were quickly elected to political office and honored as Oregon Native Sons. This chapter looks at the prominence and acceptance of nineteenth-century Jewish Oregonians in terms of both human capital and local context. I establish patterns in the backgrounds and migration routes that brought these individuals to Oregon and explore the ways in which they participated in the enterprise of pioneering, arguing that these activities fostered their acceptance and rise to prominence in a variety of Oregon towns.

Chapter Two, "Go West Young Mensch: Composition of a Community," moves beyond the pioneers to look more broadly at the migration patterns that brought Jews to Oregon up through the early twentieth century. It focuses on the ways in which these patterns shaped communal development in Portland, the only city in the state with a community large enough to support multiple Jewish institutions and sub-communities. American Jewish historians have consistently told a story of waves of immigration: first the Sephardim, then the Germans, then— in an overwhelming flood—the East Europeans. Yet this story is not an accurate reflection of western Jewish history, where

American-born Sephardim and German immigrants arrived together, followed soon after by Poseners (from eastern Prussia, which culturally bridged the gap between Germany and Eastern Europe), and where East European migrants arrived relatively late, in modest numbers, and were joined by a substantial influx of immigrant Sephardim from the Mediterranean Basin. Oregon's Jewish population is a microcosm of the Jewish migration patterns and diversity characteristic of the West. This chapter demonstrates how these particular patterns of migration played an important role in shaping the communities' social, cultural, and institutional development.[11]

Chapter Three focuses on one Portland institution, Neighborhood House, a settlement house founded in 1905 by the Portland section of the National Council of Jewish Women (NCJW). Neighborhood House was created to serve the needs of the immigrant Jewish population of South Portland. Over time, it came to serve a more diverse local population, and to function as an important public face of the Jewish community. Considered by many to be the heart of Jewish Portland, an examination of Neighborhood House provides another window into relationships among groups within the Jewish community, and also allows a glimpse of relations between Jews and other ethnic groups in Portland. Oral histories illuminate the ways in which patrons, volunteers, and clients perceived the house and one another.[12] The mid-twentieth century shift in the house's mission away from service to the Jewish community and toward the broader population of the area is reflective of a shift in neighborhood demographics, and opens up possibilities for exploring Jewish residential patterns in the broader city and relationships with non-Jewish residents of the South Portland area.

The relationship between Jewish and non-Jewish Oregonians is explored further in Chapter Four, "A Jewish Vote? Class, Ethnicity, and Politics." This essay expands on themes introduced in the first three chapters by focusing on the pioneer establishment, the new immigrants of the South Portland neighborhood, and their engagement in civic issues in the first several decades of the twentieth century. Here, the focus goes beyond the level of progressive civic involvement embodied by Neighborhood House to look at political leadership and at Jewish voting on hotly-contested ballot initiatives. This analysis provides insight into Jewish identity by examining issues and candidates that appealed to South Portland Jews on an ethnic/religious basis and those that led them to forge class-based alliances.

In exploring these issues, Chapter Four examines how the long-standing acceptance of Jews in Oregon shaped their attitudes toward political participation and leadership. The essay then shifts from leadership to community engagement in support of both candidates and causes. Under what circumstances did Jewish Oregonians embrace initiatives or candidates as their own? Did the Jewish workers and small shopkeepers of South Portland tend to vote like their counterparts in other neighborhoods or like their better established coreligionists? To what extent did a collective ethnic/religious identity connect Jews to causes that others of similar occupational or class background did not embrace? When the organized community did take a stand—as it did against the Compulsory School Bill in 1922—how did it connect that stand to Jewish values? This essay demonstrates that, despite a professed aversion to ethnic voting and clear differences in class position, the Jewish community did unify around some causes and became increasingly inclined to support ethnic candidates over time.

Chapter Five shifts from local to international causes and politics, examining Zionism and anti-Zionism among Jewish Oregonians. Although most American Jews came to embrace Zionism by the mid-twentieth century, the movement was very contentious earlier in the century. Historians have demonstrated that Jewish opposition to Zionism was particularly strong in the West, both because of the ethnic composition of western Jewish communities and because their high level of acculturation led them to dismiss the need for a homeland other than America. Yet anti-Zionism did not have nearly as strong a following in Portland as in San Francisco or Seattle. This essay explores the sources of Zionist strength and anti-Zionist weakness in Portland, and demonstrates that support for Israel became in Portland, as it was in most American Jewish communities, an increasingly central part of Jewish identity.[13]

Along with Zionism and Israel, liberalism became a central touchstone for American Jewish communities in the mid-twentieth century. Central to Jewish liberalism is what some historians have called a "minority consciousness" or "minority identification." Chapter Six, "The Color of the Community," explores the relationships between Jews and other ethnic and racial minority groups in Oregon, providing a context and history for the local embrace of racial liberalism in the mid-twentieth century. This exploration, beginning with the pioneer era and extending into the 1960s, provides an opportunity to connect to the much debated question of Jewish "whiteness" and to examine how ethnic identity played out in the diverse western landscape. It provides a window on the ways in which local prejudices shaped engagement with national discussions about the Jewish relationship to the Civil Rights Movement, and discusses the impact of increasing anti-Semitism on local Jewish engagement in these issues, weighing evidence of Jewish acceptance against that of anti-Semitism and analyzing local Jewish attitudes toward other racial and ethnic minorities.[14] What were the limits of Jewish acceptance and inclusion, and how did these change over the course of the early to mid-twentieth century? How did Jewish Oregonians respond to restrictions? When did they identify with the white majority and when did they choose to ally themselves with minority groups? What were the ways in which these identities were affected by the influx of new groups, including Japanese Americans early in the century and African Americans during and after World War II?

When I attend historical or Jewish studies conferences in places such as Boston or New York City, I frequently get puzzled questions. Eastern colleagues, responding to the title of my talk or to my institutional affiliation, will ask me, "Oregon? Are there Jews in Oregon?" or "Is there really much of a Jewish history in Oregon?" Such questions echo those that I sometimes get from East Coast friends or relatives, wondering how I like living in a place that they see as utterly remote from Jewish life. Even in the early twenty-first century, as western Jewry continues to grow faster than Jewish communities elsewhere, and decades after Los Angeles replaced Chicago as America's second largest Jewish community, the East Coast and New York-centric vision of American Jewish history dominates. Many remain convinced that Jewish authenticity resides only in the East, and that to put Jewish and Oregonian in the same phrase is somehow oxymoronic.

Yet Jewish Oregonians and Jewish westerners have long embraced both parts of their identities and seen them as compatible, even harmonious. They point out the early election of Jews to public office and the broad acceptance of Jewish pioneers in the mid-nineteenth century. At the same time, they (often reluctantly) recall professional and social exclusions that intruded a century later and admit that, despite the frequent proclamations that Oregon has been a Promised Land, the history is not untroubled. Thus, just as easterners often are surprised by Oregonians' stories of acceptance in a western landscape not usually associated with Jews, Jewish Oregonians have difficulty reconciling the positive pioneer stories with later accounts of prejudice and exclusions.

Taken together, the six chapters in this volume provide an opportunity to explore those aspects of Oregon Jewish history that surprise both the insiders and the outsiders. They aim not only to chart the historical development of Jewish community in Oregon over its first century, but also to explain the complex and evolving religious, ethnic, and regional identities of Jewish Oregonians, and their place in the state's ethnic landscape.

Understanding these stories requires analysis of both the region's Jewish communities and the context in which they developed. When I first began working on the Jewish West in the 1990s, my attention was largely directed toward the former. As I traced the migration of Jews to Oregon in the late-nineteenth century, I was far more interested in the migrants than in the region to which they were migrating. Thus, when I saw that nineteenth-century Jews were quickly elected to public office, I was convinced that the explanation lay in the types of migrants who came to the West. It seemed reasonable to think that there was a certain amount of self-selection: people most rooted in traditional practice would be less likely to move to remote areas, I reasoned. It seemed likely that those Jews who decided to venture to, say, Burns, in eastern Oregon in the nineteenth century, would be individuals who were open to interaction and engagement with non-Jews, and that this could account for their activities.

Over time, I began to pay more attention to place. Although migrants' backgrounds and attitudes toward others certainly contributed to their early engagement and prominence, the emerging literature on race and ethnicity in the West made clear that the region's ethnic landscape—particularly anxieties about Native American and Asian "others"—led to a more inclusive definition of "white" and played a key role in fostering Jewish acceptance. Likewise, understanding the economic development of the region helps to explain the ways in which the timing of Jewish arrival and their particular occupational profile fostered their inclusion.

Understanding the Oregon Jewish experience—or any regional ethnic experience—requires analysis of both group and setting. I began this project as an American Jewish historian interested in learning more about the experience of Jews who happened to live in Oregon. Over time, I have become a western historian, as interested in the place and context as in the specific ethnic communities that initially drew my attention. In many ways, my trajectory is similar to that of many of the individuals whose stories appear in these pages. Often, they initially identified as Jews who had come to make their homes in Oregon; over time, many came to embrace their identity as Oregonians. In these chapters, I aim to understand both the Jewish and the Oregonian aspects of their histories, and to explore the ways in which they complement, contradict and complicate their stories.

CHAPTER I

Pioneers and Native Sons

On March 26, 1896, Gervais, Oregon, "was enthusiastic over the arrival home of her native son, McKinley Mitchell," after his nomination to the state legislature as a Republican. "The people en masse met him at the depot and welcomed him with addresses and the firing of anvils," reported the *Daily Capital Journal*. Although Mitchell's journey had been short—Gervais is located only fifteen miles from the state capital in Salem—"a procession was formed and he was escorted home amid much enthusiasm."[1]

The warm reception is not surprising. Gervais was a small town[2] and Mitchell seemed to be a rising star in the Republican Party. A "native son" of Oregon, Mitchell was born in Oregon City in 1858, and had resided in the area since age two.[3] The eldest son of a pioneer of 1849 or 1850,[4] Mitchell attended public school in Gervais, opening his store in 1879. By the time he was twenty-two, Mitchell was serving as postmaster, and a year later he was elected to the Gervais

Gervais welcomes McKinley Mitchell home. *Daily Capital Journal*, Salem, Oregon, March 26, 1896. Credit: Historic Oregon Newspapers, http:// oregonnews.uoregon.edu

> **Mitchell at Home.**
>
> GERVAIS, Or., March 26.—Gervais was enthusiastic over the arrival home of her native son, McKinley Mitchell, who, Tuesday, was nominated as representative from this section. The people en masse met him at the depot and welcomed him with addresses and the firing of anvils. A procession was formed and he was escorted home amid much enthusiasm.

city council, a position he held well into the 1890s (although it is not clear whether this service was continuous or intermittent).[5] In 1884, he served as a delegate to the state Republican convention.[6] During these years, Mitchell engaged in several different enterprises in addition to his general merchandise store, including grain and hops dealing, warehousing, and editing a newspaper.[7] He may also have operated as an insurance agent during the 1890s.[8] After the turn of the century, while continuing the Gervais business, he moved to Portland and added branches in Portland and Hubbard. At some point, he also acquired a 147-acre farm in Yamhill County.[9]

In 1896, after the impromptu parade in Gervais, Mitchell campaigned for the legislative seat by linking himself with his more prominent namesakes, Republicans William McKinley, the presidential nominee, and incumbent US Senator John Mitchell, with a button reading, "McKinley for president, Mitchell for senator, and McKinley Mitchell for both."[10] Once elected, McKinley Mitchell played a key role in the heated contest over Oregon's US Senate seat during the 1897 state legislative session. He defected from the John Mitchell faction during the "hold up session," when the Senator's supporters blocked legislative activity rather than concede the seat.[11] After a long delay, Senator Mitchell's chief intra-party rival, Joseph Simon, a Jewish Portland lawyer, won the Senate seat.[12] In the wake of the dispute, the Gervais favorite son was portrayed by the Salem *Capital Journal* as willing to break with the warring factions and dedicated to serving the people rather than a party leader.[13] Although his later activities seem to have focused more on his business enterprises than on politics, he again served as a delegate to the state Republican convention in 1900.[14] He was active in native sons' organizations, attending meetings of the Sons and Daughters of Oregon Pioneers in Champoeg.[15]

During his period of peak political involvement in the 1890s, Mitchell was mentioned with some frequency in the regional press.[16] In addition to his political activities, newspaper accounts occasionally took note of his business dealings, and the Salem press frequently recorded his visits to the city. Striking in this coverage is what is never mentioned: that McKinley Mitchell was a Jew. Mitchell's Jewish identity was not unknown to the community. When his father, Isaac, died in

1882, the *Willamette Farmer* noted this passing of "one of the pioneers of the State," and reported that "his remains were brought to this city yesterday and interred in the Jewish cemetery."[17] When James Moore, an assistant to pioneering western historian Hubert Howe Bancroft, sought McKinley Mitchell out in 1885 for a "dictation" (oral history), Moore noted that he "is a Jew, but quite intelligent," and that "for a Jew [he] was well liked and stood very high in his community."[18] A 1928 regional history listed the elder Mitchell as the founder of one of the first Jewish businesses in the Portland area.[19] Although there was no local synagogue to join in the Gervais/Salem area at the time, it appears that Mitchell did continue to identify Jewishly. For example, he chose a Jewish bride, the former Hattie Scheier, whom he married at Congregation Beth Israel in San Francisco in 1891. When his sister, Sarah, married in Gervais, a rabbi was brought to officiate.[20] On his death in 1936, although he was not buried in a Jewish cemetery, Mitchell bequeathed one hundred dollars each to Portland congregation Ahavai Sholem [sic] and Neighborhood House, the settlement house run by the Portland section of the National Council of Jewish Women.[21]

The details of McKinley Mitchell's life are few, yet they offer intriguing glimpses into the ways in which Jewish pioneers and native sons interacted with and were viewed by fellow Oregonians in the mid- to late-nineteenth century. Jews were distinctive among the larger population, not only for their religious/ethnic identity, but also for their occupational profile: like Mitchell, nearly all Jewish Oregonians in this era made their living as merchants. Yet, despite a few notable anti-Semitic incidents, neither their religious/ethnic identity nor their occupational particularity prevented Jewish Oregonians from being accepted as town leaders, civic boosters, and neighbors. Even when they attained local prominence, their Jewishness was, apparently, not considered notable. Contemporaneous press accounts and retrospectives in pioneer histories generally fail to mention Jewish identity as a marker of distinction.

In some ways, the Oregon experience was reflective of the broader experience of Jews in communities outside the major metropolitan Jewish centers. As historian Hasia Diner has pointed out, the fact that Jews did hold political office, both elected and appointed, wherever they settled indicated much about their place in the world of politics. In cities of every size and in small towns serving as the mercantile hubs of agricultural areas, Jewish men took advantage of political opportunities. Particularly in small communities at their early stages of economic development, Jewish men, most of whom made a living as merchants, stepped forward to help govern their communities.[22]

Jewish political activity in small communities reflects both their desire to engage as citizens, and their neighbors' acceptance of them. Yet this pattern was particularly pronounced in western states such as Oregon; indeed, nearly half of the examples Diner cites to support her claim were of Oregonians.[23] Although Jews played similar economic roles in the American South and West, and were elected to positions of local leadership in both regions, the level of acceptance in the West was far greater than in the South, where Jews "remained outsiders," in the mid- to late-nineteenth century, precisely the period when Jewish Oregonians were finding great acceptance.[24]

Several factors contributed to this phenomenon. Clearly, it was significant that Jews arrived in Oregon as pioneers, rather than entering after settlement into a preexisting hierarchy. Jewish pioneers came prepared with a skill set that launched them into positions critical to developing frontier communities. As experienced merchants in communities made up largely of farmers, ranchers, or miners, they played essential roles, marketing and distributing goods, providing credit, and building towns.[25] On mining frontiers, where single men dominated, the propensity of Jews to establish families helped to provide an additional level of stability to the social order. In frontier communities where Native Americans, and, later, Asian immigrants, were seen as threats to civilization and racial order, Jews benefited from a broad, inclusive, pan-European definition of whiteness.[26] All these factors led to a high level of acceptance of Jews as respected citizens and full members of the community.

PIONEER BEGINNINGS

The importance of early arrival in shaping Jewish experience in the West cannot be overstated. Although there is no evidence of Jews among the pioneers who travelled the Oregon Trail in the early to mid-1840s, pioneer Jews began to arrive as early as 1849—when even Portland, with a population of 821 (three-quarters of them men), was more a village than a city (or, as historian Carl Abbott comments, "more like a giant fraternity house than a real community").[27] Many localities in the Willamette Valley, the primary destination of the Oregon Trail pioneers, were still unorganized settlements rather than incorporated towns. In the even more sparsely settled, arid areas of Eastern Oregon and in some mining districts, many towns would not be founded until well after statehood in 1859. Yet early in the 1850s, Jewish communities were established in Jacksonville, where Jewish pioneers arrived with the initial rush of prospectors, as well as in Portland. The first Jewish service in what would become the state took place in Jacksonville in 1856. Two years later, the first lasting congregation, Beth Israel, was organized in Portland. In these towns and in many others throughout the state, Jews were counted among the key regional founders and builders.

As pioneers, these early arriving Jews endured challenges and shared experiences common to the era, beginning with their journey west. Brothers Louis and Jacob Fleischner were unusual among Jewish pioneers in opting for the overland route. After spending a brief period in New York and several years in Philadelphia, Louis was joined by his brother, and the two made their way to Iowa, where they operated a store for three years. In 1852, they followed the trail from Iowa to Oregon, suffering many of its notorious hardships, including cholera.[28] More typically, Jewish pioneers chose the sea route, traveling from an eastern port to Panama, crossing the isthmus, and then boarding a second ship, usually bound for San Francisco. Although the sea journey was considered less harrowing than the overland route, it did not always go smoothly. Louis Fleischner's future business partner, Jacob Mayer, Mayer's wife, and their children had a particularly difficult passage. Starting from New Orleans, Mayer and his family set off for the isthmus in 1850. The passage from Panama to San Francisco took four months under nightmarish conditions. One hundred days out of Panama, food and water supplies were dangerously low, and the party faced starvation until they were able to purchase— with Mayer's remaining funds—biscuits from a Boston ship.[29] Most journeys were not as trying as the Fleischners' and Mayers', but, like all pioneers, early arriving Jews had to contend with difficult passages, slow communications, and challenging supply routes as they reached the region and established their businesses.

Although operating a dry goods or clothing store is not an occupation traditionally associated with danger (aside from financial risk), these pioneer merchants faced challenges unique to the frontier. Henry Heppner, an immigrant from Posen in eastern Prussia, started his western career as a store clerk in Shasta, California, but soon became involved in packing goods from supply hubs to mining towns throughout the Northwest, including Idaho, Montana, and British Columbia. On several occasions, his pack trains were captured by Native Americans, as part of the larger conflict over the encroachment of white settlers on Indian lands.[30] Louis Fleischner likewise operated a pack train to mining communities, leaving his brother Jacob to tend their Albany store. Sigmund Heilner ran a pack business as well in the early 1860s, on a route that took him inland from Portland as far as Montana.[31]

Simply operating a store in a remote Oregon town often meant braving frequent trips over poor roads—as well as occasional long distance travel—just to keep shops supplied with the latest goods. Merchants such as Samuel Rothchild of Pendleton and Julius Durkheimer, who had stores in Canyon City, Prairie City, and Burns, traveled to Portland or San Francisco to supply their shops on a regular basis, occasionally even making buying trips to New York City.[32] Just the trip from Burns to the closest railroad depot was 150 miles over rough roads impassable during winter; such communities, explained Julius Durkheimer's son Sylvan, were "on the fringe of civilization."[33]

Like their fellow pioneers, some early Jewish settlers participated in the region's Indian wars, which continued into the 1870s. Sigmund Heilner was one of several Jewish pioneers involved in the Rogue River Indian War of 1855-56. Sigmund had recently arrived in the mining community of Althouse Creek when the war began, and took part in a supply mission to bring arms and ammunition to the militia during the conflict. Although the details of his involvement are unclear, he was recognized by fellow pioneers in Baker as a Rogue River Indian War veteran.[34] Like many Willamette Valley pioneers, Albany resident Louis Fleischner volunteered in the Rogue River Indian War, earning the nickname (although probably not the actual rank of) "colonel."[35] During the same time period, Nathan Cohen served with Company F of the first Oregon mounted volunteers in the Yakima War in Washington Territory.[36] A more detailed account of military service can be found in the story of Bernard Goldsmith, an associate of the Heilner brothers in Althouse Creek and, before that, in Crescent City. According to Hubert Howe Bancroft's account, Goldsmith served as a first lieutenant of a volunteer militia group, as well as serving under Colonel Buchanan during the army's attack on Big Meadows. Bancroft not only credits Goldsmith with fighting, but also with mediating "with the savages" and presenting their grievances to government officials.[37]

Two decades later, in Eastern Oregon, pioneer Samuel Rothchild played his part in the conflict between Indians and his fellow encroaching white settlers.[38] Rothchild had come to Baker in 1872, and moved on to Pendleton in 1874. His clothing store was well established in the spring of 1878, when Bannock and Paiute Indians—desperate for food due to confinement on their reservation and the government's failure to fulfill its promises to supply them—began advancing along a traditional migration route toward the town. Coming only a year after the Nez Perce War, this move was met with much anxiety on the part of the settlers, who believed Indians to be "on the warpath."[39] Rothchild joined others in his community in making preparations and volunteered as part of the local militia. He was injured in a skirmish, taking a bullet to the leg.

In a state where participation in conflicts with Native Americans was considered a defining experience, weathering such trials marked Jewish settlers as authentic Oregonians and fostered their inclusion in pioneer society. Even those who did not fight could play a role in these conflicts. In Jacksonville, the Brunner brothers' store—the town's first brick building and Oregon Territory's second—served as a shelter for local settlers during the Rogue Indian conflict.[40] In 1878, as Rothchild fought near Pendleton, Harry Heppner donated materials to shore up a fort in Heppner and supply those who had to take refuge from the conflict there.[41] In Eastern Oregon, soon after returning from her honeymoon in 1889, Delia Fried Durkheimer found herself hiding in a miner's cave with the two other Canyon City "women residents of repute" (prostitutes were housed in a separate, nearby cave) in anticipation of a conflict with Paiute Indians.[42]

Along with such shared experiences, another key to the ready acceptance of Jewish merchants in pioneer Oregon was the fact that they were generally well acculturated at the time of their arrival; ready to jump into business and civic affairs. A few were born in America. Samson H. Friendly was born in New York in 1840. He spent two years in California before arriving in Eugene in 1865 (only three years after the town's incorporation) and establishing a general merchandise store and a warehouse for agricultural goods. Within a few decades, he was one of Eugene's leading citizens, having served as a city councilman, mayor, and regent of the University of Oregon.[43] Eastern Oregon pioneer Julius Durkheimer was born in Philadelphia in 1857 to German parents who had immigrated years earlier. He arrived in Portland with his family, sailing around the Horn, in the early 1860s. In 1874, he left the family in Portland and joined the Bamberger and Frank merchandising operation in Baker as a bookkeeper.[44]

As native born Americans, Friendly and Durkheimer were exceptional; most Jews who arrived in the mid-nineteenth century were immigrants. Still, they were not usually greenhorns. Their sojourns elsewhere in the United States, often in small towns or in the countryside, helped to prepare them for the frontier. Most importantly, they arrived relatively acculturated and able to speak English—as reflected in the records of the organizations they founded, which were all kept in English.[45] Many had years of experience peddling or marketing in rural America.

In this, the Mitchells of Gervais were fairly typical. McKinley's father, Isaac, had migrated to the United States from Poland in the late 1830s, at age twelve.[46] After spending time in New Orleans and California, Mitchell arrived in Oregon City by 1850, and immediately went into business in partnership with a coreligionist.[47] Likewise, Samuel Rothchild's family emigrated from Wurttemberg to the United States in 1852, when he was a boy. The family settled as farmers in

Kentucky, where Samuel attended school and began his career as a merchant, before moving to Oregon in the early 1870s.⁴⁸ And Kaufman Durkheimer, Julius's father, spent twenty-six years in Philadelphia before making the journey west.

Others immigrated as adults, but spent years in eastern cities, southern towns, or California mining regions before arriving in Oregon. Jacksonville pioneer Morris Mensor spent several years working in New York before making his way to Southern Oregon via San Francisco and Crescent City.⁴⁹ Samuel Adolph, born in Prussia in 1835, arrived in America in 1855. Adolph soon enlisted and spent eight years in the US Army, rising to the rank of lieutenant; the 1860 census found him at Fort Laramie. After marrying in Denver and following "the mining excitement" to Idaho, Adolph arrived in Salem in 1867, establishing that city's first brewery, and eventually serving on Salem's city council.⁵⁰ Austrian Adolf Wolf had arrived in the United States in 1863, coming to Portland three years later and then opening the first store in Independence, Polk County, where he lived for over a decade. Later, he moved to Silverton, where he ran for city council in 1888 and briefly served after a disputed election.⁵¹ In 1891, he erected a substantial building housing his general merchandise store in that town's center.⁵²

Similarly, the earliest Portland merchants arrived around 1850, after spending years elsewhere in the United States. Lewis May, who reached Portland in 1849, had been in the country for nearly a decade, living principally in Shreveport, Louisiana. His Portland business partner, Jacob Goldsmith, also a German, had resided in San Francisco before coming north. Jacob Mayer, who would later become one of the three principles in the largest of the Jewish dry goods businesses in Portland, Fleischner, Mayer & Co. (1875), had considerable experience in America before his arrival. The 1860 census shows Mayer and his wife Mary living in Portland with their six children whose birthplaces are evidence of the family's travels. The eldest, Josephine (who later married Mayer's partner and prominent Oregonian Solomon Hirsch), was born in Louisiana in 1848, as was her sister Clementine. Both children were with their parents on the harrowing sea voyage from New Orleans to Panama, and from there to San Francisco, where Ben was born in 1852. Daughters Bertha (1853) and Rosa (1855) were also born in California. By 1859, when Marcus was born, the family was residing in Portland. Another well acculturated immigrant was Bernard Goldsmith, who emigrated from Bavaria at age sixteen in 1848 and apprenticed in a cousin's jewelry store in New York before making his way west. Two years later, Bernard was in San Francisco, where a family friend helped him gain passage to Sacramento. Before settling in Portland in 1861, he had not only fought in Southern Oregon's Indian wars, but had operated a pack train between California mining towns, and run stores in the Northern California towns of Crescent City and Yreka, Southern Oregon, and British Columbia. Just eight years after his arrival in Portland, Goldsmith would be elected mayor.

CREATION OF COMMUNITY

As Goldsmith's story suggests, behind many of the stories of individual arrivals were family strategies. Often, an older brother arrived first, working a number of years in the United States to establish himself and pave the way for brothers, cousins, nephews—and eventually a bride—to follow. In other cases, direct immigrants to Oregon were joined by siblings who had tarried elsewhere. Such was the case with the Hirsch brothers. Leopold, the eldest, came from Wurttemberg, Germany, to Oregon in 1851, and established a store in Salem. Two years later, brothers J.B. and Mayer—who served in 1860 on Salem's first city council—joined him. [53] Edward and Solomon, both of whom would later serve in the state senate, were next, arriving in 1858. Solomon's route was indirect—he spent four years clerking in New York, New Haven, and Rochester, New Hampshire before his arrival in Oregon. [54]

The Heilner family reflects a similar pattern of family strategy and indirect migration. Seligmann was the pioneer older brother, migrating from Bavaria to the United States in 1845. After several years in the East, Seligmann followed the gold rush to California in 1849. A few years later, he opened a dry goods store in the Northern California town of Crescent City with coreligionist Julius Simonsfeld. [55] Seligmann's younger brother Sigmund followed him to America in 1853, staying with friends on the East Coast, until his father's concerns about Seligmann's situation and the dangers of the West could be addressed. Finally, in late 1854, permission was granted, and Sigmund sailed to Panama, crossed the isthmus, and sailed again for San Francisco. The brothers then proceeded to Southern Oregon, arriving just in time for

Heppner & Blackman store, Heppner, Oregon, 1900. Credit: Oregon Jewish Museum

Sigmund to participate in the Rogue Indian War. Over the next several years, Sigmund operated a dry goods store in Browntown, participated with his brother in a Southern Oregon mining venture, operated a packing business out of Portland, opened a general merchandise store in the mining camp of Sparta, and eventually settled in Baker.[56]

Jewish pioneers drew together to set up businesses, most frequently general merchandise or dry goods stores. As in the case of the Heilners, partnerships were often based on family relationships. Henry Heppner's store in Heppner (the town named for him) was run for a period of time by his brother-in-law, Henry Blackman and his nephew, Phill Cohn.[57] In early Jacksonville, at least four sets of Jewish brothers operated businesses, including Samuel, Lippman, Ben, Isaac, and Solomon Sachs's Temple of Fashion, which operated from the early 1860s until 1875.[58] Brothers Abraham and Newman Fisher partnered for a period of time with their brother-in-law, Morris Mensor, in a mercantile business in Jacksonville, and Mensor's brother-in-law, Lipman Coleman clerked there.[59] In Portland, brothers Simon and Jacob Blumauer established a store on Front Street in 1851; the following year three brothers and two cousins from the Haas family opened a grocery business.⁶⁰

When business partners were not brothers or cousins sharing a last name, it is difficult to determine whether they had pre-existing relationships before forming these partnerships or simply met on site and joined forces. Such appears to be the case with McKinley's father, Isaac Mitchell, who partnered with one of the Dusenberry brothers, also from Poland, in Oregon City to form one of the first Jewish businesses in the state. Similarly, Jacob Goldsmith and Lewis May, usually recognized as the first Jewish settlers in Portland, arrived in 1849 and opened a general merchandise business together, but it is not clear whether the two had a connection prior to meeting up in Portland. Although both were German, May had spent nearly a decade in Louisiana, while Goldsmith arrived via San Francisco.⁶¹

Both familial relationships and business partnerships connected early settlers to chains of Jewish suppliers and merchants, creating regional networks. Thus, Mitchell's Oregon City partner, Dusenberry, went on to operate a business with his brothers in The Dalles. One of their employees, Benjamin Burgunder, later went into partnership in Washington Territory with Schwabacher Brothers, a major San Francisco-based Jewish firm.⁶² Perhaps that connection was made through Isaac Bloch, a Schwabacher uncle who ran a general merchandise and assay office in The Dalles by the early 1860s.⁶³ One Schwabacher in-law, Bailey Gatzert, after proving himself by operating stores in Portland and Wallula, Washington Territory, settled in Seattle, where he ran the state's largest merchandising operation and, in 1875, became mayor of that city.⁶⁴

Stints in remote outposts could provide not only training for young men, but also discipline. When Ben Selling found his cousin and trainee paying more attention to young ladies and card playing than to business, he sent him to Joseph, in Eastern Oregon, admonishing him that he was being sent "to get you away from bad company and try to make a man of you. . . . You are not up in the country for your *health* . . . but to make and *save* money. It will not be long before your father and mother will depend entirely on their children for support."⁶⁵ [Emphasis in original.]

Fleischner, Mayer & Co., recognized as "the largest manufacturer of and dealer in dry goods in the Pacific northwest [sic]" in a 1903 publication, evolved out of a series of partnerships that launched the careers of several of Oregon's most prominent Jewish pioneers and native sons.[66] Louis Fleischner, who had traveled overland with his brother in 1852, moved on from his Albany business and packing operation to settle in Portland in 1864 and enter a partnership with Solomon Hirsch and Alexander Schlussel.[67] Hirsch, one of the five brothers based in Salem, had previously run businesses in nearby Silverton and Dallas. The three partners purchased the Haas Brothers' pioneer merchandising business, and renamed it L. Fleischner & Co. In the meantime, Mayer, arriving from San Francisco with his expanding family, established a dry goods business in Portland in 1857. In 1875, he merged with L. Fleischner & Co., and Fleischner, Mayer & Co. was born. In subsequent years, Fleischner's nephews Isaac and Marcus (Max), native Oregonians, were brought into the business when Louis stepped down; Solomon Hirsch married Mayer's eldest daughter, Josephine; and Mark Mayer succeeded his father. In addition to being recognized as key founders of Jewish institutions in Portland, including Congregation Beth Israel, the First Hebrew Benevolent Society, and B'nai B'rith, principles Solomon Hirsch, Isaac Fleischner, and Jacob Mayer are widely mentioned in pioneer and native son histories as key founders and builders of Portland.[68] Solomon Hirsch had an extensive political career, serving in the Oregon state house and senate in the 1870s and 1880s, including three terms as president of the senate, and as ambassador to Turkey; partner Louis Fleischner served a term as state treasurer.

The link between merchandising operations and politics was not coincidental: Jewish business establishments were critical to town development and therefore propelled men such as Hirsch and Fleischner into positions of civic and political leadership. Jewish pioneers fostered a sense of growth and permanence in new towns, and their buildings—often among a town's first brick structures—literally placed them on the map. Such was the case with the Muller store, which occupied Jacksonville's first brick building, built by a pair of Jewish bothers. [69] As Max Muller reminded customers in an 1862 advertisement, "Do not forget the place—the Brick Store heretofore occupied by Brunner & Bro."[70] In 1864, Muller would be elected mayor.[71] Among Simon Blumauer's claims to fame was that he built the second brick building in Portland, in 1855, and the first three-story brick building—accomplishments that, along with the success of his merchandising partnership, likely led to his election to Portland city council in 1876 and his recognition in the inaugural volume of *Oregon Native Son*.[72] Such local and pioneer histories make clear that Oregonians considered the construction of these buildings an important marker of local development, recording the first, second, and even the third brick building constructed in each town. These volumes often featured pictures of the buildings as major landmarks. For example, the 1898 Souvenir Edition of the *Morning Democrat*, celebrating the history of Baker, Grant, Harney, Malheur, and Union counties in Eastern Oregon, called Baker's M. Weil & Co. building "one of the most substantial brick buildings in town," featured a picture of the "Heilner Block," and noted Gorham and Rothchild's "very substantial, two story stone structure," in North Powder.[73] The Adolph building, erected by Salem brewer Samuel Adolph and a partner in 1880, was hailed in the local press as "one of the finest buildings in the city," and housed Adolph's saloon, "the finest and best furnished north of San Francisco."[74] In Portland, historian Robert Scott Cline estimates that nearly a third of the 146 merchants in 1860 were Jewish, and that seven of the thirty-three brick buildings standing in Portland by 1870 had been built by Jewish merchants.[75] In Jacksonville, according to historian Robert Levinson, six of nine merchants in 1873 were Jewish, and, although

HEILNER BLOCK.

S. A. HEILNER.

Like many pioneer publications, the 1898 Souvenir Edition of Baker City's *Morning Democrat* featured several pictures of Jewish pioneers and their stores.

there was considerable transiency, Jews consistently formed a majority of that town's merchant class during the first thirty-five years of its
existence.[76]

As they built their businesses and the brick buildings to house them,
Jewish pioneers also established families. Young men were dominant
among the early migrants, particularly among those who engaged in
frontier activities such as packing, or who were drawn to Browntown
and other similar, hardscrabble settlements. Even in Portland, single
men dominated in the early years.[77] As both individuals and towns
became more established, family strategies turned toward marriage.
Jewish men in remote locations drew on their familial and business
networks to identify potential mates, and their marriages are evidence
of the connections among coreligionists across the state and beyond.
Sigmund Heilner, by then residing in the eastern mining camp of
Sparta, returned to Portland to marry Clara Neuberger in 1874, before
settling with his new bride in Baker, where the Neuberger-Heilner Bank
became the first bank in the city.[78] Julius Durkheimer's bride, Delia,
who had waited out the Indian conflict in a cave near Canyon City, was
the daughter of Willamette Valley pioneer Moses Fried.[79] Although it is
not clear how the pair became acquainted, it seems likely that they met
in Portland, where Delia's family attended holiday services and Julius
made purchasing trips timed to coincide with holidays. Carl Adler of
Astoria met Laura Hirsch, Salem native and daughter of Solomon, on a
trip to the state capital.[80] And Pendleton's Samuel Rothchild journeyed
to Portland in 1880 to marry Hannah Wurzweiler, probably a relative
of one of Rothchild's associates.[81]

In seeking a partner for marriage, many pioneers looked beyond
the state's borders. Even for the Oregon-born, younger generation, San
Francisco remained the major hub for commerce, and many Jewish
merchants made regular trips to the city to supply their stores and, when
the time came, to find a bride. Like McKinley Mitchell, I.N. Fleischner,
also the son of a pioneer, found his bride, Tessie Goslinsky, in San
Francisco in 1887.[82] Even farther afield, Portland businessman Simon
Blumauer married Mollie Radelsheimer in New York in 1853; he had
resided there in 1847 and 1848, although it is not clear whether he had
met his future wife then.[83] Among immigrants, brides were sometimes

sought from even more distant points; Aaron Meier, for example, married Jeannette Hirsch while visiting his family in Bavaria.[84]

As Jewish pioneers in towns across the state formed businesses, built brick buildings to house their stores, and established families, they often did so in close proximity to one another. Despite their isolation and small size, many of the towns that drew the pioneers were home to small clusters of coreligionists during the period of early settlement. Jacksonville is a classic example. A mining town, Jacksonville boomed suddenly after the discovery of gold nearby in 1851. A year later, at least seven young Jewish men were living there.[85] By 1860, the Jewish community included at least one family—the Mensors, husband Morris, wife Matilda, and the three children, ages three, two, and eleven months—along with several single men, among them Matilda's brothers Newman and Abraham Fisher.[86] Tight ties among Jacksonville's Jews are demonstrated not only in their evolving business partnerships, but also in residential choices. The 1860 census, for example, shows the two Fisher brothers and M. Rosenberg, a clerk, living together with the Mensor family. As late as 1870, a decade after the gold fever had run its course, the Mensors, the Caro brothers, the Fisher brothers (now each living with his own family), Muller (with his wife and young son), the Solomon brothers, and some of the Sachs brothers were still residing in Jacksonville, closely clustered occupationally and residentially. Of the thirteen adult men listed in the 1870 census who could be positively identified as Jews, six were dry goods merchants, two grocers, four either grocery or dry goods clerks, and one a barkeeper. All these men lived—and presumably worked—in buildings that were in close proximity, often next door to one another.[87] Several, including Morris Mensor and Max Muller, remained in Jacksonville until their deaths.[88]

Even in tiny Gervais in the agricultural Willamette Valley, the Mitchells were part of a small cluster of Jewish merchants. The 1880 census shows several Jewish merchants living near the Mitchells. The Kaminsky family, including wife Henrietta Hirsch Kaminsky, eight children, and two boarders (one of whom clerked in the store), also originated in Poland/Prussia. A few doors down from the Kaminsky household were the Goodmans, also with eight children and two boarders, headed by merchant Neuman, a native of Prussia.[89] When

Carl Adler and his wife, Laura Hirsch Adler, moved to Baker, they settled in a house on the same block as her sister.

Even where formal partnerships were not undertaken, Jewish pioneers in isolated locales forged critical, long-lasting connections. For example, during their time in the Browntown mining camp, the lives of the Heilner brothers intersected with those of the Goldsmith brothers. Both sets of brothers ran stores in Browntown, and, while visiting family in Germany in 1859, Bernard Goldsmith and Seligmann Heilner (aka E.D. Cohen) met to discuss a possible partnership (although, apparently, this did not come into being). The following year, when Sigmund Heilner sojourned briefly in Portland, he lived with Goldsmith.[90]

Although boomtowns such as Jacksonville occasionally contained a minyan (quorum) of ten Jewish men needed for a religious service, Portland was the only city in the state with a community sufficiently large to form lasting synagogues with purpose-built structures. Even there, the transiency of the early settlers likely delayed this development; the persistence rate for Jews in Portland between 1853 and 1860 was only 33 percent.[91] There were enough men for a minyan in Portland as early as 1853, but it was not until five years later that Congregation Beth Israel was founded with an initial membership of twenty-one men.[92] By 1859, they had purchased a lot, and, in the spring of 1861, they laid the cornerstone for a new building large enough to seat two hundred. Within four years, they would have to expand it.[93]

No other communities could come close to Portland, but formal organizations did coalesce in a few of the smaller localities, most often beginning with a burial society. This was the case in the Willamette Valley town of Albany, where the desire to establish a cemetery led in 1878 to the organization of a congregation that drew members from towns as far away as Eugene, some 30 miles upstream, for its annual meeting.[94] Neither Eugene nor Salem (25 miles downstream from Albany) had formal congregations with regular services until the 1930s. In Pendleton, a small congregation briefly organized in 1879, elected officers, and held services in a rented room, but there is no evidence that it persisted.[95]

In the absence of formal organizations, clusters of Jews often marked religious rituals together, with families gathering for holiday services in isolated small towns. In Jacksonville, where the first known

Jewish religious service in Oregon was held in 1856, holiday services took place in the Odd Fellows Hall, led by one of the local merchants.[96] Similarly, the cluster of Baker Jewish families rented the Elks Hall for their services.[97] An alternative to holding services on site was to travel to a larger community for the holiday. Merchants often arranged purchasing trips to Portland or San Francisco to coincide with the holidays, so that their families could celebrate there. Willamette Valley settler Moses Fried, for example, closed his store for two weeks each year so that the family could celebrate the High Holidays as part of Congregation Beth Israel in Portland.[98]

It is difficult to determine the extent to which individuals and families in such scattered settlements observed home-based religious traditions. It is likely that those who opted to seek their fortunes in remote locations, where the requisites for traditional observance were lacking, were individuals who were, at the least, flexible about their practice—particularly so during a period in their lives when they were mobile and unmarried. As a congregational history of Portland's Temple Beth Israel explains, "before 1858, engaged in a tough struggle for survival, the Jewish pioneers paused only occasionally to give thought to their Religion. They remembered their Faith when the High Holydays approached or when crucial moments in their personal lives demanded solemnization [sic]."[99] In contrast to communities such as Cincinnati and San Francisco, where congregations formed quickly, the Jewish men who found their way to Portland did not meet to establish a congregation until they married and began forming families.[100] The lack of formal organizations and limited evidence of even informal practice in remote locales suggests that this simply was not a priority. An exhaustive search by the biographer of East Oregonian Samuel Rothchild, for example, found almost no information whatsoever about his religious practice, although we do know that his marriage was performed by a rabbi in Portland.[101] According to oral accounts, services were held in Jacksonville, although their frequency is uncertain. Historian Robert Levinson was only able to speculate about whether life cycle rituals were held there—with the exception of funerals. He states unequivocally that "the weddings that occurred wholly within the faith" were held in San Francisco, with only one exception, and none are known to have taken place in Jacksonville.[102] Leo Adler recalled that, during his boyhood at the turn of the century, the fifteen or twenty Jewish families who lived in Baker "met in some lodge hall and everybody brought some food and they would have beer," on Sunday nights, yet there were no regular services and he "had no chance to learn about the Jewish religion."[103]

Scattered evidence of observance in small towns did appear in the form of newspaper notices about the availability of matzah for Passover or store closures on high holidays. Such announcements can be found in papers from Jacksonville to Astoria. Some focused on individual stores, such as the annual notice in the *East Oregonian*, beginning in 1883, that Pendleton's Dusenbery & Co. would close for the High Holidays.[104] Others, including an 1877 story in the *Daily Astorian*, explained that all the stores owned by "Hebrews" would be closed.[105] Such advertisements offer clues about both the extent and the limits of Jewish ritual observance. For example, the announcement that Dusenbery & Co. would close for the High Holidays—and the absence of similar notices for the other Jewish owned stores in Pendleton— implies that the others remained open.[106] Also suggestive is an 1872 notice in Jacksonville's *Oregon Sentinel*. It explained that Yom Kippur would be observed on Saturday the twelfth of October, and informed residents that, because "our Hebrew citizens" would be observing the fast, "their places of business will all be closed on that day."[107] Interestingly, this provides evidence of both the general observance of the High Holiday among Jewish merchants in Jacksonville, and of their non-observance of the Sabbath. If Jewish businesses had generally closed on Saturdays, special notice about this particular Saturday

Small town newspapers noted the availability of matzah for Passover. The *Daily Astorian*, April 19, 1881. Credit: Historic Oregon Newspapers, http:// oregonnews. uoregon.edu

—The festival of the Passover is strictly observed in Astoria, by our Jewish residents. We are under special obligation to Mrs. I. Bergman for the compliment of a share of the matzos and honey to be found at her hospitable board.

would not have been necessary. It is also notable that, although information about the availability of *matzot* for Passover was published in many localities, advertisements for other specialty food products, such as kosher meat, are not in evidence. After an exhaustive search of Pendleton area records, Rothchild's biographer was able to find "no other information of any kind" beyond a handful of newspaper announcements to "shed light on the degree to which Pendleton Jews in the nineteenth century practiced the Jewish religion."[108]

Personal accounts offer similarly fragmentary evidence about religious observance (or lack thereof). For example, Adalbert Bettman, son of pioneers who lived in Eugene from 1879 to 1897 reported only minimal Jewish ritual observance during his boyhood. Portland's Rabbi Jacob Bloch visited the community periodically to perform life cycle rituals such as circumcisions, weddings, and funerals, but "Bloch never conducted any services for Sabbaths or holidays in Eugene, since the early Jewish families in Eugene came to Portland fairly often." Although the Jewish merchants "probably closed their stores" on Yom Kippur, Bettman recalled a gathering, but no services. Until they moved to Portland, his family did not hold a seder on Passover.[109] And, despite the fact that Jewish pioneers' hope to be buried in a Jewish cemetery often served as an impetus to community organization, Salem brewer Samuel Adolph was buried in Salem's Odd Fellows cemetery in 1893, rather than the Portland Jewish cemetery (as originally announced)

Julius, Delia, and Sylvan Durkheimer, c. 1915
Credit: Oregon Jewish Museum

Durkheimer's general store, 1891. Credit: Oregon Jewish Museum

or the Albany cemetery shared by Salem and other mid-valley Jewish communities.[110]

The difficulty of religious observance in remote towns clearly spurred migration to Portland and other larger Jewish centers. Several accounts suggest that wives, in particular, pushed families to relocate to Portland as their families grew. Burns merchant Julius Durkheimer promised his bride, Delia Fried, who did not relish the idea of becoming "an Eastern Oregonian in a primitive community" that they would return to the Willamette Valley within a decade. Although Julius "didn't feel the pull to bring him to services," his wife was "more religiously inclined," according to their son.[111] In 1896, after Julius's term as mayor ended, the family sold its business and moved to Portland. There, they moved in with Delia's parents, who had relocated to the city from Hubbard in rural Marion County in 1880. Delia's brother, Leo Friede [sic], also relocated to Portland after living in the small Eastern Oregon community of Prineville from 1881 to 1889.[112] Likewise, Lehman Blum, who ran a store, managed a bank, and rented out the brick buildings he built in Pendleton, left Eastern Oregon for Portland in 1891, after thirteen years.[113] Along with the commercial promise of the rapidly expanding city, the opportunity to be part of a larger Jewish

Morris Mensor, owner of the
New York Store, Jacksonville,
Oregon, c. 1880.
Credit: Oregon Jewish Museum

community was a motivator in many of
these moves. Certainly this was the case
for a number of families, including the
Bettmans and Frieds, who had journeyed
to Portland to celebrate holidays for years.

The movement from small towns to
Portland was not, of course, unique to
Jews. Mining towns such as Jacksonville
that had boomed after mineral strikes,
dwindled rapidly when deposits were
exhausted. Moreover, Portland grew far
more quickly than the rest of the state
in the final decades of the nineteenth
century; while only about 10 percent of
Oregonians lived in there in 1880, over 20
percent resided there by century's end.[114]
Jewish settlement patterns were an exag-
gerated version of these broader regional trends. Lee Shai Weissbach's
study of small Jewish communities demonstrates that the revival of
small Jewish communities that took place in other parts of the country
in the late nineteenth century was not felt in the West.[115] Small Jewish
clusters, including those in the Willamette Valley and Eastern Oregon
declined in these decades, and in some cases vanished altogether. In
the valley, the Frieds' move to Portland presaged those of other Jewish
families. By the time McKinley Mitchell was elected to the state legislature in the mid-1890s, his was the sole Jewish family remaining in
Gervais and they would decamp to Portland after the turn of the century.[116] By 1895, many small valley towns had only one Jewish family
or individual, nearly always a merchant, such as L. Jacobs in Detroit,
the Wolf family in Silverton, or peddler M. Ostrow in Aurora.[117] After
the departure of the Frieds, Hubbard's only Jewish family was led by
I. Isaacson, who worked as a station agent.[118] A few pioneer Jewish
families, including the Mensors in Jacksonville or the Friendly family
in Eugene, remained for decades. Yet the lack of Jewish community in
these locales took a toll; in a number of cases, families that resided for
long periods in remote locales ultimately lost their Jewish identities.

A JEWISH PRESENCE: VIEWS FROM OUTSIDE

Clustering of families and Jewish businesses created Jewish space in many Oregon towns, but how visible was that presence to non-Jews?

Certainly, Jewish names were prominent on storefronts and in advertisements in the local papers, yet, since many non-Jews had similar, often German-sounding names, which stores were Jewish may not have been readily apparent. For example, in 1862, readers of Jacksonville's *Oregon Sentinel* would have found their news coverage framed by prominent advertisements for the Sachs Brothers and Max Muller stores, both selling clothing as well as groceries. Neither these, nor those for other small town Jewish stores such as Durkheimer's in Burns, indicated the owner's religious origins or advertised specifically Jewish products, although a few, including Morris Mensor's Jacksonville business, used the tag "New York store" or "New York prices," a common marker of Jewish stores across the country.

Still, residents of these towns—and readers of local newspapers—would have been aware of the presence of Jews in their communities. Indeed, in Portland—and perhaps elsewhere as well—it was not uncommon for Jewish communities to invite their non-Jewish neighbors to participate in significant celebrations. When Portland congregations dedicated new synagogue buildings in 1869 and 1889, many non-Jewish local dignitaries were in attendance. A huge crowd "estimated to be two-thirds Christian" attended a Portland Purim gala in 1884. Several months later, when the community marked the hundredth birthday of Jewish philanthropist Moses Montefiore in 1884, crowds packed the New

Like many small town newspapers, Jacksonville's *Oregon Sentinel* featured regular ads from Jewish merchants like the Sachs Brothers and Max Muller. *Oregon Sentinel*, Jacksonville, Oregon, December 13, 1862. Credit: Historic Oregon Newspapers, http://oregonnews.uoregon.edu

Market Theater, and dignitaries included local Christian ministers, the British Vice-Consul, and a federal judge.[119]

In the secular press, Oregonians from across the state would have seen the occasional mentions of Jewish holidays, as when the *Daily Astorian* informed readers in April of 1881 that "The festival of the Passover is strictly observed in Astoria, by our Jewish residents," and recognized Mrs. I. Bergman "for the compliment of a share of the matzos and honey to be found at her hospitable board."[120] The same week, Jacksonville's newspaper noted that "This is the season of unleavened bread among our Jewish brethren," and informed those interested that Mrs. E. Jacobs had a supply of matzah. Five years later, members of the Jewish community placed a notice of appreciation for Mrs. Jacobs' "bountiful supply of matzos. She always remembers us every year at this time."[121]

Unlike the information about the availability of *matzot*, High Holiday notices were aimed primarily at the non-Jewish community, to inform readers of upcoming store closures. Thus, in October 1872, Jacksonville's *Sentinel* indicated that *"Yum Kippur,* or 'Long Day'" [sic] would be observed on the coming Saturday "by our Hebrew citizens," and that "their places of business will be closed on that day."[122] Similarly, the *Daily Astorian* noted on September 11, 1877 that Rosh Hashanah had been observed a few days before by "our Hebrew fellow citizens," and that their "day of atonement (Yom Kippur)" was coming the following Monday. "These days are always rigidly observed by the Hebrews everywhere," explained the notice, "and we suppose all their business houses in this city will be closed on that day. Persons interested will remember this and act accordingly."[123] Such notices rarely listed the businesses to be closed by name, suggesting that local residents knew which stores were Jewish.[124]

In addition to practical information about store closures, local newspapers sometimes provided readers more explanation, apparently aiming to educate them about Jewish tradition. For example, in 1868, an *Oregon Sentinel* notice about Yom Kippur explained that the holiday had begun at sunset the previous day and would continue until "starlight this evening." "It is kept as a day of atonement and repentance for the transgressions of the past year," the article continued, "one on which a kind of moral balance sheet is struck and a new leaf in the book of life turned over."[125] An 1880 *Sentinel* article, after explaining the "Jewish feast of the Purim," lamented that so few in Jacksonville had celebrated the recent holiday. The piece connected the poor showing for Purim to a falling off in holiday observance in the population in general, observing enigmatically that "the observance of religious holidays, both among Jews and Gentiles on this coast is growing beautifully less every year."[126] In 1885, the *Daily Morning Astorian*, under the headline "Pesach" presented an explanation of the Passover holiday, written expressly for that publication by H.W.—most likely Herman Wise, a German Jew who settled in the city in the 1870s, and would serve as its mayor after the turn of the century. Beginning with the story of the Jews' slavery in Egypt and oppression by the Pharaoh, the article linked specific elements of the story to ritual practices of the holiday and explicated in some detail the dietary restrictions. "Matzos or unleavened bread is used during Passover; nor are the Jews allowed to drink liquor, beer, or use anything sour, nor rice, flour, oatmeal, etc., etc. Matzos is used instead, which, by the way, makes excellent pancakes or dumplings." The article went on to explain customs such as the cleaning the house of "chomez" and selling it to a gentile neighbor, and the rituals of the Seder.[127] Even when inaccurate, as when Jacksonville's *Democratic Times* conflated Passover and Yom Kippur, reporting that Jews would eat matzah during the Yom Kippur fast, the intention was clearly to educate.[128]

Occasional human interest or social stories commented positively on Jewish tradition or culture. For example, in 1898, Salem's *Daily Capital Journal* reported on "A Valentine Wedding" between Samuel Adolph's daughter, Miss Eva Adolph, and Mr. Isidor Greenbaum, conducted by a Rabbi Levin:

The ceremony in the Hebrew was translated into English, and was very impressive and followed by some wise words of admonition to the newly made man and wife. . . . Miss Eva was attired in a charming dark green travelling suit trimmed with lace and wearing a beautiful coiffure of orange blossoms. Mr. and Mrs. Greenbaum are well known to all Salemites, the bride being a native of the Capital City and the groom having lived here since he was 19 years old. They are a well matched couple. . . . "[129]

In other human interest stories, individuals were identified as Jewish, but only incidentally. An interesting example comes from Jacksonville's *Oregon Sentinel* in 1867. Headlined "Love Under Difficulties," the article told of the elopement of two young people to Jacksonville, a young man, and a "girl about fifteen or sixteen years old—the daughter of a rich old Hebrew in Siskiyou county." The girl's father tried to have the prospective groom arrested for kidnapping, but the crisis was averted when the young couple agreed to meet with the father. Aside from identifying the father as a "Hebrew," the article make no further mention of religion, focusing instead on the passion of the couple for one another and wishing them success in marrying "the next time they run away."[130]

Along with what did appear in local papers about Jewish communities, it is interesting to note what did not: with few exceptions, the Oregon press did not note the Jewishness of local personalities who appeared in their pages. For example, Julius Durkheimer's stores in Baker, Prairie City, Canyon City, and, later, Burns, and his service as that town's mayor, made him a prominent figure in Eastern Oregon. In addition to his frequent advertisements in the *Grant County News*, he was mentioned in occasional news stories reporting his buying trips or store openings. Yet the local papers did not label him in these stories as a Jew. Only when the *Morning Oregonian* posted a notice in 1900 that Mrs. Julius Durkheimer, by then living in Portland, was serving as secretary of the Hebrew Ladies Sewing Society was the connection made.[131] Similarly, McKinley Mitchell, mentioned frequently in the press for his political activities, most often in the Salem papers, was not identified as a Jew; nor was Sigmund Heilner in the many stories about his activities in the Jacksonville, Canyon City, or Salem press, spanning over a thirty-year period. A search in the *Historic Oregon Newspapers* digital collection, which includes a wide variety of newspapers from towns and cities across the state, shows no articles about any of nine different Oregon mayors that identify them as Jewish.[132] For prominent statewide figures, the pattern is the same, with exceptions only when the Jewish connection was germane to the article, as when Ben Selling was elected to the board of the Hebrew Benevolent Association or working on a campaign to raise money for relief of Jewish refugees.[133] Even in their obituaries, Jewish identity was evident only when interment in a Jewish cemetery was mentioned, as in the

1895 obituary of former Portland mayor Philip Wasserman, indicating that he would be buried at the "Beth Israel (Jewish) cemetery." Six years later, after the death of Wasserman's predecessor, Bernard Goldsmith, the lengthy, front page obituary noted his background as a German immigrant, and detailed many achievements and contributions, but did not identify him as Jewish.[134] Only when public figures who had also been Jewish communal leaders passed away were their activities within the community lauded in obituaries, as was the case in the 1902 obituary for Solomon Hirsch.[135]

The practice of not identifying Jews in the press is particularly notable because it seems at odds both with practice elsewhere at the time and locally in later periods. After the turn of the century, the Portland section of the National Council of Jewish Women would launch a campaign to persuade the Portland press to discontinue their practice of specifying the religious affiliation of suspects and criminals.[136] And in many parts of the country, it was common for prominent Jews to be identified as such when their names appeared in print. Although coming at the end of the period in question here, the election of Joseph Simon to the Senate provides a useful test case for understanding how local practices compared with those elsewhere. Senator John Mitchell's political enemies were so determined to defeat him that they prevented the state legislature from meeting during the 1896 session. (US Senators were, at the time, elected by state legislatures.) Not until 1898 did the legislature convene and, after a bitter struggle, select Simon over Mitchell. The long-delayed decision, when it finally came in October 1898, made national news.[137]

A number of newspapers across the country reported Simon's victory, often including the information that he was Jewish. In some cases, the reference came in passing, as part of a short biography of Simon, as in the *Omaha Daily Bee*'s story, mentioning that "Mr. Simon is a Hebrew and was born in Germany." The *Salt Lake Herald*, the *Los Angeles Herald*, the *Kansas City Journal*, Sacramento's *Record Union*, and the Reynoldsville, Pennsylvania *Star* all described Simon as "a Hebrew" or "of Hebrew parentage." The *Vermont Phoenix* identified him as a Jew and the *Globe-Republican* of Dodge City, Kansas headlined the story "A Hebrew Senator." A series of other papers reported that Simon was the fourth Jew elected to the Senate, either as part of a larger story or as a separate, stand-alone story. For example, the *Times* of Washington, DC, headlined the story "Oregon's new Senator," with a sub-heading reading "Mr. Simon the Fourth Jewish Member of the Upper House," and included an entire paragraph, both in its morning and evening editions, on this topic. The *Semi-Weekly Interior Journal* of Stanford, Kentucky reported erroneously in a stand-alone brief that Simon was the third Jewish senator. Both the *Salt Lake Herald* and the *National Tribune* of Washington, DC, reported the fourth Jew story.[138]

Locally, of course, Oregon papers covered the story of the contentious election closely. Salem's *Daily Capital Journal*, for example, published numerous articles throughout the controversy, announced the decision on the front page, and ran a lengthy biography of Simon, mentioning his German origins, but not his Jewish identity. Neither Simon's identity as the fourth Jew elected to the Senate, nor the fact that he had served in state government along with a number of coreligionists—including two serving in that 1897 session, Ben Selling and McKinley Mitchell (who initially supported Simon's rival, but later shifted his allegiance to his coreligionist and therefore became a critical vote in Simon's favor)—was reported in these stories.[139] This was typical of the Oregon press: a search of the Oregon newspaper database for "Joseph Simon" paired with "Israelite," "Hebrew," or "Jew" yields only one story pairing these terms, a *Capital Journal* article published several weeks after the dispute was resolved. The story came in response to articles from other papers that had erroneously reported that Simon was the second Jew ever elected to the Senate. In correcting the story, the *Journal* explained,

> when first elected US Senator Joseph Simon was reported to be the second Jew ever elected to the US Senate. Now he has grown to be the fourth—the others are Jonas and Benjamin of Louisiana, and Yulee of Florida. It is likely there are others in the US Senate who belong to the class called Jews. Strictly speaking, Senator Simon is not so much of a Jew as many public men not descended from the Hebrew race. In Portland he has fraternized more with Americans than with Jews.[140]

The *Journal's* framing of the story is intriguing. The paper chose not to identify Simon as a Jew in its ongoing coverage—although his identity would have been commonly known. Although Simon was not a central figure in Jewish communal life, he clearly identified as part of the Jewish community—the son of a charter member of Congregation Beth Israel and a longtime member himself, Simon also belonged to the elite Jewish Concordia Club, and provided free legal services to organizations including the congregation and the National Council of Jewish Women.[141] Faced with the widely reported story about Simon being the fourth (or second) Jewish Senator, the paper responded by trying to distance the Senator-elect from his Jewish background. The *Journal's* explanation comes in its suggestion that Simon "is not so much of a Jew as many public men not descended from the Hebrew race." This implies a negative understanding, that Jewishness was about character and association more than background, and that, based on that understanding, Simon (and presumably Selling and the other prominent Jewish leaders in Oregon) was "not so much of a Jew." "Jew" is associated with a negative stereotype, but, apparently, not one that applied to the Oregon public figures who happened to be Jewish.

It is possible to flesh out this understanding and broaden it by placing it in the larger context of discourse about Jews in Oregon, beginning in the pioneer period.[142] A survey of the use of the terms "Jewish" and "Hebrew" in the digital Oregon historic newspaper database demonstrates that, most often, articles that mentioned Jews were either referencing Biblical figures, or reporting on faraway places. Stories of the persecution of Jews abroad appeared with some frequency. Often, these were straight news stories, but on occasion they were combined with condemnations of the treatment or defense of the Jews. For example, Portland's *New Northwest* in May 1877 printed a story originating in Washington, DC, on "the outrages upon the Jews in Roumania," and urged intervention on their behalf. It continued, "The Jews form a large portion of our community and having among them many men of highest intellectual ability, they are quite an element of strength."[143] Similarly, in 1878 the *East Oregonian* reprinted a letter from a southern Jewish lawyer responding to an anti-Semitic slur. The "open letter" proclaimed pride in the writer's Jewish "lineage and race."[144]

Such items were reinforced by occasional feature pieces that painted a positive picture of Jews. In November 1880, Pendleton's *East Oregonian* published a lecture that Benjamin I. Cohen had delivered in Portland on Jewish history in America. Starting with colonial America, the half-page piece provided an overview of the topic, focusing particularly on Jewish contributions to the country.[145] Similarly, an 1872 *Willamette Farmer* article titled "Intelligence of the Jews," described Jews as high achieving, intelligent, moral, and contributing citizens.[146] More equivocal was a piece appearing in Canyon City's *Grant County News* in 1880. Titled "Jews in Europe," the column characterized the "Jewish mind" as "expansive," and claimed that this quality was the cause of both Jewish "eminence and antagonism." Attributing to Jews a "passion" to "do something and to be something," the piece explained that, where restricted, Jews grew frustrated, but, where fields were open to them, they found success, concluding, "In the long run, it may be confidently predicted that everything that favors civilization will favor the Jew."[147]

Of course, there were exceptions to this positive treatment. Certainly one of the earliest and most notorious was the attack by Thomas J. Dryer, publisher of the *Oregonian*, on alleged Jewish influence on politics in 1858. Following on the heels of his unsuccessful run for the territorial legislature, Dryer attacked his opponents, claiming,

> the Jews in Oregon, but more particularly in this city, have assumed an importance that no other sect has ever dared to assume in a free country. They have leagued together by uniting their entire numerical strength to control the ballot boxes at our election . . .
>
> They have assumed to control the commercial interest of the whole country by a secret combination. . . . The history of the Jews is but a history of a great variety of ways and means adopted by them to obtain money and power. They as a nation or tribe produce nothing, nor do nothing unless they are the exclusive gainers thereby.
>
> Do you know of a Jew who ever drove an ox team across the plains, or engaged in an Indian war to defend the homes and firesides of our citizens on this coast or on any other frontier?[148]

Notably, the rival *Oregon Statesman* took Dryer to task for his tirade, calling him "an ignoramus . . . a man without integrity or honor," and defended Jews as "men of honesty and integrity." Portland's *Weekly Times* also attacked Dryer.[149] Community historians generally portray this incident as anomalous, and emphasize the general acceptance of Jews and absence of anti-Semitism during the pioneer period, as does Lowenstein.[150] Still, it is clear that Dryer's would not have been the only anti-Semitic voice in Oregon. For example, as was the case nationally, the R.G. Dun credit-rating agency (later Dun & Bradstreet), often defamed Jewish businessmen, and their reports on Jewish Oregonians are studded with negative stereotypes. Their write up on Aaron Meier, for example, depicted him as "shrewd, close, calculating, and considered tricky."[151]

Dryer's suggestion that Jews were not true pioneers was countered not only by competing newspapers, but also by pioneer associations in the decades following the incident. The Oregon Pioneer Association, founded in 1873, considered "all comers to original Oregon prior to February 14, 1859" (the date of Oregon statehood) to be pioneers. Pioneers, and their children, the "native sons and daughters," took great pride in the role they had played "in shaping the history of the state."[152] Organizations such as the Pioneer Association, Native Sons and Daughters of Oregon, and the Indian War Veterans were devoted to recording the history of their struggles in the wilderness, a struggle so epic that it had "no parallel . . . in all the history of mankind . . . since the going forth of our first parents from the Garden of Eden."[153] As the pioneer generation began to pass at the end of the nineteenth century, both statewide organizations and local societies set about honoring and celebrating their achievements in commemorative volumes filled with biographies of notable pioneers, native sons, and veterans.

The inclusion of Jews among the ranks of pioneers and native sons is evident in these tomes. The inaugural volume of *Oregon Native Son*, for example, featured biographies of thirty-four Native Oregonians and one hundred pioneers. Of those pioneers, fully a quarter (twenty-six) were immigrants (although only about 10 percent of the 1860 population in Oregon was foreign born). Among the immigrants were natives of Canada, England, Germany, Scotland, Ireland, Switzerland,

HERMAN ROTHCHILD.

❀ ❀ ❀

GORHAM & ROTHCHILD.

The above firm, who carry a general line of merchandise at North Powder, Union County, is both well known and well patronized, owing to the first-class goods carried, together with low prices and the large assortment to select from. They occupy a very substantial two-story stone structure, 30x60 feet, and have three grain warehouses with a capacity of about six thousand square feet. They are heavy buyers and shippers of grain, and also operate a chop and feed mill, with a daily capacity of fifteen tons. The members of the firm are H. O. Gorham and Herman Rothchild.

Mr. Gorham is a native of Kentucky, coming here in 1866. He has always taken an active interest in the welfare of this section, and being a man of great practical ability, has easily accumulated a competency. He is president and a large stockholder of the North Powder Milling Co., and also operates one of the largest farms in the valley. He is married to Miss Annie Neeson, and is the father of a large and interesting family.

Mr. Herman Rothchild, the active manager of the store, is one of those genial whole-souled chaps it does one good to meet, and who infuse new life into you with a simple shake of the hand. His affability and good nature make him a general favorite, and his friends are legion. Mr. Rothchild was born in the Black Forest in Germany, came to this country at the age of 22, locating in Kentucky, where he spent a year. Moving then to Oregon, he located at Pendleton for 2½ years, since which he has resided here. He takes an active interest in politics, being an earnest Democrat, but has never allowed his name to be mentioned for any office. He is unmarried, and the fault is his own. This, we believe, is the only objectionable feature he possesses in the minds of the fair sex.

Profiles of merchants, such as Herman Rothchild, frequently appeared in publications celebrating the pioneer past. Credit: 1898 Souvernir Edition, *Morning Democrat*

Belgium, Spain, Bohemia, and Cuba. Nearly a fifth of the immigrants (five), or 5 percent of the total number of profiled pioneers were Jewish—a striking number, given that the percentage of Jews among the pioneers was probably well under half a percent (as late as 1877, the first year for which we have a count of Jews in Oregon, they made up only about 0.5 percent of the population). It is particularly notable that Sol Blumauer, a founder and "grand trustee" of the Native Sons of Oregon, was elected that organization's second Grand President in 1899; biographies of both of his parents were included among the pioneer profiles in the publication's first volume.[154]

Profiles in pioneer histories followed the same pattern found in news coverage—Jewish identity generally went unmentioned except where it was listed among the individuals' various community contributions. Typical was the profile of Herman Rothchild in an 1898 publication celebrating Eastern Oregon. Documenting the history of each of five counties, and featuring pictures and profiles of individuals and businesses, the publication included this short biography:

> Mr. Herman Rothchild, the active manager of the store, is one of those genial whole-souled chaps it does one good to meet, and who infuse new life into you with a simple shake of the hand. His affability and good nature make him a general favorite and his friends are legion. Mr. Rothchild was born in the Black Forest in Germany, came to this country at the age of 22, locating in Kentucky, where he spent a year. Moving then to Oregon, he located at Pendleton for 2 ½ years, since which he has resided here [North Powder]. He takes an active interest in politics, being an earnest Democrat, but has never allowed his name to be mentioned for any office. He is unmarried, and the fault is his own. This, we believe, is the only objectionable feature he possesses in the minds of the fair sex.[155]

The same publication featured a picture and profile of Sigmund Heilner, praising him as successful, a hard worker, and a man with "unblemished" reputation, whose "word is considered as good as his bond."[156] Likewise, the profile of Native Sons Grand President Sol Blumauer did not mention his Jewish identity, although the article on Sol's father, Simon, in the same publication indicated that the latter was the president of Temple Beth Israel for twenty-five years. Sol's mother, Mollie Blumauer was called "one of the mothers of our state," and was not identified as Jewish.[157]

Similar were the entries for I.N. Fleischner, Edward Hirsch, and Jacob Mayer in *Portrait and Biographical Record of the Willamette Valley, Oregon*, published in 1903, and featuring over 1,500 pages of pioneer and native son profiles. Fleischner, son of overland pioneer Jacob, was praised for his business success and progressive civic spirit, with no mention whatsoever of his Jewish identity.[158] Likewise, Edward Hirsch's profile mentioned nothing of his religion, instead focusing on his business and political achievements.[159] The lengthy profile of Jacob Mayer detailed his harrowing sea voyage from Panama, as well as the history of his various business partnerships and civic leadership in organizations ranging from the Chamber of Commerce to the YMCA and the Oregon Historical Society. The only indication of Jewish identity was that, among the many organizations listed were several that were Jewish, including the Hebrew Benevolent Society of San Francisco, the B'nai B'rith, and Congregation Beth Israel.[160]

Exceptional was the profile of Solomon Hirsch in the Willamette Valley volume, published just after his death in 1903. When Hirsch's biography appeared in *Oregon Native* Son just four years earlier, the focus was exclusively on his business and political achievements, without any mention of Jewish identity or activities.[161] The posthumous profile, however, added to the usual catalog of achievements by quoting at length from the eulogy delivered by Rabbi Stephen Wise specifically addressing Hirsch's Jewish and American identities:

> I would say that his love of the race and religious fellowship whence he was sprung rivaled his devotion to his adopted country. If rivalry there was between his attachment to his mother-faith and his loyalty to his fatherland, it was a rivalry that tended to deepen his attachment and strengthen his loyalty at one and the same time. So faithfully did he cherish the religion of his fathers that I have long thought that, if he was ambitious, it was because he hoped to serve his people by representing them honorably and worthily in public life. Eagerly he welcomed every opportunity to win and merit the world's respect for the Jew. . . . The religion he professed impelled him to nobility of action.[162]

Despite the rabbi's emphasis on Hirsch's Jewish identity driving his actions, the framing of newspaper and local history profiles of prominent Jews suggests that, in most cases in Oregon public discourse, Jewish public figures were regarded as products of the same pioneering experience that shaped their non-Jewish counterparts. Rather than being a critical force shaping their development as the rabbi asserted, Jewish ties, if mentioned at all, were listed as civic contributions, not formative experiences.

Thus, the critical influence on the profiled pioneers was not religion but the frontier. Profiles detailed frontier experiences including the Fleischner brothers' crossing "the plains to Oregon in an oxcart"; Mayer's harrowing sea voyage and near starvation; and Simon Blumauer's role in saving desperate Oregon Trail pioneers in 1852.[163] Experiences mining, packing, and fighting in Indian wars were often recounted. And, on the few occasions when Jews as a group were discussed, the histories framed their experiences as part of the larger story of pioneering and state building. For example, a long *Oregon Native Son* article on "Portland, Oregon. Its Founders and Early Business Men," included a picture captioned "Simon Blumauer, Pioneer of 1852," and a paragraph mentioning that Goldsmith and May were the first merchants "of the Jewish race" in the city, and highlighting Blumauer's key role.[164] Perhaps most telling is a 1900 article in *Oregon Native Son* titled "Shematic Emmigration to the Pacific Northwest" [sic]. In keeping with the publication's practice of marking "firsts" in Oregon history, the article took note of the first Jewish settlers, first stores, first peddler, first Jewish woman, first Jewish child born, first marriage, first Jewish congregation, etc. In addition to marking these firsts, the article commented,

> In later years numbers of others came. Many of them are quite wealthy and are identified with some of the leading enterprises on the coast. Some of them have received high honors at the hands of their fellow citizens. Among them being Hon. Sol Hirsch, ex-minister to Turkey, and Joseph Simon, at present a United States senator from Oregon.[165]

The inclusion of individual Jewish Oregonians as pioneers and native sons and of Jewish communal experiences into these formulations of regional firsts is revealing. It suggests an awareness of Jewish presence and identity, without an emphasis on difference. It contrasts sharply with the framing of the role of minority groups such as Chinese, African American, and Native American Oregonians. Whereas Jewish pioneers and native sons were included as part of the story of the development of the frontier, the state, its cities, and its economy, other racial minority groups were portrayed as anomalies, impediments, or otherwise apart from the pioneer story. No members of these groups were counted among the native sons or pioneers profiled in these commemorative volumes.[166]

Acceptance as fellow pioneers—as fellow white citizens—was also signaled in the extensive inclusion of Jews in fraternal organizations. Jews were members and leaders, not only of pioneer and native son organizations, but also of fraternal groups, as was the case throughout the West. Mention of these (most often Masonic) ties are ubiquitous in the pioneer and native son profiles, and in obituaries. Indeed, Portland's first two Jewish settlers, Jacob Goldsmith and Lewis May, were among the founders of that city's first Masonic lodge in 1850.[167] Jacob Mayer's profile in the Willamette Valley volume notes his long standing Masonic connections, including a term as "grand master of the Grand Lodge of Oregon." Solomon Hirsch was cited as one of only two Oregonians so universally esteemed that they were "made Masons 'at sight,'" without the usual secret ballot.[168] The obituary of former Jacksonville mayor, Max Muller, a founding member and "trusted leader" of the local lodge of the Ancient Order of United Workman, is particularly interesting, in its passing reference to his Jewish identity: "Through long years of the most intimate association in the lodge room, on the street, or within his home, we learned to look upon him, not as a father in Israel, but as a father in Workmanship."[169] Here, as in the *Capital Journal*'s characterization of Simon as "not so much of a Jew," the obituary recognized, but minimized, Muller's Jewish identity, instead emphasizing his qualities as a pioneer, "useful citizen" and "trusted leader."

Like Max Muller in Jacksonville, Bernard Goldsmith, elected mayor of Portland in 1869, was likely seen less as a Jew than as a frontiersman, packtrain operator, cattle rancher, Indian fighter, railroad developer, and Masonic brother. For white Oregonians, the struggle of the pioneer in the wilderness was the central historical experience that defined belonging. Even today, a golden pioneer stands atop the state Capitol building as the emblem of the iconic Oregonian. Nineteenth-century Jewish migrants—despite the fact that most were immigrants—began to arrive in Oregon in time to play their part as white, American pioneers. While the majority of them did not travel the Oregon Trail, fight in the Indian Wars, or run supply routes through the wilderness, some did, and they were embraced for these roles. Many more participated in the crucial work of erecting towns—in many cases, quite literally building the permanent structures that were regarded as the visible signs of "civilization" in this remote "wilderness." Arrival and participation in pioneer society and in the early days of statehood fostered acceptance and paved the way for civic and political leadership. Although Oregonians, like most Americans, likely carried negative stereotypes about Jews in the abstract, the involvement of Jewish settlers in the pioneering process led them to be seen as "not so much of a Jew" and more as fellow citizens.

CHAPTER 2

Go West, Young Mensch
Composition of a Community

In popular memory, the Portland Jewish community of the early to mid-twentieth century was divided by ethnicity. On the one hand, Reform Temple Beth Israel was where "all Jews established at that time" affiliated, according to Adelaide Lowenson Selling. In her account, that "established" group was defined as much by national origin as by class: "As far as I can recall there were no Russian, Lithuanians, they were all German Jews."[1] Likewise, Fannie Kenin Friedman, daughter of East European immigrants, remembered that, although she attended the temple's Sunday school, she was definitely regarded as coming "from the wrong side of the tracks," due to her ethnic and class background.[2] Miriam Aiken, who came of age in the Beth Israel community in the 1910s, noted that potential suitors "were not supposed to be any other than a German background," and that when East Europeans did begin to join Beth Israel, they were welcomed "maybe with one arm, but not with both."[3]

Such divisions were prominent in the memories of many seniors interviewed in the 1970s by a group of oral historians led by Shirley Tanzer. Whether talking about individual families or congregations, ethnic tags such as "German," "East European," or "Polish" were frequently used. Conflicts between Germans and East Europeans figured prominently in these accounts, often with an emphasis on German exclusivity. As late as the mid-1950s, recalled Ernie Bonyhadi, "the real hostility in Portland between German Jews and those that came from Russia and Poland and Eastern Europe," was still palpable, with the latter resenting what they viewed as snobbery on the part of the Germans.[4]

Reflecting these oral accounts, intergroup tensions emerge as a key theme in community histories. Most notably, Steven Lowenstein's *The Jews of Oregon, 1850–1950*, which draws heavily on the Tanzer interviews, emphasizes conflict between Germans and East Europeans:

> Jews arrived in Portland from Eastern Europe carrying their worldly possessions in gunny sacks and old valises. The men were swarthy and often bearded, the women dressed in the old ways. They were frightened and poor but strangely defiant and proud. The resident, decorum-loving German Jews cringed at their sheer numbers and their "backwardness" and orthodoxy. They wondered whether the Eastern Europeans could ever become Americans and whether the success they had fought so hard to achieve would be undermined and tarnished by these new arrivals. To the Germans they appeared "clannish" and as the immigrants crowded into South Portland, it acquired the feel of a European ghetto.[5]

Such depictions reflect a classic trope. The story of German–East European rivalry is a key component of a historical understanding of American Jewish history as the tale of three migrations: first the Sephardim (pre-dating settlement of the western United States), then the Germans, then—in an overwhelming flood—the East Europeans. The three-migrations framework both periodizes American Jewish history and provides the central plot conflict: the tension between the quickly assimilating Germans and their poorer, more religious, less sophisticated, politically suspect, and later-arriving East European cousins who were resistant to assimilation. Long accepted as the standard, this plotline has been called into question in recent years, most notably by historian Hasia Diner, who argues that the contrast between waves of German and East European immigrants has been exaggerated, and that it is more reasonable to think in terms of a "century of migration" spanning from the 1820s to the 1920s.[6] As Diner points out, the traditional chronology is "overly simplistic," ignoring, for example, that many of the "Germans" arriving in the mid-nineteenth century from eastern Prussia were, culturally, religiously, and even linguistically, quite similar to those from the East, or that many East Europeans also arrived prior to 1880.

Although western community histories often echo the traditional chronology, the trope is particularly problematic when it is transported to the West, not because there were no ethnic tensions, but because the ethnic mix in the West was particularly complex. For example, American-born Sephardim, diverse Germans and Poles, English, and a variety of other Jewish immigrants were among the newcomers who arrived in California together, rather than in separate waves, in the wake of the Gold Rush in 1849.[7] Likewise, rather than a flood of East Europeans arriving at the turn of the century, Jewish communities in the far West experienced a much smaller and more gradual stream of newcomers, many of whom arrived after sojourns elsewhere in the country. Their numbers gradually increased in the early twentieth century, but they remained modest in comparison to the East, peaking only after the "mass migration" had ended in the 1920s. In cities including Seattle, Los Angeles, and, to a lesser extent, Portland, the East European influx was complemented by the entry of a significant wave of immigrant Sephardim from Greece and the eastern Mediterranean.

These distinctive migration patterns had a direct impact on community development. If the key conflict in American Jewish history reflected the demographic apprehensions of assimilated Germans about the mass influx of East Europeans, then it should not be surprising that a differently structured demographic history altered community dynamics.[8] Despite the tendency of both historians and community members to impose the traditional framework on the local story, the clash and struggle that form the set piece of American Jewish history were muted in the West. In reality, although there were certainly differences—and conflicts—between German American and East European Jews, a close examination demonstrates that western stories were more complex. The development of the Jewish community of Oregon is a case in point.

Indeed, despite his emphasis on conflict (including a chapter subheading titled "Discord between German and East European Jews"), Lowenstein concedes that the local clash was not as "extreme" as in the major cities of Jewish settlement. He attributes Oregon's "softer" experience to the "sensitivity and commitment of several extraordinary Jews."[9] These individuals—Ben Selling, Ida Loewenberg, and Stephen Wise—certainly deserve recognition for their contributions. Yet the analysis here will suggest that the relative harmony between German and East European Jews in Oregon can be attributed to a variety of factors, many of which are connected to migration patterns rather than the efforts of individuals.

This chapter explores the ethnic landscape of the Oregon Jewish community, with a focus on deviations from the "tale of three migrations" and their impact on internal community relations in Portland. That the focus will be on Portland is a first indication of the distinctive migration pattern in the region: whereas scholars have shown that small Jewish settlements in much of the rest of the country were bolstered by the turn-of-the-century arrival of East Europeans, and communities such as Johnstown, Pennsylvania, or those along the Ohio River Valley, were transformed by the influx, this pattern did not hold in western states, including Oregon, where the newcomers overwhelmingly settled in Portland.[10] Without such an influx, small communities around the state experienced neither the growth nor the divides between Germans and East Europeans, Reform and Orthodox so common in other parts of the country. Rather, Jewish communities in towns such as Baker, Albany, and Jacksonville, declined and, in some cases, virtually disappeared.

Thus, with a focus on Portland, this chapter examines the ways in which a classic ethnic divide between "Germans" and East Europeans features in popular memory, drawing on the oral histories conducted in the 1970s. An analysis of the real diversity hidden by assumptions about "German" migrants, with a focus on immigrants from Posen who played a key role as a bridge between German and East European communities follows. Finally, the ways in which the "mass migration" played out in Portland are explored, with an emphasis on the composition and pace of East European—and to a lesser extent, Sephardic—immigration. This analysis demonstrates the critical ways in which these migration patterns shaped internal relations—not eliminating ethnic tensions, but rendering them less severe.

ETHNIC DIVIDES?

Because conflicts within Jewish communities so often were centered on differences over liturgy, historians have often focused on men who, unlike women, had an official role as members and officers of synagogues and burial societies. Yet an examination of women's identities provides an interesting window into ethnic divisions and identities. Women who grew up in Portland during the early twentieth century perceived a strong ethnic gap between German and East European Jews. This is reflected in the transcripts from an extensive oral history project conducted in the mid-1970s.[11] These interviews provide a sense of the ways in which women who came of age in the 1910s through the 1930s perceived their Jewish identities and their relationships with others in the community. They suggest sharp differences in religious identity between those women identifying as German and those claiming East European origins, and provide evidence of ethnically based social groupings that seem to reinforce traditional depictions of German–East European conflict.

Among those women (mostly descendants of nineteenth-century pioneers) who identified as German American, there is a striking absence of traditional markers of religious identity. Of ten such women, three mentioned no synagogue affiliation at all, and even among the Beth Israel members, many characterized their formal Jewish observances and activities as limited. Adelaide Lowenson Selling recalled going to temple as a young child with her grandparents, but she "knew nothing about the festivals," and characterized her home as "not a Jewish home, it was an American home."[12] Likewise, Gladys Trachtenberg described her parents and grandparents as "totally Reformed Jews," emphasizing the absence of ritual observance in their home.[13] Several interviews mention German families that left Judaism altogether—like the prominent Hirsch family, most of whom became Christian Scientists.[14] Even Hannah Bodner, who characterized her mother as "very religious," described traveling to nearby towns for social visits with Jewish families—rather than synagogue attendance—as the dominant Sabbath ritual.[15] This emphasis on social aspects of Jewish identity recurs in several accounts. Selling, for example, while highlighting friendships with non-Jews, also noted the strength of the social network of Reform Jewish families in Portland: "At that time, most of my friends were from the Jewish group. I don't know why, something had to do with the neighborhood, of course, something had to do with the Beth Israel Sunday School."[16]

The emphasis on Jewish social interaction was reinforced at Temple Beth Israel by the rabbinical leadership. Gladys Trachtenberg's account of one of Rabbi Jonah Wise's (1907–26) Sunday services at Temple Beth Israel vividly captures the way in which temple attendance reinforced social and class ties:

> *Gladys:* I still remember Jonah Wise trying an experiment of having services on Sunday mornings in hopes that he could get the fellows in too, as well as the old ladies and I remember one Sunday all of us came up from religious school to attend the services.. . . I don't remember how it happened, but his robe came apart, the hook must have come unhooked or something and here he was in his golf knickers, and of course, everybody burst out laughing and some of the men, including my father were in theirs also.

> *Interviewer:* I just wondered if you remembered his sermons.

> *Gladys:* Jonah—oh, he gave marvelous sermons, but he didn't speak much on Judaism at that time, except as it was related to literature. He was a marvelous scholar of English literature. Outstanding.[17]

Wise's successor, Rabbi Henry Berkowitz (1928–49), was remembered for his efforts to create an exclusive social bond among the temple's teens.[18] For example, he did not allow temple teens to bring dates from the other congregations to their socials. Felice Lauterstein Dreisen recalled,

> Rabbi Berkowitz was very profoundly determined and proud of Reform Judaism and he said, "my children are Reform Jews, and I want them to be raised as Reform Jews. I want them to be proud and to understand and to live their lives as Reform Jews and I don't want it dissipated." He not only definitely discouraged, but often prohibited [social contact with others] . . . [so] that when we had an Octagonal Party, we members of Temple Beth Israel, were we to say "Rabbi, I have a date with Johnny Shmul from Temple Neveh Zedek, can I bring him to the party?" "No," he said, "you date somebody from Temple

Beth Israel. This is where you belong." You couldn't bring a Christian date, God forbid, to an Octagonal Party. By the same token you couldn't bring somebody from the Ahavai Sholom either.[19]

Because temple families tended to be of German origin, these congregational boundaries were often expressed in ethnic terms. As Trachtenberg explained, "Let's face it, before World War II, the Portland German Jews were the biggest bunch of snobs that ever lived."[20] The emphasis on cultivating Jewish *social* ties among this group spawned several exclusively German social clubs early in the century. Yet these did open up to the expanding ranks of second-generation East European professionals—some of whom began affiliating with the temple in the 1920s and 1930s.[21] Octagonal Club member Dreisen, for example, was the daughter of a German American mother and a Russian father.

Beth Israel rabbis Stephen Wise, Jonah Wise, and Henry Berkowitz encouraged not only social cohesion among temple members, but also an ethic of service to the larger community. Stephen Wise's efforts in this regard were legendary.[22] Girls from families with a strong service ethic saw the commitment to public service as inseparable from Jewish identity. For example, Trachtenberg's Reform family was involved in extensive service activities throughout the city. Most prominent was her maternal aunt, Ida Loewenberg, at the center of Jewish service activity in Portland as the director of the social settlement, Neighborhood House. She used social ties to recruit some of the most prominent Portland Jews as volunteers for the numerous classes and other services offered at the settlement house.[23] Trachtenberg's perception of service as an outgrowth of Jewish identity is clear in her interview: "There was a strong feeling of pride in being Jewish and in being prominent and being active and contributing in every way humanly possible to society and to the growth of Portland. Yes, they were proud that they were Jews."[24] The women of the Portland section of the National Council of Jewish Women (NCJW) and the Neighborhood House board overwhelmingly came from temple families, and service through Neighborhood House was common among temple women.

The focus on social cohesion and community service among German Americans who had grown up at Beth Israel was quite different from the accounts of East European informants, nearly all of whom were affiliated with one of South Portland's more traditional shuls. The majority of women (thirteen of twenty) identifying as East European grew up in families affiliated with Shaarie Torah, Portland's first and largest Orthodox synagogue. Five women came from families affiliated with Neveh Zedek, five with the smaller Orthodox congregation Kesser Israel, and one with the Conservative Ahavai Sholom.[25]

Although Neveh Zedek was quite progressive in outlook and embraced some of the social and community activities emphasized at Temple Beth Israel, the Orthodox shuls had a more strictly religious orientation. Rabbi Joseph Fain (formerly Faivusovitch), leader of Shaarie Torah for thirty years, saw the shul as strictly a place of worship and refused to allow the building to be used even for weddings, arguing that the shul "is a place where you go and you *daven* [pray] and that's it."[26] Despite Rabbi Fain's focus on Shaarie Torah as a house of prayer, women saw it as a social center as well. Sadie Horenstein characterized Shaarie Torah as "the life of every Jew in South Portland," emphasizing the strong sense of community and the greetings and conversations during services.[27] While socializing during services — particularly in the separate women's section — helped to create strong friendships, Shaarie Torah lacked the formal social and educational opportunities for youth that characterized Beth Israel. Shaarie Torah's lack of religious school and youth organizations was typical of the South Portland congregations. Instead, the social and Jewish educational needs of South Portland children were served by Neighborhood House, and the pan-congregational Hebrew school located there.

Whereas Jewish identity among temple women was often expressed in terms of social networks and service, it was characterized by a more pervasive, all-encompassing lifestyle for the children of East Europeans growing up in South Portland. Frances Schnitzer Bricker recalled a dense network of family ties in the neighborhood, and a life that centered on Jewish identity and activities at Shaarie Torah and Neighborhood House. "We practically grew up in shul," she remembered.[28] Likewise, Frieda Gass Cohn depicted South Portland as a thriving and self-contained Jewish neighborhood.[29] The council women who came to Neighborhood House as volunteers were clearly outsiders to this world, marked by their class standing and, often, by ethnicity. As Gertrude Bachman recalled of her sewing teachers, "the women, they called them the German women."[30]

These accounts make clear, that, if grouped based on family origins, there were definite differences in experience and outlook between those claiming German origins and those identifying as East European. This provides evidence for those who characterize Portland's as a Jewish community with a classic German–East European schism. Yet, there was also overlap and evidence of blurring of ethnic lines, as women from the first East European families to move into temple society bridged the gap. Beginning in the 1920s, these women would provide the leadership for Zionist women's activities in Portland that would bring East European and German Jewish women together in common purpose.

Marguerite Swett Dilsheimer and Carrie Bromberg Hervin came from families that bridged German and East European religious institutions. The Swetts and Brombergs were among the earliest arriving and most assimilated of the East European Jews, and the men in these families were among the first to become active in community-wide organizations such as B'nai B'rith. Although Dilsheimer's grandfather and Bromberg's father were both among the leaders of Ahavai Sholom, these women attended the temple and associated primarily with German Jews. Women from both families followed affiliation patterns typical of temple women, including joining the NCJW.

A similar case was that of Fanny Kenin Friedman, the daughter of Latvian immigrants, who describes her father as "early assimilated," and recalls few contacts with Jews as she grew up in Portland.[31] Although she went to the temple's Sunday school, she associated primarily with her Christian neighbors—and was even included in their Christmas celebrations. Fanny (from the "wrong side of the tracks") did not become part of the Beth Israel social group. However, it is likely that those early social contacts—as well as her family's rather secular and civic-minded posture (her brother served on the school board from 1932 to 1942 and was a state senator from 1938 to 1942)—contributed to her involvement in voluntary organizations usually associated with German Jewish women, including the NCJW.

In addition to family background, Friedman's educational experience also facilitated her move into the socially conscious voluntary associations founded by German Jewish women. A graduate of Reed College, Friedman became a professional social worker, whose career included a number of years with the Works Progress Administration during the Depression and as an administrator of the Japanese relocation during World War II. Higher education and professional work experience helped draw second-generation women out of South Portland and into broader Jewish and civic organizations. Marguerite Swett Dilsheimer, active in all manner of Jewish organizations, was, like Friedman, a college graduate. Edith Schnitzer Goodwin, also a social worker, was involved in diverse civic organizations, serving as a Democratic precinct committeewoman and as a member of Portland's Election Board and of the League of Women Voters, an organization that also drew Friedman.

The experience of Estelle Director Sholkoff demonstrates the ways in which class allowed such women to bridge the ethnic divide. Her parents, who arrived as part of an interconnected group from the Chartorysk area of Russia in 1908, were "very orthodox, very traditional,"[32] and initially took up residence in South Portland, where they attended classes at Neighborhood House. They held memberships at Shaarie Torah and Neveh Zedek, her father attending the former alone and the latter with her mother, who preferred it because it had family seating. As her father moved from peddling to store ownership and the family moved out of the core South Portland area, Estelle shifted her activities from Neighborhood House to the B'nai B'rith Center, an institution that had more purely athletic and social functions, without the social service component central to Neighborhood House. Sholkoff went on to study at Reed College and the University of Washington, and as an adult retained membership at Shaarie Torah while also joining the temple.[33]

According to Kathryn Kahn Blumenfeld, a third-generation German Jew who spent her teen years in Portland as part of the temple community, a number of former South Portlanders were moving into the temple community during the interwar years. Teens would partake in the social and cultural activities available through the Octagonal Club when parents who belonged to one of the South Portland congregations took an additional membership at the temple: "They still belonged and kept their old membership but they wanted their children

to be members of Temple Beth Israel, so there was a transition beginning during those days of my teens."[34]

Women from the German/Reform side of the divide rarely crossed
these boundaries. An exception was Paula Heller Lauterstein. Daughter
of Rabbi Henry Nathan Heller, who served a Reform congregation in
Copenhagen, and later Portland's Conservative Neveh Zedek congregation, Lauterstein was apparently able to move as freely between the
Eastern European and the German, the traditional and the Reform, as
her father. Marrying an upwardly mobile East European Jew, Paula
was greatly involved in Beth Israel society and a religiously devout
Reform Jew.

Paula Lauterstein and other women like her were instrumental in
founding Hadassah in Portland. Unlike the NCJW, which began to
attract upwardly mobile women of East European background only
as their families affiliated with the temple, Hadassah became a broad-
based, community-wide organization for Jewish women in Portland.
For Lauterstein, Hadassah provided an outlet for the commitment to
service that was so inculcated at the temple, in a form that tapped her
profound commitment to a Jewish identity that was not fully expressed
there. Zionism attracted service-oriented Beth Israel women—such as
Ida Loewenberg and her sister, Zerlina, a librarian—and appealed
just as strongly to the daughters of Orthodox immigrants, with more
than half of those interviewed mentioning Zionism as one of their primary activities. Indeed, Hadassah emerged in the 1930s as the first
community-wide women's organization that propelled women of East
European origin into positions of leadership. By uniting Jewish women
from various segments of society in the crusade for Zionism, Hadassah
succeeded in creating a unity of purpose that set it apart from the other
Jewish women's organizations in Portland. In contrast to the congregational sisterhoods, the NCJW, and Neighborhood House (all of which
served to highlight and reinforce the gap between immigrants, ethnics,
and natives), Hadassah bridged those gaps and would become a basis
for common identity among Jewish women in Portland.

In some ways, then, women's accounts of the Portland Jewish community in the early twentieth century reinforce the popular vision of
a German–East European divide. However, they also reveal a more
complicated reality. Despite the boundaries articulated in these oral

histories, there is also evidence of a softening in the interwar period. The experiences of women from families like the Schnitzers, Swetts, and Friedmans suggest that groupings were not fixed solely on ethnic origin, but were also shaped by factors including education, wealth, profession, and civic experiences. Moreover, a closer examination of each side of the divide reveals that the "German" and "East European" categories themselves are misleading.

POSENERS: A BRIDGE BETWEEN

In the familiar tale of three migrations, phase two centers on the "German immigrants" of the mid-nineteenth century. Theirs is a story of young men breaking free of the economic and residential restrictions of German society and venturing out into the American hinterland. Beginning as peddlers, these newcomers eventually built stores, supply networks, and, in some cases, merchandising empires. Both by predisposition and as a result of living scattered in American communities, these Germans, while often maintaining some religious practices, were open to American life and enthusiastically embraced their new identity as Americans.

Yet the German-ness of the mid-nineteenth-century migration has been overstated in this popular version of events: "'Germans' made up perhaps a slim majority of the Jewish immigrants" of this period, argues Hasia Diner. In reality, she claims, the migration was far more diverse in origin—and therefore in cultural background—than has previously been understood.[35] Even among those carrying German papers, there was far more variation in cultural and religious outlook than is implied in the traditional contrast between "modern" Germans and "traditional" East Europeans, for the simple reason that the partition of Poland in the late eighteenth century brought many Polish Jews under Prussian rule. Diner particularly notes the important role of Prussian Jews from former Polish territories, such as Posen, where a relatively traditional East European population was experiencing rapid Germanization in the nineteenth century.[36]

The diversity of immigrant Jews during the "German" period has long been noted by historians of western Jewry. Norton Stern and William Kramer argued as early as the mid-1970s that "German" was a misnomer for nineteenth-century California Jewish communities. In

"The Major Role of Polish Jews in the Pioneer West," and several subsequent articles, Stern and Kramer argued that the "German" immigration to California was overwhelmingly made up of Prussian Jews from Posen, who, they claimed, "were culturally Polish Jews."[37] Likewise, Rudolf Glanz argued in the early 1980s that Poseners were "represented in a much larger proportion [within the German migration], at a number of points constituting a majority, and even the only Jewish subgroup in certain places."[38]

Although it is clear that many of Oregon's earliest Jewish settlers were Bavarian, Poseners played an important role, particularly in Portland, where they had close ties with, but were not fully integrated into, the German community. Poseners also had strong connections to the early arriving East Europeans, before there were sufficient numbers to establish separate East European institutions. Interestingly, Poseners are rarely recognized as a distinct group in community histories—at times, they are grouped with the Germans, but at others they are designated "Poles." In reality, despite ties to both groups, it appears they were fully part of neither the German nor the East European community. Rather, they might be seen as a bridge between the two—a role that significantly shaped internal community relations.

Some studies have suggested that Poseners were the dominant early group in many, if not most, nineteenth-century western Jewish communities,[39] but this was not the case in Portland. The city's early Jewish community was composed primarily of Jews from southern Germany: in 1860, the overwhelming majority of foreign-born Jews in Portland were from Bavaria and surrounding areas.[40] Then, beginning in the mid-1860s, there was an influx of Jewish immigrants from Prussia, many of whom were undoubtedly from Posen.[41] By 1880, Prussian Jews outnumbered southern Germans among foreign-born Jews in Portland by a small margin.[42] This arrival of Poseners after the Bavarians and other southern Germans were already established reflects national patterns noted by historians of the German emigration.[43]

The cultural position of the Poseners has been debated among western historians. While Stern and Kramer emphasize the Polish-ness of Posen Jews, Alan Levenson depicts Jewish Poseners as walking a middle path, maintaining religious traditionalism while embracing a German identity.[44] German identity was adopted voluntarily by many Jews in Posen because they saw Prussian authorities and German culture as more attractive than the Polish alternative. German culture and language was also imposed via mandatory Prussian schooling for Jewish children during the nineteenth century. According to Rudolf Glanz, although this Germanization led to a decline in Yiddish language and culture, religious reform was less marked.[45] Similarly, Avraham Barkai, in his work on the German Jewish immigration, characterizes these Jews as a group between—relatively eastern in their religious outlook, but attracted to and increasingly adopting German language and culture.[46]

The Germanization that took place in Posen allowed Jewish immigrants from the region to blend with those from other German regions once they reached America. Indeed, their success in blending was sufficient to obscure their role in many historical accounts of the period, where they have often not been distinguished from other Germans. Some historians characterize these immigrants as East Europeans who "masked" their true identity by presenting themselves as Germans, while others claim they were able to blend into the German migration because they had experienced genuine acculturation in Posen.[47] For example, Glanz argues that the Poseners fit in comfortably with Germans—except in the area of religion, where Poseners tended to prefer the *minhag Polin* (Polish religious ritual). He explains, "German education allowed Poseners interaction with German Jews in America; on the other hand, their religious training constituted a link with the masses of immigrants from Russian Poland and Russia."[48]

The institutions established by immigrant Jews illustrate both the unity and the divisions between these groups. For example, differences in religious ritual were key to the establishment of competing congregations in San Francisco, with Poseners joining with Jews from England, Poland, Russia, and various other locales to form Sherith Israel, while Bavarians combined with French and some American-born Jews at Emanu-El.[49] In many smaller communities, however, the Poseners threw their lot in with the Germans, creating unified congregations based on German tradition.[50] In Portland, where both groups were present in sizeable numbers by the mid-1860s, available records strongly suggest that immigrants from Posen had embraced a German

identity. Yet, while expressing their identification with German language and culture through the institutions they created, the Poseners
remained a distinct ethnic group within the Jewish community, closely
tied to—yet not fully integrated into—the Bavarian community.

To understand internal community relations in Portland, it is important to first recognize that a large majority of Jewish immigrants arriving in the nineteenth century, regardless of regional origin, had resided
elsewhere in the United States. By the time they arrived in Portland,
most Jewish immigrants from South Germany, Posen, or even Russia
had lived for several years in the American Midwest, South, or West,
often in communities with very small Jewish populations.[51] Historians
have argued about the degree to which Jews from Posen shared a common culture and language with southern Germans, but migrants to
Portland from both groups shared another language: English.[52] Their
experience living in the United States prior to arrival in Portland likely
helped to mute differences between the groups that might have been
more apparent had they come directly from Europe.

Bavarian and other southern Germans formed the city's first congregation, Beth Israel, in 1858. Until 1869, Beth Israel was Portland's sole
congregation, and, as such, it served both the southern German majority and the substantial minority from Prussia and the few from Poland
who arrived in the 1860s.[53] Several early Prussian settlers remained
Beth Israel members, but Poseners led a splinter group that left Beth
Israel in 1869 to form Ahavai Sholom, and hired fellow Posener Julius
Eckman as their first rabbi. Of the eight founders of Ahavai Sholom,
four were former Beth Israel members, and all eight listed "Prussia" as
their birthplace in the census.[54] Clearly, this was regarded within the
community as a split along ethnic lines: Beth Israel came to be known
as the "German" synagogue, and Ahavai Sholom as the "Polish."[55]

It would be tempting to assume—based on the work of Barkai,
Glanz, and others—that this split must have been rooted in the different religious outlooks of "German" and "Polish" factions. Yet the contrast between the two congregations was not that stark. For example,
although Beth Israel fully embraced Reform Judaism in the final decade
of the nineteenth century, the congregation's attitude toward Reform
during the 1870s and 1880s was, at best, mixed. On the one hand,
members found Posener rabbi Julius Eckman too traditional for their

liking. On the other, Bavarian-born rabbi Mayer May, a staunch advocate of Reform who served the Beth Israel from 1872 to 1880, created tremendous controversy and was eventually ousted—after shooting at a leader of the Conservative faction during an altercation on the streets of Portland.[56] Although Beth Israel affiliated with the Reform movement's Board of Delegates of American Israelites in 1865, it resisted adopting the *minhag America*—the American Reform ritual—until 1895.[57]

Just as Beth Israel in the 1870s and 1880s was not a congregation that was eagerly embracing reforms, Ahavai Sholom was far from being the stereotypical *"Poylishe* shul." Rather, Ahavai Sholom's development supports the notion that its Posener founders were far more German than Polish in their religious, cultural, and linguistic orientation. From its founding, Ahavai Sholom adopted the *minhag Ashkenaz* (German ritual) that was used at Beth Israel.[58] German and English—not Yiddish—were the languages used for sermons and lectures. Although English was the official language of the congregation and the 1889 constitution mandated that all officers be able to read and write in English, the congregation continued to offer lectures in German through the end of the nineteenth century.[59]

The choice of Julius Eckman as Ahavai Sholom's first rabbi is telling. Although Eckman was born in Posen, he can hardly be considered a traditionally oriented leader. Studying in Berlin under Leopold Zunz, Eckman sought a middle way between tradition and reform. Eckman fought to preserve Hebrew in the service and voiced staunch opposition to Reform innovations such as permitting worshipers to ride to services on the Sabbath, yet he also endorsed measures to modernize the service, including the use of a choir and an organ.[60] Eckman's outstanding speaking ability in German and English was one of the primary reasons that liberal congregations in the South and West, including Ahavai Sholom, saw him as an attractive leader.[61] It was only after serving various congregations in the South, as well as brief tenures at San Francisco's Emanu-El and Portland's Beth Israel, that Eckman came to Ahavai Sholom. While the congregation engaged one traditionalist (some said "fanatic") during the tumultuous 1880s, at least two of the rabbis serving Ahavai Sholom during the 1880s were German trained and had served congregations in the American South or West.[62]

The integration of the sermon into services was only one of the many modern reforms immediately embraced at Ahavai Sholom. A choir was part of the dedication service and became a regular feature of services from the congregation's founding.[63] Indeed, the congregation's first building was designed with a choir in mind.[64] The congregation's emphasis on "modern" services continued through the end of the century, when newspaper notices revealed a regular Friday night lecture program, the use of a choir in weekly and High Holiday services, and lecture topics such as "Judaism As a Positive and Universalistic Religion." David Solis-Cohen, known for his liberal views expressed in lectures with titles such as "Can a Person Be a Jew without Believing in a Supreme Being?" was a frequent speaker, delivering High Holiday and regular Shabbat sermons with some frequency.[65]

In addition to speaking regularly at Ahavai Sholom, Solis-Cohen (of the prominent Sephardic Philadelphia family) held memberships at both Beth Israel and Ahavai Sholom—a pattern of joint membership that was not uncommon.[66] While there were chilly relations between the two congregations immediately after the split, closer ties soon were revived and continued into the twentieth century. By the turn of the century, Beth Israel's Rabbi Stephen Wise made it a practice to lecture at Ahavai Sholom on the second day of Rosh Hashanah, since his own congregation observed only the first day. Wise also gave the dedicatory sermon at the opening of Ahavai Sholom's new building in 1904. The two congregations held occasional joint services, as they did after the assassination of President McKinley in 1901. A decade later, prominent members of both congregations were key players in the creation of a building fund aimed at creating a Jewish cultural and recreational center in Portland.[67]

Although it is impossible from the existing records to create a complete picture of the ritual practices of these two congregations during the nineteenth century, glimpses in congregational histories, records, and newspaper notices do not suggest stark differences. Both congregations used the German *minhag*, advertised similar types of lectures and sermons, emphasized decorum and order in the service, and even followed the same pattern of emphasizing the use of English, supplemented by occasional German lectures. Although differences in religious sensibilities did exist (evidenced most clearly by the fact that

Eckman suited Ahavai Sholom but not Beth Israel), they were relatively subtle until the 1890s, at which point the two congregations began to move in contrasting directions—Beth Israel more self-consciously embracing Reform Judaism just as Ahavai Sholom briefly fused with a Russian congregation and began defining itself as Conservative.

The key difference between the two congregations in the first several decades, then, seems to be based on a combination of ethnic identity and class rather than ritual or even language. In 1880, approximately ten years after the split, the ethnic divide between the two congregations was clear: while 33.7 percent of the city's Jewish population was born in Prussia, Prussians made up only 14.9 percent of Beth Israel's membership. Over 40 percent of Beth Israel members were South German–born, about 50 percent higher than the percentage of South Germans among the total Jewish population.[68] These numbers suggest that origin was one—but not the only—factor influencing congregational affiliation. Wealth was the other. The two were highly correlated; in part because of their earlier arrival in the city, the South Germans tended to be far more financially successful than their Prussian-born counterparts. The Poseners who remained Beth Israel members after the split—men such as Julius Loewenberg, whose mansion, a replica of a Prussian castle, stood at the foot of Washington Park—tended to be part of the economic elite.[69] At the same time, there were a few exceptional successful South Germans who joined Ahavai Sholom.[70]

As with the synagogues, the pattern of affiliation in community organizations suggests strong, but porous, lines of ethnic identification. For example, William Toll's analysis of fraternal organizations demonstrates that Prussians and South Germans joined together to form Portland's first B'nai B'rith lodge, Oregon Lodge 65, founded in 1866. According to Toll, this indicated that "whereas the synagogues might divide along regional lines, the members of the lodge overlooked those cleavages in their desire to join a modern organization with mutual insurance services."[71] Later, additional lodges were founded that attracted new generations of immigrants or native-born Portlanders, but Lodge 65 remained the province of early arriving South Germans and Poseners, suggesting that these ethnic ties did continue to resonate even as mixing in other arenas increased.

In contrast to the ethnically diverse B'nai B'rith lodge, the exclusive Concordia Club catered solely to the South Germans.[72] Even those Poseners and Poles who joined the city's economic elite were not welcome in the club—not even Julius Loewenberg, one of Portland's wealthiest merchants, a Beth Israel member, and husband of a Bavarian woman. The ethnic exclusivity of the Concordia Club was echoed in a new B'nai B'rith lodge made up primarily of second-generation South Germans, established in the final decade of the nineteenth century. [73]

It is interesting that these increasing social distinctions between South Germans and Poseners coincided with the arrival of larger numbers of Russian Jews. While the South Germans of the Concordia Club and Beth Israel kept their distance, the level of interaction between the Poseners and the newcomers was far greater. From its founding, Ahavai Sholom had included a small number of Russian- and Polish-born Jews. During the period when the elite Concordia Club took shape in the late 1880s, larger numbers of Russian Jews began arriving in Portland, in a flow that would increase the total population of the Jewish community more than tenfold by World War I.[74] The vanguard of this group quickly created links with established members of Ahavai Sholom. That the newly arriving Russians looked to Ahavai Sholom rather than to Beth Israel for social, religious, and business connections is an indication of the middle place that the congregation occupied in terms of the class status, regional origin, and, by the 1890s, religious orientation.

Although ethnicity seemed to be a key factor defining that middle place in the late nineteenth century, religious orientation became increasingly important. While Poseners' ethnic difference was enough to disqualify them from Concordia Club membership (even when they were wealthy members of Beth Israel), in most discussions of community relations, the Poseners do not appear as a distinct group.[75] Descendants of Poseners (who, like the Loewenberg sisters, were raised at Temple Beth Israel) became indistinguishable from other sons and daughters of mid-nineteenth-century pioneers. Women from these families joined the NCJW, the temple sisterhood, and were likely thought of as "Germans." In some cases, individuals redefined themselves ethnically, perhaps as a way of distancing themselves from the East European newcomers. For example, Gervais's McKinley Mitchell, a native Oregonian born in 1858, was listed in the 1860, 1870, and 1880 censuses as Michael Mitchell, son of Polish immigrants. By 1880, however, his first name had been changed to the more American "McKinley," and by 1900 he had transformed his father into a Russian and his mother a German. In the 1910 census, he listed both parents as Germans, and in 1920, he apparently told the census taker that they were German-speaking Europeans.[76]

Those who remained at Ahavai Sholom seemed more removed from that elite group and more connected with the Russians. The decisions made by the two congregations in the wake of a pair of fires in 1923 illustrate the contrast.[77] Temple Beth Israel opted to build its new structure in a tony Northwest neighborhood that was home to many of its members. Ahavai Sholom debated three options: to rebuild on the old site (near, but not in, the South Portland neighborhood), to fuse with Neveh Zedek Talmud Torah, or to build on the East Side, where many of its congregants were, by then, residing.[78] Although the choice was made to remain on the old site, consideration of a merger with Neveh Zedek is evidence of the continuing close ties between Ahavai Sholom's membership and the most progressive of the immigrant Russian congregations. Although Ahavai Sholom was founded squarely in the "German" period and by a group that included many who identified as German Americans, it remained a cultural bridge, softening the distance between the two "waves" of migrants. Interestingly, Ahavai Sholom would play a similar role in connecting with the growing Sephardic community in the 1920s—lacking a Sunday school of their own, many Sephardic families sent their children to the Ahavai Sholom Sunday school.[79]

"MASS MIGRATION" IN PORTLAND

In August 1899, Congregation Talmud Torah in Portland, Oregon, placed an advertisement for High Holiday services in the *American Hebrew News*. The services, according to the notice, would be led by the "Reverend Dr. M. Mosessohnn . . . with the assistance of a well-trained choir, under the leadership of David N. Mosessohn," and would include "musical selections from Sultzer, Weintraub, Love, Minkowsky and other Jewish church musical celebrities" and "sermons in English and German."[80]

The tone of the services described in this advertisement would not be at all surprising for a late-nineteenth-century Reform German American congregation such as Portland's Beth Israel, or for its sister (and heavily Posener) congregation, Ahavai Sholom. However, Congregation Talmud Torah was neither a Reform synagogue nor a congregation of "German" Americans. Rather, it was one of two congregations of immigrant Russian Jews founded in Portland in the 1890s. The portrait of religious observance at both Talmud Torah and its sister congregation Neveh Zedek emerging from newspaper articles and advertisements in the 1890s is striking in the emphasis on order and orchestrated music, and the absence of Yiddish. They provide a sharp contrast to accounts of religious services in the synagogues of Russian immigrants elsewhere in America, where "irritating noise," and "commotion," were sources of embarrassment to established American Jews.[81]

Examination of these congregations provides a glimpse into the religious orientation and identities of early arriving Russians and helps explain the relative cohesion among ethnic groups in Portland's Jewish community. Just as Ahavai Sholom and the Posener immigrants helped bridge the fabled gap between Germans and Russians, the particular migration stream that brought Russian Jews to Portland also served to mitigate conflict. Many Russian Jewish immigrants to Portland in the 1880s and 1890s already had experience in America, and therefore, like the mid-nineteenth-century pioneers, were already English speakers when they arrived in the Rose City (as Portland became known in late 1880s). Moreover, many came from the South Pale, where Jewish communities were less insular and more exposed to modernization efforts than those in other parts of the Pale. In addition, a number were veterans of the Jewish colonization movement, and had spent several years or more in frontier communities or agricultural settlements in America. This group quickly assumed leadership positions within Portland's emerging immigrant community and played a key role in creating institutions that were modernist in outlook. Like the Poseners, they served as a bridge between the established community and the more traditional, less assimilated East Europeans who would follow them.

Isaac Swett, son of an Am Olam member who had traveled to Oregon hoping to establish a communal, agrarian settlement, became one of the most prominent men of this group. Joining Ahavai Sholom, Swett became a congregational leader as well as a prominent B'nai B'rith activist. Swett's activities demonstrate the potential for ethnic fluidity in Jewish Portland. A Russian arriving in the United States during the period of mass migration, Swett became secretary of the "Posener" synagogue, led a brief merger in the mid-1890s between it and one of the "Russian" synagogues, and later, was a key force in the B'nai B'rith Building Association that brought Germans, Prussians, Poles, and Russians together in a community-wide effort. Swett's wife, Julia, served as president of the local section of NCJW—a group strongly associated with the elite German American women of Temple Beth Israel.

Likewise, Isaac Gevurtz, another early arriving East European who easily crossed boundaries, served as president of Ahavai Sholom in the 1890s when it merged with the "Russian" congregation Neveh Zedek. Gevurtz had arrived in the United States in 1860, settling first in San Francisco as a cigar manufacturer. After losing his business in the Panic of 1873 and divorcing his first wife, he moved to Portland with his three sons and established a furniture business in the early 1880s. Shortly thereafter, he married Cacelie Gerson, of German Jewish origin. By the turn of the century, Gevurtz held joint memberships in Ahavai Sholom and Beth Israel.[82]

The affinity between Ahavai Sholom and the Russian congregation Neveh Zedek, which led to their brief merger in the mid-1890s, appears to have been due less to a shared East European or traditional outlook than to a mutual interest in modernization, driven by individuals including Swett and Gevurtz. Neveh Zedek embraced the same modern practices that prevailed at Ahavai Sholom, including the use of a choir, instrumental music, and English (and sometimes German) language sermons, and even held Sunday services in addition to those on the Sabbath. Advertisements from the 1890s described services as "orchestrated" and "well-ordered," revealing a clear effort to identify the congregation as modern. Although the merger dissolved within a few years, Neveh Zedek continued on this modernist path. Neveh Zedek remained a Conservative congregation in the twentieth century, ultimately merging again with Ahavai Sholom in the post–World War II period to form Neveh Shalom.

The development of congregations such as Neveh Zedek (and sister congregation, Talmud Torah, which merged with Neveh Zedek in 1902) reflects distinctive western migration patterns that shaped Portland's immigrant Jewish community at the turn of the century.[83] Portland's relatively remote location was key to this selective migration. Migrants choosing Portland tended to share occupational, cultural, and religious orientations that helped ease their transition to the Rose City, reinforcing a relatively modernist outlook and limiting conflict with the established community. Distance slowed the influx of newcomers to Portland, and this, coupled with the historic acceptance of Jews in the city, meant that established Jews worried less about a possible anti-Semitic backlash than did their counterparts in the East. Cultural conflicts were also reduced because East European immigrants to Portland often had sojourned in other American cities and had begun the process of adaptation to their new country prior to their arrival in Portland.

Because Portland's economy was far less industrialized than economies of the East and Midwest, it drew migrants hoping to enter the commercial sector rather than those seeking factory work. Like the city's German Jews, later-arriving East Europeans tended to gravitate toward trade, often starting out as junk dealers or in other types of petty merchandising. Although there were significant differences in the scale of their enterprises, the two groups, in contrast to their counterparts in the East, were unlikely to meet as factory owners and laborers on opposing sides in labor struggles.

In his analysis of the occupational profiles of immigrant Jews in Seattle, Portland, Charleston, and Galveston, William Toll shows that far fewer were found in the industrial sector and far more in trade than in eastern cities. In the four cities, "only 22.5 percent of East European men were skilled workers, while over 60 percent were proprietors or clerks in settled locations." Toll demonstrates that of East Europeans in the peripheral cities in 1900, 35.4 percent and 27.2 percent, respectively, held high white-collar or low white-collar positions—50 percent more than worked in such occupations in New York. Likewise, roughly half the percentage of Portland men worked in skilled or semiskilled occupations as in New York. This distinct occupational distribution, Toll suggests, means that "either immigrant merchants selectively left the ports of entry, or the skilled workers who resettled in cities such as Portland or Charleston opened junk shops, secondhand stores and groceries."[84]

Analysis of the regional origins of Portland Jews suggests the former. Despite popular accounts that suggest that the choice of destination within the United States was dictated by chance, in fact, a systematic self-selection process, based on occupation and personal connections, was at work. Portland lacked the industrial and craft positions abundant in many eastern and midwestern cities, but it provided trade-oriented newcomers excellent opportunities. While some individuals transferred craft skills learned in Russia or elsewhere in America directly to Portland, a larger number used their experience in trade and their family connections to establish merchandising businesses.[85] Newcomers often entered the trade sector as junk dealers and peddlers, gradually building up more substantial businesses as merchants dealing in a wide variety of goods.[86] Many of these families established diverse retail and wholesale businesses. For example, after spending eight years in North Dakota, Marcus Gale arrived in Portland in 1890 and began peddling. The 1910 Portland City Directory listed him as the owner of two businesses on Third Street in Portland. Moress Barde followed the same occupational trajectory— beginning as a junk dealer in 1900, he had opened a plumbing supply business by 1910.[87] Likewise, Sam Schnitzer, who arrived in Portland in 1905, was listed in the 1910 city directory as a peddler. By 1920, he moved from peddling scrap metal with a horse and wagon to establishing the Alaska Junk Company, from which he built a major shipping company and the legendary Schnitzer fortune.[88] Such examples demonstrate that many Portland newcomers were not tailors who turned to trade in response to local conditions. Rather, they were individuals who chose Portland because their skills matched opportunities in the local economy.

Once the immigrants discovered business opportunities in Portland, word spread to extended family, resulting in chain migrations. A Nudelman family history illustrates both the immigrants' concentration in trade, and family connections that helped to support newcomers:

> Joseph [Nudelman] opened a meat market with Joe Steinberg. . . . Son Hymen left school to be the delivery boy. Joseph's brother Sam went into the grocery business in the store-room next door to the meat market. Maurice worked in the grocery store. . . . In 1904, Jacob Levitt had some problems with his business in Wisconsin and Joseph went there to help them out. They shipped all the merchandise to Portland where Levitt opened and successfully operated a general store. Uncle Barde was in the scrap metal business and Uncle Bromberg was in the picture framing business and sometime later bought a dry-goods store. Uncles Phillip and Samuel were in the cartage business. Some years later Phillip purchased and ran a feed store.[89]

Clusters of Portland families from small towns in the Russian Pale are evidence of the chain migrations that led siblings, cousins and others to follow the early migrants from their home towns to Portland. Many hailed from the southern areas of the Jewish Pale in Russia, in contrast with Jewish migrants to eastern industrial cities, who were more likely to come from the northern Pale.[90] For example, at least seven families from the neighboring towns of Chartorysk, Vladimirets, and Steppan, in the southwest's Volhynia Province, followed a relative, known to descendants as Fetter (uncle) Fox directly to Portland.[91] Estelle Director Sholkoff's account of Fox's efforts is typical: "My dad came to Portland because his older brother was here. . . . His name was Shiah Director . . . and the reason that Shiah came to Portland was that there was a man called 'Vetter [sic] Fox.' I guess he was the uncle of all the people in the area."[92] In addition to this group from Volhynia Province, another cluster of at least twelve families originated in Odessa, with additional families hailing from smaller towns near that cosmopolitan Black Sea city. Many in the Volhynia group came directly to Portland on arrival in the United States; others, including many of those from Odessa, migrated in a more gradual manner, with at least thirty-one family groups residing for a period in midwestern or western states prior to their arrival in Portland in 1890s.[93]

Regional and occupational backgrounds were mutually reinforcing and may have shaped not only the economic trajectories of arriving immigrants, but also their orientation toward the broader community. Jews from the southern Pale were much more likely than those from the north to be merchants, most often dealing in agricultural goods. [94] Accustomed to close contact with suppliers and consumers among the non-Jewish population and hailing from regions with less dense Jewish populations, they may have been more comfortable with peripheral destinations and less-concentrated Jewish populations.[95] For these migrants, occupational and communal backgrounds likely eased their transition to Portland.

Such experiences were reinforced for the many "gradual" or "step" migrants by sojourns in America, just as had been the case for the mid-nineteenth-century German migrants. For example, among the early Russian migrants were a number of families who had tried farming in the United States prior to arrival in Portland. The largest—and ultimately most influential—group of such migrants was a contingent of settlers who arrived in Oregon via North Dakota. At least eighteen Portland families settled in the Dakotas during the 1880s prior to relocating to the Rose City,[96] including at least fourteen families from of the Painted Woods farm colony.[97] Similarly, Leon Swett came to Oregon as a member of the idealistic Am Olam group to establish New Odessa, a communal agrarian colony in Southern Oregon. Although Swett left the group when it reached Oregon, he expressed his commitment to their "back to the soil" motto by taking up farming outside of Portland.[98]

Other future Portlanders resided first in places as diverse as New Jersey, New Mexico, and Missouri. For example, the Labby family briefly resided in New Jersey's agricultural Woodbine Colony before migrating to Portland.[99] As Manly Labby reported in an oral history, when his father decided to leave Woodbine he "tossed a coin to decide whether we would go to Oregon or Argentina."[100] The elder Labby's reasons for limiting his choices to Oregon and Argentina are not clear, but it seems significant that he apparently did not consider the major industrial metropolitan areas of New York or Philadelphia, each within a few hours of Woodbine. Although his decision-making process seems crude, it suggests that individuals considering Oregon made conscious decisions to look to the frontier.

The migration from North Dakota and other rural settings to Portland represented the end of the agrarian experiment for most of these families, with very few attempting farming in Oregon after the dissolution of the short-lived New Odessa Colony in Southern Oregon.[101] Yet the experiences of Jewish immigrant families who lived first in cities, towns, and rural areas of the South, Midwest, and West helped to shape their adaptation to Portland and the development of Jewish community there. This reinforces the critical point that many early members of Portland's Russian Jewish community were not greenhorns. Whether they settled first in rural North Dakota, California, New Mexico, or Minnesota, these migrants made their initial adjustment to America *prior* to their arrival in Portland—and they made that adjustment in places where Jewish infrastructure and community were limited. As a result, many were able to speak English. They had encountered American officials ranging from land claim officers to schoolteachers to bankers. They had experience negotiating train schedules, grain markets, and bank loans.

Those who joined in the Jewish agricultural settlements of North Dakota demonstrate the range of experiences that such gradual migrants brought to Portland. At Painted Woods Colony, the Dellar, Katz, Nudelman, Bromberg, and Lauterstein families had ample opportunity to learn about American business and government practices. Arriving in North Dakota in the spring of 1882, the first group of twenty-two families took up homestead claims and purchased railroad land for the colony. Although locals perceived the colonists as hopelessly foreign and inept, and protested their attempt to cluster in a village rather than settling on scattered homesteads, many of the settlers did succeed in proving their claims and adapting to the requirements of their new situation. In 1887, "in accordance with a call issued by the county clerk under instructions from the county board," the colonists elected Joseph Nudelman, Solomon Dellar, and another colonist to the school board. They also became involved in local issues such as the annexation of their township by McClean County. In 1888, the colonists platted a township (to be known as Nudelman, North Dakota) and filed their plans with the McClean County Register of Deeds.[102] Thus, while the concentrated settlement at Painted Woods helped shelter these immigrants and provide them a mutually supportive group experience, it also provided early opportunities for them to get involved in civic affairs. In times of need, Painted Woods colonists learned to tap into the support of the established Jewish community. Their chief sponsor, St. Paul Reform rabbi Judah Wechsler, visited the colony and helped resolve disputes with neighbors on several occasions.[103]

The Russian Jewish immigration to Portland, while never rivaling the flood of migrants to eastern Jewish communities, was substantial. Portland's Jewish community as a whole topped eight thousand by the end of the 1910s (roughly 3 percent of the city's total population) and approximately six thousand of these lived in the immigrant district in South Portland.[104] This made Jews one of the larger and more visible minority groups in Portland—there were about half as many Italians in the city, and the African American, Chinese, and Japanese populations each numbered under two thousand.[105]

The South Portland neighborhood sported a full array of shops catering to the Jewish immigrants, a vibrant settlement house, and at least four synagogues.[106] By the 1970s, many former residents looked back nostalgically on a neighborhood that they characterize as insular and traditional.[107] Yet the emphasis on orthodoxy and traditionalism in such reminiscences is relative. Critical examination of the institutions created in South Portland in the 1890s demonstrates that the foundation laid by the early arriving Russians at the turn of the century was notable for its level of acculturation and emphasis on modernity. The background shared by many of the immigrants and, particularly, by the leadership group that included a number of colony veterans, set the tone for Portland's Russian Jewish community and its institutions.

The disproportionate number of immigrants who hailed from Odessa came from an environment that was cosmopolitan and multiethnic. The Jewish community of Odessa was therefore among the most modern in the Pale of Settlement. Many of Odessa's Jews attended Russian schools and were exposed to the Haskalah (Jewish enlightenment) movement. Indeed the Jewish agrarian movement that spawned Painted Woods, North Dakota, and similar experiments originated in Odessa. Indications of such modernist outlooks *prior to migration* appear in several oral histories.[108] Although these oral histories also demonstrate that many Jewish immigrants to Portland in this period were quite traditional in religious practice, the early presence of an unusually large proportion of Jews from the Odessa area helped infuse Portland's first Russian Jewish institutions with a distinctly modernist outlook.

Examination of synagogue development creates a clear picture of an immigrant Jewish community that was relatively acculturated. Despite community historians' emphasis on the traditionalism of the new immigrants,[109] the first congregations that the Russians founded, Neveh Zedek and Talmud Torah, clearly made efforts to demonstrate modernism over traditionalism. Newspaper coverage of services and events at Neveh Zedek suggest a tone and ritual that was relatively progressive. For example, advertisements in the 1890s in the *American Hebrew News* reveal practices including a choir and a sermon in English, and are strikingly similar to ads for Ahavai Sholom. Services are described as well-ordered and carefully orchestrated—a clear message that the congregation had rejected more traditional forms that were often seen by acculturated American Jews as disorderly and cacophonous. A High Holiday advertisement from September 1894 boasted, "Congregation Neveh Zedek Reverend Bluestein officiating, has his choir of young men thoroughly under good practice and the services . . . will be conducted in good form."[110] The following year, the paper noted that the choir sang "all the concerted numbers in perfect time and precision," and that the Yom Kippur High Holiday service included an English-language sermon by David Solis-Cohen.[111] When a new Torah was dedicated at Neveh Zedek in 1895, the service included violin solos by the rabbi's son.[112] According to notices published in 1900, services at Neveh Zedek were being held on Friday evenings, Saturday mornings, and *Sunday* mornings. An English-language sermon was the highlight of the Sunday services.[113]

Neveh Zedek's modern style was echoed in a second Russian congregation, Talmud Torah, also founded during the 1890s. It published similar notices in the *American Hebrew News* prior to merging with Neveh Zedek in 1902. In 1899, when Talmud Torah dedicated its new building, the list of speakers included the ubiquitous Solis-Cohen, who had delivered a lecture as part of the High Holiday services the previous year.[114] Speakers at the dedication, the newspaper announced, would "address the audience in English and German," but not Yiddish.

[115] Talmud Torah tried to reach out to the established community, advertising its "Channukah [*sic*]" ball in 1899 as "a swell affair" that "should be patronized by everyone as it is deserving of support by all our liberal co-religionists."[116] Like Neveh Zedek, Talmud Torah congregation had a choir by 1899, which, it advertised, was training to perform a variety of musical selections for the High Holiday services.[117]

Such unorthodox proceedings at the first Russian synagogues in Portland are evidence of the distinct path this community was traveling in comparison to eastern Jewish communities, where Orthodox congregations dominated in the early years of the migration. As Gerald Sorin notes, "by 1890 . . . the majority of Jewish congregations were Orthodox. And by 1910, 90 percent of more than two thousand synagogues in America called themselves Orthodox."[118] Yet in Portland, the first Orthodox congregation was not founded until 1902, when a group broke away from Neveh Zedek to form Shaarie Torah.[119]

To understand the development of the first Russian congregations in the 1890s, one must look again at the North Dakota colony veterans who were among their founders.[120] Their Reform Jewish sponsors — and certainly their Christian neighbors — depicted the North Dakota colonists as traditional in their religious practice and outlook, but evidence suggests that they, like their counterparts in other Jewish colonies, were far more open to modern religious practices than most East European immigrants.[121] Rabbi Benjamin Papermaster, a Kovno native recruited to serve as spiritual leader to a North Dakota community, found that it "consisted chiefly of younger men and women who were anxious to adjust themselves to a new life in this country, and when they discovered that in this young rabbi they had one who had liberal views in the practice of Judaism, they were happy and enthusiastic."[122] Such *relative* liberalism in religious views among agricultural colonists can be attributed to factors including the secular orientation of the ideological leadership of the "back to the soil" movement, the realities of frontier life, and the regional roots of the movement in the South Pale, where a variety of religious reforms had advanced further than in the North.[123] Indeed, Rabbi Papermaster made the connection between the regional origin and religious orientation of his North Dakota congregation, noting that one North Dakota community consisted of sixty Jewish families, "mostly from the Ukraine," who liked his "liberal" views.[124] This is not to say that all settlers were reformers or that orthodox religious practice was completely discarded. Indeed, there is evidence of colonists going to great lengths to obtain kosher meat, for example.[125] But frontier settlements required flexibility. Individuals opting to leave well-established communities might have been those who had already accepted change or those who shared some degree of flexibility. These factors help explain the rapid embrace of modern practices in Portland's pioneer congregations.

Rabbinical leadership further shaped this modernist outlook. Odessa-born Nehemiah Mosessohn, who served as rabbi first at Talmud Torah and later at the unified Neveh Zedek Talmud Torah, considered himself a "rebel from orthodoxy." Prior to arrival in Portland, he had served congregations in Dallas (Texas) and Oakland. In Oregon he attended the University of Oregon School of Law and founded and edited Portland's *Jewish Tribune* from 1902 to 1919, which served as the sole press outlet for the entire Jewish community.[126] A later Neveh Zedek Talmud Torah rabbi, Henry Nathan Heller, had served previously at a Reform temple in Denmark.[127] Max Levin, one of Talmud Torah's spiritual leaders, had spent nearly a decade in Kansas prior to his arrival in Portland.[128]

Although the arrival of more traditional immigrants in Portland after the turn of the century led to the establishment of several Orthodox congregations, the foundations built by these liberal leaders of the late-nineteenth-century influx continued to shape key institutions. For example, although the founders of Shaarie Torah were seeking a more traditional approach to Judaism, they, too, were relatively acculturated. The first president of Shaarie Torah was Joseph Nudelman, an Odessa native who had spent nearly two decades farming, mining, and ranching in the American West, prior to settling in Portland in 1899.[129] Nudelman and his family retained close ties through marriage and business to prominent Neveh Zedek families.[130]

The Portland Hebrew School, incorporated in 1913 and based at South Portland's Neighborhood House, was indicative of broader impact of this modernist outlook on the South Portland community.[131] Supported by the two Conservative congregations (Ahavai Sholom and Neveh Zedek Talmud Torah) and the Reform Temple, the school was designed as a modern educational institution serving South Portland's

Conservative and Orthodox families. By the 1920s, it was a meeting ground for children from the various South Portland congregations and, like Neighborhood House, served as an agent of Americanization.[132]

From its founding, the school saw its mission in terms of modernization of Jewish education, Americanization, and cultural Zionism. Israel Bromberg, a Painted Woods veteran and lifelong Zionist, became the first chairman of the board.[133] Bromberg, with his devotion to cultural Judaism, Hebrew study, Zionism, and modern learning, was in many ways representative of the type of Jew from the South Pale who became involved in the agricultural colonization movement. His daughter describes him as a learned man, devoted to Judaism and to the ideals of the enlightenment:

> He very avidly embraced every opportunity to get possession of or have access to reading all these different books other than just the traditional Hebraic literature, the Torah, the Talmud and all those sort of things. His interests were very broad. He was interested not only in what our prophets said but what Roman philosophers, the Greek philosophers said, but in any country's outstanding men of thought and intelligence and in his subsequent writings he would refer to them and make reference to the various writers, the historians.[134]

Bromberg's modernist outlook strongly shaped the school, seen by its directors as "not so much a setting for religious instruction but a vehicle for instilling in their children and grandchildren an appreciation for a culture, which could contribute to their moral stability in a very mobile secular society."[135] This modern outlook at the primary institution for Jewish education among Portland's orthodox children is striking, and speaks to broader community identity.

After the turn of the century, and particularly by the 1910s, increasing numbers of direct migrants were making their way to Portland. Unlike many of their predecessors who had sojourned elsewhere in America, these newcomers were following earlier arriving relatives and townspeople, enabling them to proceed directly from their port of entry to their final destination of Portland. As Hansa Brill Shapiro, who arrived in Oregon in late 1906, put it, "We came right straight to

Portland, Oregon. We left Russia for America, and we chose our own America and instead of New York we chose Portland, Oregon."[136] Not surprisingly, these migrants tended to be more traditional in terms of both religion and culture—and the community was now in a position to meet the needs of such migrants. For example, kosher food was readily available and Orthodox synagogues using the Russian ritual were being established. Arriving more directly from Europe, the new-comers were Yiddish speakers, and many took advantage of English and other classes that Neighborhood House offered.

The more traditional orientation of the newcomers is evident in the synagogues they established. Many joined Shaarie Torah, where Rabbi Fain, who served from 1916 to 1946, emerged as the dean of Oregon Orthodox rabbis. As the migration swelled, two new Orthodox shuls, Linath Hazedek (1914) and Kesser Israel (1916), were founded, as well as a Sephardic congregation, Ahavath Achim (1910).[137] Popular memory paints these congregations and the South Portland commu-nity as strictly Orthodox and, at times, very old world. Lowenstein describes Shaarie Torah as retaining "the Orthodox forms from the old country." Augusta ("Gussie") Kirshner Reinhardt, whose family belonged first to Shaarie Torah and later to Kesser Israel, described the neighborhood as like a "shtetl" and remembered men being called from the streets to attend daily minyan.[138] Manly Labby recalled that "the customs and life style of the people in this congregation [Shaarie Torah] were completely in keeping with the life my family had lived in Russia."[139] And Frances Schnitzer Bricker, whose father attended Shaarie Torah (and sometimes helped to complete a minyan at Kesser Israel, across the street from their house), spoke of "Jewishness" as "a deep thing" when she was growing up: "The house and the activities all revolved in Jewishness."[140]

The new congregations undoubtedly served a more traditional population and prided themselves on the maintenance of orthodoxy. Yet, as at many congregations, individual members represented a range in personal practice. For example, Mollie Blumenthal recalled that though her father belonged to Kesser Israel and served as that congre-gation's secretary, he was not particularly religious: "My mother never did keep kosher. . . . My father only got religious when he thought he was dying . . . then he got terribly religious . . . but otherwise, fasting on the holidays, he didn't go for things like that."[141] Among the congregants at Shaarie Torah were colony veterans, including Joseph Nudelman, who had spent two decades in the West before helping to found the congregation. Families such as the Nudelmans and Labbys (who had chosen between Oregon and Argentina) gravitated toward traditional congregations when they were available, but were, apparently, willing to compromise when they were not. Thus, it appears that among the Orthodox—as among other migrants to remote locales— self-selection took place favoring those who were more flexible in their practice, and that this had an impact on the congregations that formed in Portland. The oral history of Rachel Fain Schneider, the daughter of Rabbi Fain, is revealing, as she makes comparisons between western orthodoxy and that in the East and Midwest. Schneider recalled that her father would frequently host visiting dignitaries from the East, and that, even as the daughter of the leading Orthodox rabbi in the community, she was unfamiliar with traditional expectations:

> When it came time to say goodbye, without thinking, I said "It's so nice to meet you, sir" and the hand [of the visitor] didn't come up and I felt about yea big, but I talked to my Dad and he said "Well, that's the difference between your East and West and you just don't do those things [shake hands with a man]."[142]

Schneider had a similar experience when she accompanied her father to a rabbinical conference in Chicago. There—unlike at home in Portland—he required her to leave her purse in the hotel when they went to another rabbi's house for Shabbat dinner, saying "Here, you don't do it [carry anything on Shabbat]." Her father suggested that she just put her lipstick in her pocket—but she ended up being criticized at the dinner even for that. Schneider concluded of her father, "In comparison to the rabbis that I met back East and middle west and in Portland that came visiting, he was a very broad-minded man. He didn't object to dates, providing, of course, if he knew who you were going with, or swimming, or dancing. Back East, forget it."[143] That Rabbi Fain encouraged the Orthodox community to send their children to the progressive-minded Hebrew School at Neighborhood House is evidence of what his daughter called his "broad-mindedness"—and

appears to have been fairly characteristic of Portland's Orthodox community, even after the arrival of the more traditional direct migrants.

Such an attitude, rooted largely in the selective migration pattern that brought newcomers to the South Portland neighborhood,
contributed to a relatively cohesive community. For example, within
a generation, by 1918, Jews of German, Polish, and Russian descent
unified their separate B'nai B'rith lodges.[144] Even earlier, going back
to the 1890s, a series of English-language newspapers had served the
entire Jewish community, reporting on events at all the community's
institutions and frequently advocating cooperation among the various
groups.[145] Leading newcomers worked together with old-timers—and
often took leadership roles—in a variety of projects, including the B'nai
B'rith Building Association, the unified Hebrew school, and, particularly, the numerous Zionist organizations that blossomed in Portland
shortly after the turn of the century.[146]

The relatively harmonious relations between established "German"
families and East Europeans in Portland, noted in several histories, has
been attributed to both a Jewish occupational structure that minimized
class tensions and a few extraordinary individuals who led the effort
to welcome and integrate the newcomers.[147] Yet the immigrants' background and prior experiences in America and Europe were also key
factors. Overlapping groups of colony veterans, immigrants who had
resided elsewhere in America, and immigrants from the southern provinces of the Pale moved quickly from leadership of immigrant institutions to larger, community-wide endeavors, and gaps between them
and early arriving Germans were bridged by the Poseners.

SEPHARDIM: THE *OTHER* TURN-OF-THE-CENTURY MIGRANTS

The ethnic mix of Portland's Jewish community was further complicated by the presence of a small but significant Sephardic population.
Although Sephardim are generally thought of as the country's earliest
wave of Jewish immigrants, arriving in colonial times, with the exception of a few American-born Sephardim such as David Solis-Cohen,
the Portland Sephardic community began arriving after the turn of
the twentieth century. Cultural differences between Germans and East
Europeans were actually less profound than those between these groups
and the Sephardim, who generally spoke Ladino (an archaic form of

Spanish written with Hebrew letters, also known as Judeo-Spanish) rather than Yiddish, and whose rituals, foods, and home practices were distinctive. Indeed, when the first Sephardim arrived in Portland and Seattle, the established community sometimes questioned whether they were really Jewish.[148] Despite this gulf, Sephardic informants—generally from the second generation—emphasize acceptance and integration in accounts of their experiences growing up in South Portland.

Sephardim are usually overlooked in national discussions of turn-of-the-century immigration because their numbers were tiny in comparison to those of East Europeans. On the West Coast, although the latter still outnumbered the former, the direct Sephardic immigration in this period was more significant in relative terms. Those Sephardim who came to Portland were part of a larger wave that brought immigrants from the Ottoman Empire, principally from Marmara, Rodosto, and Rhodes, to Seattle. Beginning with two pioneers who arrived in that city in 1902, Seattle's Sephardic population grew to over two thousand by the 1920s, making it the second-largest Sephardic community in the United States, after New York. By that time, it boasted three congregations based on the three main geographic origins.[149]

The first Sephardim to settle in Portland arrived from Seattle in 1909, and by 1910 there were sufficient numbers for a minyan. Twelve attended High Holiday services that year, with the community rapidly increasing in subsequent years—to forty in 1911, and eighty in 1912, when it was (briefly) the second largest on the West Coast.[150] Another

Mayo & Hasson was one of many small Sephardic businesses, n.d. Credit: Oregon Jewish Museum wave from Rhodes (by then under Italian rule) would arrive as refugees in the late 1930s. Although that group attempted to set up a separate congregation, as had their counterparts in Seattle, the size of the Portland community was not sufficient to support multiple institutions, and by 1915, the group reunited. Calling themselves Ahavath Achim (Brotherly Love), perhaps as a hopeful gesture, the group formally founded a synagogue in 1916. Indeed, they had difficulty supporting even one congregation and relied on the financial assistance of the established community, most notably Ben Selling. They met in the B'nai B'rith Building until they purchased a site, built, and, in 1930, dedicated their building. Even then, they were not able to afford a rabbi, instead bringing in readers and cantors, mostly from Seattle. Of particular note was Seattle cantor Jack Maimon, who conducted High Holiday and Purim services for the congregation for over fifty years, beginning in 1933.

Like their counterparts in Seattle and their Ashkenazic predecessors, Portland's Sephardic community concentrated in the trade sector. Connected groups of relatives and others sharing hometown origins established homes and businesses in close proximity to one another, principally in South Portland. For example, Joy Babani Russell's parents, both from Istanbul, arrived in Seattle just before the World War I and subsequently moved to Portland, residing next door to and operating a fish market with the Policar family.[151] Particularly notable was the Menashe family, consisting of seven brothers from Rhodes who operated a row of stores near one another.[152] Unlike the first wave of East European immigrants, who had often spent years in the United States before arriving in Portland, these Sephardim came more directly to the Pacific Northwest (although a number spent time in Seattle before relocating to Portland).

As new and relatively unacculturated immigrants with a language and religious tradition that set them apart, it is not surprising that the Sephardim turned to one another for community, establishing their own synagogue and social network. As Joy Babani Russell, born in Portland in 1924, explained, "There were a lot of Ashkenazim there [in South Portland] at that time. They were not familiar to us in their ways and we, of course, were not familiar to them."[153] Especially for

Nessim Menashe at his shoe store, c. 1916.   Policar family celebrating Sukkot, 1910.
Credit: Oregon Jewish Museum   Credit: Oregon Jewish Museum

the adult immigrants "there was not a free mingling," according to Beulah Menashe Schauffer.[154] Joanna Kapalota Menashe, who was born in Turkey in 1907 and came to Portland as David Menashe's wife, recalled keeping "very much to ourselves." Mirroring responses from East Europeans who tended to perceive the diverse South Portland neighborhood as shtetl-like, Kapalota Menashe recalled that "all of the neighborhood, between ten blocks they were all Spanish Jewish. All of us were together."[155]

Despite such perceptions, there is strong evidence of fluid relationships, particularly among the younger generation. Even Kapalota Menashe, despite her assertion that she socialized primarily with other Sephardic Jews, was a member of both Hadassah and the Ahavai Sholom sisterhood.[156] Interestingly, Ahavai Sholom, which played such a crucial role as a bridge between the established "German" community and the East Europeans, played a similar central role in bridging the gap with Sephardim. Because the Sephardic congregation could not support its own religious school, many Sephardic families sent their children to the Ahavai Sholom Sunday school. This was the case with many members of the extended Menashe family, and was likely the reason Joanna Kapalota Menashe became involved in that congregation's sisterhood. Mixing in both public school and Sunday school—as well as at Neighborhood House or the B'nai B'rith Center—with other Jewish children, the younger generation tended to report a sense of belonging in the larger Jewish community. Harry Policar, whose family moved from Seattle to Portland in the mid-1910s, while he was still a boy, reported that relations between Sephardim and Ashkenazim were "wonderful! It never apparently made a difference. I never felt there was a difference. We were Jews and they were Jews and that's it." Policar recalled no social discrimination until he experienced it in a college fraternity.[157]

In their emphasis on harmonious relations, Policar and others draw distinctions between experiences in Portland and Seattle. Seattle had a Sephardic community large enough to support more of its own social, educational and religious institutions, fostering exclusivity. In contrast, Portland Sephardim—and especially their children—necessarily mixed more with the broader Jewish community. As Policar explained,

> In Seattle there was a large immigrant Sephardic community, much bigger than the group in Portland. The Seattle Sephardic community was much more locked into itself. There were enough of them that they did not have to go outside of their own circle to satisfy many of their needs. In a way, they lived isolated from the Ashkenazy [sic] and so a large schism developed between the two groups. In Portland there were not so many Sephardim. The people next door to us were usually Jewish, but not necessarily Sephardic, and we didn't care. They were our friends. We children didn't ask; our parents didn't complain; our neighbors were Jewish and that was sufficient. As I grew up, most of my friends were not Sephardic.[158]

Toinette Rosenberg Menashe, an Ashkenazi Jew who married into the Menashe family, drew a similar conclusion about the "fluidity" in Portland:

> Apparently in Seattle it was very structured, I mean with whom you associated. Sort of interesting, because as I said, my husband is from a Sephardic background and there always has been a small Sephardic synagogue in Portland and there were only about sixty families.

Whereas in Seattle—which I think was the third or fourth largest Sephardic community in the country and they were sent there for fishing which is similar to what they had done in Rhodes—but my husband's family settled in Portland. But his parents wanted the boys to have a religious school education which their synagogue did not have, so they were sent to Ahavai Sholom—most of the Sephardic kids were at that synagogue. But they were just kids—we didn't think anything different. Whereas in Seattle, there was so much prejudice between and against German Jews, Russian Jews, and Sephardic Jews and what not—so everybody moved in their own community but this wasn't true in Portland.[159]

Toinette met her future husband, Victor Menashe, in the Ahavai Sholom Sunday school.

COMPOSITION OF A COMMUNITY

Individuals, whether from Germany, Posen, the South Pale, Poland, or the Mediterranean Basin, were drawn to remote, commercially under-developed, yet rapidly growing locales in the United States that offered them opportunities. Willingness to pioneer in areas that were Jewishly underdeveloped and experiences gained while sojourning in the American hinterland created some common ground between newcomers and the established Jewish community. Although the early-twentieth-century migrants established a Jewish neighborhood in Portland that had an East European flavor as well as Sephardic hues, the distance between their values, aspirations, and even religious rituals and those of their established coreligionists was less pronounced than was the case in many eastern Jewish communities. Furthermore, the gap that did exist between Jews of varying backgrounds was bridged by the presence of Ahavai Sholom, a congregation expressing the sensibilities of its Posener founders, who, although sometimes emphatically asserting their German identities, also had clear affinities with these East European newcomers—and later reached out to Sephardim as well.

Portland's Jewish community was a product of the particular mechanics of the migration streams that brought Jews west, mechanics that differed from the classic tale of three migrations. Because of its distinct location and economy, Portland drew immigrants selectively, appealing to many who had prior experience in the American hinterland and who shared regional and occupational backgrounds that eased their adaptation to Portland. These immigrants chose their own America in Portland, creating a history that profoundly shaped Portland's Jewish community.

CHAPTER 3

The Heart of the Community
Neighborhood House

> The most important social institution in South Portland was
> Neighborhood House. . . . It touched the life of virtually every
> Jewish immigrant in South Portland. It was the social anchor of the
> neighborhood, and it sought to meet every need that was not being
> addressed elsewhere.
> —Steven Lowenstein, *The Jews of Oregon*

> Everybody was at the Neighborhood House, because everybody
> more or less lived in that area. There was a certain something; it was
> almost like going home.
> —Mary Friedman Rosenberg

At the turn of the century, South Portland was the heart of the Jewish community, and Neighborhood House was the heart of South Portland. Founded in 1905 by the Portland Section of the National Council of Jewish Women (NCJW), Neighborhood House offered a broad range of opportunities. For the American-born, privileged women of the council, it provided a "rare and socially acceptable opportunity for Jewish upper-class women to be responsible directly and in control of significant work outside the home."[1] For the immigrant newcomers, it provided an array of educational, recreational, and social opportunities, as well as serving as a clearinghouse for philanthropic aid. In a Jewish community rich in organizational life, Neighborhood House stood out as a focal point, providing an institutional center for South Portland's immigrant community, as well as a point of contact between that community and the established, Reform Jews who created and ran it.

The settlement also served as a point of contact between the Jewish community and the larger city. For the women of the council, activities at the house provided not only an opportunity to interface with their coreligionists, but also an entrée into the women's club and social service network in Portland. From the outset, they envisioned the settlement as part of the citywide response to urban issues, with its leaders participating actively with non-Jewish partners in this work. For immigrant Jews, Neighborhood House provided opportunities to interact both with their coreligionists and with the area's non-Jews. Although many perceived it to be an exclusively Jewish institution, the settlement's clientele was, in fact, quite mixed.

Neighborhood House was created in response to the growing number of immigrant Jews who began arriving in Portland in larger (although still relatively moderate) numbers only after 1900. As over a million poured into East Coast ports, the Portland Jewish community grew by only four thousand—counting both new arrivals and natural increase—between 1878 and 1910. Moreover, among those East Europeans who did arrive in the Rose City prior to 1900, many were not new immigrants at all, having spent years in the interior as merchants or farmers before finding their way to Portland. Only after the turn of the century did a substantial group of direct immigrants began to arrive from Eastern Europe, often following relatives who had earlier established themselves in Portland. Others were sent to the Rose City by the Industrial Removal Office, which aimed to spread arriving Jewish immigrants across the country to lessen the concentration in New York. In comparison to the flood arriving in eastern cities, or to the growing number destined for Los Angeles, Portland experienced only a modest influx, adding approximately seven thousand to the total Jewish population between 1910 and 1927.[2]

Yet for established community members, the migration—and the prospect that greater numbers of migrants might soon arrive—created a sense of urgency. Despite the relative security Portland Jews had long enjoyed, they experienced anxieties about the immigrants similar to those of their counterparts across the country. Perceiving the East

Europeans as backward, superstitious, and disturbingly foreign, they feared they might prove an embarrassment or a burden, undermining the high status of the Jewish community as a whole. Quickly reforming the immigrants and assisting them in adopting American customs, language, dress, and decorum would help inoculate the entire Jewish community against potential backlash.

Their response was also motivated by altruism. Like their mothers, who had devoted themselves to the Hebrew Ladies Benevolent Society, the young women who would become the animating force behind Neighborhood House were committed to service. They believed that, by guiding the immigrants in their embrace of American ways, equipping them with useful skills, and providing a nurturing environment for their children, they would pave the way for the newcomers to become self-supporting, contributing, and accepted members of society.

The Portland NCJW section that created Neighborhood House was part of a national organization that grew out of the Jewish Women's Congress at the Chicago World's Fair in 1893.[3] Combining the impulses of clubwomen and social welfare workers, the NCJW dedicated itself to "becoming Jewishly educated, fighting anti-Semitism and assimilation, and solving society's problems through social reform work. It further assumed that participation in this work would bring Jewish women together, transforming division into harmony."[4] In this, the group tapped a growing appetite among middle- and upper-class women for civic engagement consistent with gender norms and with their Jewish identities. While sharing the philanthropic impulse of their immigrant mothers, this new generation of Jewish women was secularly educated and outward looking. Many were graduates of the same private schools as their Christian peers and inspired by Progressive social reformers such as Jane Addams. Unlike their mothers, they were not inclined to focus inwardly on mutual aid. Rather, they embraced a philanthropic program that served their less fortunate coreligionists while expanding their own public role, both within the Jewish community and in the larger civic arena.

Enacting programs that frequently revolved around the establishment of settlement houses, American women in this period expanded the female sphere, creating an agenda that envisioned assimilated women as mothers, and immigrants as "members of their extended family."⁵ Under this model, American women went beyond raising and dispensing charity, instead embracing a model of "personal service," which called on them to actively engage with and serve as guides for their impoverished, immigrant protégés. The National Council of Jewish Women—like the Sisterhoods of Personal Service that were founded at major Reform synagogues in New York and San Francisco in the same time period—provided a specifically Jewish way of participating in these activities, emphasizing the historic connection between Judaism and social justice, and the traditional link between women and charity.⁶ At the same time, they provided Jewish women with an entrée into the larger network of women's organizations and social service networks in the city.

In Portland, the transition from communal self-help to this more outward-looking model was relatively smooth. As historian William Toll explains, "In western cities, where Jewish women had had prominence during the pioneer generation, sisterhood and council work provided an opportunity to modernize rather than create the Jewish women's public role."⁷ Certainly, the integration happened quickly. As early as 1899, the Portland NCJW section joined Oregon's Federation of Women's Clubs, and NCJW members were among those who helped establish Portland's City Federation of Women's Clubs. From that point, the Portland Section was "recognized . . . as an important Jewish voice on issues of civic welfare," according to community historian Steven Lowenstein.⁸ In 1905, the section participated in Women's Club efforts to prepare for the Lewis and Clark Exposition.

This integration of council chapters into broader women's networks was a direct result of council demographics. Nationally, the council tended to attract young, Reform, native-born women of German background. The group that coalesced at Temple Beth Israel in Portland in 1896 was typical. Nearly 80 percent of the charter members belonged to Beth Israel, as did at least thirteen of the sixteen officers.⁹ Although the early leaders of the council were very prominent, affluent women of an older generation, including Matilda ("Tillie") Selling (wife of Ben, prominent Jewish philanthropist and Oregon politician), Jeanette Meier (wife of Aaron and mother of future governor Julius Meier), and Josephine Hirsch (wife of Solomon, a state Republican Party leader), the vast majority of members, 70 percent, were under forty years of age.[10] Like many middle- and upper-class American women of their generation, they had the leisure time to pursue service activities. Fully a quarter of them were single, and those who were married tended to have far fewer children than their mothers and often had live-in servants.[11]

Ida Loewenberg, the woman who became the face of Neighborhood House in 1912 when she began her thirty-two-year tenure as head-worker, was among this younger group of women. Born in Portland in 1872 to parents who had arrived in the United States while in their teens, she was the daughter of privilege, attended by servants, study-ing at elite Portland private schools and spending her eighteenth year with her mother and siblings on a grand tour of Europe while her father constructed a castle-like home in Portland. She was twenty-four when she became a charter member of the Portland NCJW section in 1896. A year later, her fortunes would change when her father suffered financial losses as a result of the national economic crisis of 1893 to 1897; in 1899, he passed away. The family's new economic circum-stance led two of the three sisters to seek professional training, and both devoted their careers to serving the South Portland neighborhood, Ida at Neighborhood House as headworker and Zerlina as librarian at the local public library branch.[12] Despite her changed fortunes, Ida remained well connected socially and was able to leverage those con-nections to support the settlement. As her niece, Gladys Trachtenberg, recalled, "My aunt, being of pioneer stock, was able to get money per-sonally from the most prominent people in Portland, people like the Failing family, the Corbetts, Mr. Joseph Keow who was a very promi-nent lawyer and married one of the Thompsons."[13]

Although Loewenberg's changed economic circumstances and long tenure as a professional worker at Neighborhood House make her story exceptional, her confident engagement in elite civic and social circles was not. In western cities, women's role in transforming "settle-ments of transient men into stable communities,"[14] has been widely recognized by historians. Jewish merchants had been able, in Portland and elsewhere in the West, to gain prominence as civic and business pioneers. Their daughters, like the Loewenberg sisters, attended private

Ida Loewenberg at Neighborhood House, c. 1930. Credit: Oregon Jewish Museum

(often Christian) schools and counted the daughters of the city's leading families among their close friends. These women grew up with a strong identity "not as an insular, stigmatized minority, but as the heirs of a mercantile elite." According to historian William Toll, "Assimilation to western standards of religious pluralism led them to transform their Jewish work from communal benevolence into participation in the wider world of club women."[15]

As was the case nationally, the Portland NCJW section initially focused on Jewish learning, featuring study circles, readings, and lectures, as well as entertainment, often by group members. For the first several years, social service activities were limited, consisting primarily of the provision of vocational education and sewing classes for South Portland residents. In 1900, however, the arrival of the dynamic Reform rabbi Stephen S. Wise inspired an explosion of service activities. The women studied social philanthropy, reading (at Wise's suggestion) books on immigrant social issues such as Israel Zangwill's *Children of the Ghetto*. By 1902, they were exploring the possibility of establishing a social settlement along the lines of those founded in larger cities including Chicago and New York. And in 1905, a purpose-built edifice rose in South Portland.[16]

Although the Portland section of the NCJW engaged in a broad array of programs, ranging from internally focused educational and social programming to advocating for peace and engaging in local, state, and national campaigns for various causes,[17] Neighborhood House became the group's signature initiative. The council turned over direct control of the settlement to a newly created Neighborhood House Board in 1902, but the board formally remained a part of the council, with council members taking six of its eight seats, including the position of board chair. Council women provided the bulk of the volunteer labor and coordinated programming until they hired Sadie Bloch as the first resident headworker in 1911. After Bloch's departure the following year, Ida Loewenberg took the headworker position, serving in that capacity for the next three decades. The professional staff oversaw day-to-day operations, but the council retained control of the settlement house's programming until 1955.

Neighborhood House quickly became a hive of activity. As was the case nationally for the council, there was a special focus on immigrant girls, who were thought to be particularly vulnerable. In major ports of entry, the NCJW established agents and offices to intercept single girls and track their safe passage to their destination.[18] Since Portland was not a port of entry for newcomers, such services were not needed. Instead, the council's programming for girls—initiated prior to the erection of Neighborhood House—was more domestic in orientation. As Miriam Rosenfeld, whose native-born parents were part of the German Jewish community, recalled, "The girls were taught sewing and cooking and many things that the women of the Council of Jewish Women felt that these immigrants should know in order to become, I wouldn't say assimilated, but more Americanized."[19] Tillie Selling, the wife of Portland's most prominent Jewish civic leader, personally led the sewing school from 1900 to 1933.

Neighborhood House soon added to the sewing and domestic classes, developing programs designed to aid in the adaptation of immigrants. English and citizenship classes were offered to adults, who also frequented the house to attend lectures, political meetings, and theatrical and musical productions (often featuring their children).

Neighborhood House cooking class, 1914. Neighborhood House sewing school, c.
Credit: Oregon Jewish Museum   1920. Credit: Oregon Jewish Museum

Educational and recreational programming for children expanded. Indeed, such programs multiplied so rapidly that, by 1908 the council was already discussing plans for a new, larger building. That building was quickly erected at the corner of Second and Woods, and dedicated in December 1910.[20]

As programs multiplied, the Portland group, following the national strategy of the NCJW,[21] avoided duplicating existing programs and instead created a niche by providing services not yet available in the city. When other agencies adopted programs pioneered by Neighborhood House, the group relinquished them. For example, the house's kindergarten was created in response to a need in the community. Although there had been efforts in Portland to establish free kindergartens, demand exceeded supply. After several years of discussion with kindergarten advocates, the Neighborhood House kindergarten opened in 1905. However, council continued to participate in efforts to lobby for kindergartens in public schools, and when the Portland schools did initiate a program in 1917, the Neighborhood House kindergarten was discontinued.[22] Yet, by 1925, a Christian bias in the kindergarten program at nearby Failing School led to the reinstitution of the Neighborhood House program. As Sadie Cohen Geller recalled in an oral history, her daughter came home from that kindergarten crying, "Mother, they want me to sing the Christmas carols and I won't." Geller continued, "I went to Miss Loewenberg and talked to her . . .

Neighborhood House kindergarten class, 1931. Credit: Oregon Jewish Museum

'How about starting a kindergarten?' And that's when the kindergarten at the Neighborhood House was started."[23] Despite the temporary reversal in this case, the pattern of developing and then relinquishing programs was repeated in other areas. As public schools or other service agencies began to offer kindergartens, English classes for foreigners, and manual training programs, Neighborhood House turned its attention elsewhere.

Much of the programming was driven by the council's emphasis on Americanization. Miriam Rosenfeld explained that the settlement house was "organized to help these newcomers, to Americanize them, so they would become citizens and to teach them different fields."[24] Council women, like Progressives more generally, believed that Americanization would be fostered by personal contact between immigrant clients and native-born volunteers. "Friendly visiting" would allow the volunteer (or professional social worker) to guide the immigrant in the spirit of sympathetic understanding, allowing her to serve

Neighborhood House game room, 1914. Credit: Oregon Jewish Museum

as a model to her less fortunate protégé. Simply by coming in contact with middle- and upper-class women, immigrants (and particularly immigrant girls) would begin to adopt their "American" values and learn to emulate their manners. On many occasions, Blanche Blumauer, longtime chairman[25] of the Neighborhood House Board, reminded board members that each of them "must concern herself with the work inside the house," through regular, at least monthly, visits.[26]

In some cases, personal contact went far deeper. By all accounts, Ida Loewenberg's embrace of individual service was legendary, and was central to her ability to build bonds of trust with neighbors. Loewenberg's niece, Gladys Trachtenberg, who also served as a social worker at Neighborhood House, recalled the challenges of the work:

> You walked and you walked and you walked and you climbed stairs and you never knew what you were finding when you went into these homes. You never knew what sort of social problems, what sort of economic problems, what sort of problems of adjustment and psychological problems you would run into.[27]

Children from Neighborhood House's Penny Saver Club deposit their coins, 1914.
Credit: Oregon Jewish Museum

Neighborhood House records testify to the intimate contact between the headworker and her clients. For example, the deputy district attorney from Multnomah County contacted Loewenberg in 1917 regarding domestic trouble between a neighborhood resident and his wife, writing "to ask if it is possible for you to act as the mediator for them and induce them to re-establish the home and live together."[28] A few months earlier, the Portland Department of Public Safety called Loewenberg to inquire about the situation of a teenage girl from the neighborhood who was "running wild," and whose father was suspected of trying "to sell his daughter for immoral purposes."[29] Loewenberg's intimate knowledge of the neighborhood meant that she was the one contacted when the Native Sons and Native Daughters Central Committee on Homeless Children were seeking to place adoptees within the Jewish community.[30] She was also the one to write to authorities at the Oregon State Hospital to inquire about community members who were patients there.[31] Neighborhood residents' trust in Loewenberg is demonstrated in the case of a woman desperate to avoid pregnancy in an era when even dispensing birth control *information* was illegal. According to Trachtenberg, the woman

> had so many children that she came and begged my aunt to help her. "What can I do?" said my aunt and worked with a Mrs. Spaulding who was the head R.N at the County Hospital, and she arranged for this woman to have a sterilization in the dead of night. No one ever knew about it, it was not on the records, but this was a sort of a life you were leading in those days. Fortunately, my aunt was very broad-minded.[32]

Certainly, this degree of trust and personal connection was not typical of council volunteers at Neighborhood House—Loewenberg, after all, was a full-time, professional worker. For volunteers, personal contact most often came through regular programming at the house, where council women served as sewing instructors, modeled etiquette, or met with mothers' clubs. As Blanche Blumauer, who was Portland Section president in 1905 when she began her thirty-year term as chairman of the Neighborhood House Board, explained in her first annual statement, "Through our monthly programs we have succeeded in bringing together the reform Jew and her orthodox sister, giving to both a common interest in Jewish thought, Jewish history, and Jewish woman's relationship to the non-Jewish world."[33] These personal lessons included not only formal educational training, but etiquette—as volunteer Miriam Boskovitz Aiken put it, "we taught them to eat American style."[34] In a 1912 report, headworker Sadie Bloch explained:

> The supreme test of the worth of this work is proven in the response of the neighbors, particularly those young girls who do not find their homes sufficiently attractive and environment sympathetic, and who have long felt the need of someone to bid them welcome in a social way each day or week—or when they cared to come. What means more than that, though, is the fact that someone has come into the

neighborhood from another world, as it were, whose attitude toward them is that of the friend who keenly feels and carefully practices the belief in the brotherhood of man and fatherhood of God in the true Jewish spirit.[35]

Although personal contact and service was at the core of these activities, it is important to emphasize that the interchange that took place was not on a plane of equality. Established Jews—those who resided in more affluent sections of the city, owned more prosperous businesses, and were usually members of Temple Beth Israel—extended themselves in service but limited social contact. The unequal relationship sometimes led to feelings of resentment. For example, the Mothers' Club that formed in the early 1910s initially was structured to organize women "for the good of the community." Women instructed one another (often in Yiddish) on diet, nutrition, housekeeping, gardening, the care of children's teeth, and other topics of interest. Yet the group soon disbanded "due to a patronizing feeling because of some overzealousness of the Council"—apparently stemming from the practice of having council women, but not neighborhood women, take turns providing refreshments. The group was soon reconstituted; while neighborhood women were now invited to help with refreshments, all offices were still held by council members.[36]

Council members contributed support at Neighborhood House, either financially or as volunteers, but as members of the middle and upper classes, they had their own facility for athletic, fraternal, and social activity—the B'nai B'rith Building, founded in 1914 (it later became the Jewish Community Center). As Mollie Blumenthal, a South Portland resident, recalled, "Our social life centered around the Neighborhood House, never the BB, that was like going from South Portland to Dunthorpe, going from Neighborhood House to B'nai B'rith, because that was a different element up there."[37] The B'nai B'rith Building was, according to Blumenthal, "for the ritzier Jews." As Marguerite Swett Dilsheimer explained, the B'nai B'rith Building and Neighborhood House were "entirely different":

The Neighborhood House was more social service, as I understood it, a settlement house. This [the B'nai B'rith Building] was never a settlement house. It was a community center for people who needed to meet socially. To have a gymnasium, swimming and social activities, club meetings and to bring Jewish people together. I think that was the idea, but never any welfare work, as such, except that they used that as an office later.[38]

The social distance between the two groups was most pronounced in the early years, when it reflected the sharp social divide between the immigrants and the established community and was often thought of as an ethnic divide. As early as the 1920s, however, some of the children of earlier arriving East Europeans began to enter the professions or find success in business. These individuals began to move to more affluent parts of the city and, in some cases, to join Temple Beth Israel. Women of these families often joined the NCJW, and by the late 1920s, approximately 20 percent of council members were from East European families.[39] Social distance between this rising group of East Europeans and the established German Jews remained however, as the latter continued to exclude the former from elite clubs and to oppose "intermarriage" between the groups. Still, as more women of East European parentage joined NCJW, the relationship between council women and Neighborhood House users shifted. One reflection of this was in the goals for Neighborhood House children. Whereas the council had once emphasized vocational programs, by the 1920s they had organized a Scholarship Loan Fund to assist neighborhood children to attend college.[40]

As did settlement houses elsewhere in the country, Neighborhood House came to embrace athletics and recreational activities, imbuing them with a higher purpose that was directly related to the core mission of the institution. Physical development and athletics were strongly associated with the development of American manhood and a robust citizenry, as well as being considered a bulwark against delinquency. These activities, facilitated by the addition of a gymnasium and pool in 1925, were part of a Progressive understanding of the importance of environment and a broad education in the development of children. House programs included holiday pageants, opportunities in the arts, an array of clubs, and summer camp activities, as well as athletics. Theatrical and musical programs often had a patriotic bent, such as the 1939 summer camp pageant that included titles such as "Our Own Dear Country," "The Battle Cry of Freedom," "Made in America," "Columbia Gem of the Ocean," and "Way Down South in Dixie," as well as skits and songs recognizing American diversity such as "The Kelley Boys," "From Deutchland Came," and "The Piccaninnies."[41]

As the latter titles suggest, in preaching its Americanization message, the women of Neighborhood House, like their counterparts in settlement houses across the country, made an effort to recognize diversity (although, as the final number suggests, such efforts were colored by the racial attitudes of the day). Celebrations of ethnic cultures were considered a way of lessening the gap between children and parents—a gap that was often seen as a potential contributor to delinquency.[42] Many preached the importance of "mutual respect," embracing the idea that immigrant traditions should be valued and even cultivated among the children, at least where these did not conflict directly with American ones. For Jewish settlement houses in particular, the attitude toward the traditions of clients was a complicated one. On the one hand, East European religious practice, Yiddish culture, and Zionism were regarded with a mixture of fear and disdain in many Reform circles. Jewish settlement houses often offered Sunday school programs that exposed neighborhood children to Reform ritual and practice that was foreign to—and very problematic for—their families. In asserting these Reform models, settlement workers frequently did, implicitly or explicitly, devalue more Orthodox practices. On the other hand, increasing anxieties about Jewish continuity in America led some established American Jews to regard the East Europeans as a repository of knowledge and tradition that carried the panache of authenticity. In Portland, headworker Loewenberg approached the issue carefully, stressing the need for balance between the "fear that the Jewish immigrant may not become a thorough and loyal American" and the "opposite danger, that of Americanizing him at the expense of his religion."[43] Loewenberg's concern about the issue was related to her worry about a growing estrangement, "a peculiar void, a vast gulf," between parents of the immigrant generation and their Americanized children.[44]

Outside the Jewish community, there were some who believed that Christianity was part and parcel of Americanization. Neighborhood House countered this, fending off Christian missionaries who targeted area children with their programming. An example of this occurred when the Christian content of the available kindergarten program was a key factor in the re-creation of the Neighborhood House kindergarten in 1925. In 1929, when the nearby Methodist-run Portland Settlement Center stepped up efforts to recruit area children for their Christian programming, the Neighborhood House board met with a group of Portland rabbis representing Reform, Conservative, and Orthodox congregations to discuss the situation. The group agreed on a strategy of having the rabbis urge from their pulpits "attendance at Jewish institutions and their remaining away from the Settlement Center." In addition, the group agreed that Loewenberg and Burt Treiger, head of the Hebrew School, would draft a letter "to be both tactful and expressive of a wish to attend Jewish institutions and eschew other [sic]." The letter was distributed to the community in English, Yiddish, and Ladino.[45]

Believing that Jewish identity was completely compatible with Americanization, Neighborhood House programming and leadership did more than simply fend off missionaries. Rather, leaders embraced the idea of positively promoting the maintenance of religious practice among the Jewish children of the neighborhood, albeit in a relatively progressive vein. As headworker Sadie Bloch explained,

> We always strive to bring about points of contact with our neighbors, and to encourage them, by simply being interested, to retain the traditional customs, and yet we help them to the usage of the new ones . . . . Some time ago I asked the children how many of their fathers "bench" [recite prayers] in the morning, and every hand went up instantly, but when I put the same question regarding their own gratitude to our Maker, only two hands signified that a morning prayer was repeated, so now each child has one printed on cardboard, and is rapidly learning the beautiful thoughts and wishes Mr. D. Solis-Cohen expressed in a way suitable for a child's understanding.[46]

Bloch's account is suggestive of the balance between old and new. On the one hand, she recognized the value in traditional practice and sought to encourage it. Yet she did not seek the guidance of one of

South Portland's Orthodox rabbis to supply the text, instead turning to David Solis-Cohen, a figure well known for his progressive religious attitudes.

In addition to encouragement of religious practice, Neighborhood House provided, along with English and citizenship classes, programs that *were* specifically Jewish in cultural and/or religious orientation. The settlement hosted a variety of Jewish cultural and political clubs, including some that seem at odds with the central goal of Americanization. For example, popular literary and mothers' clubs conducted their meetings in Yiddish during the 1910s.[47] Several different Zionist clubs also were based at the house, despite the fact that some in the Reform community saw Zionism as an ideology that posed a threat to Americanization.[48] Clearly, however, the longest-running and most popular of the specifically Jewish programs at the house was the Portland Hebrew School.

The Hebrew School demonstrates vividly the balancing act between assimilationist and preservationist impulses. Nationally, religious education was a common point of tension between immigrant newcomers and the established, mostly Reform, native-born community. The traditional religious education (*heder*) was viewed by the established community—and by a number of the immigrants themselves—as narrow and outdated, both in terms of curriculum and pedagogical approach. Progressives advocated educational programs that, unlike the *heder*, provided opportunities to girls as well as boys, used up-to-date teaching methods to engage students, and included a broad curriculum of Jewish history, culture, and values rather than focusing solely on the study of sacred texts. Reform temples frequently opened their Sunday schools to immigrant children, or provided programs for them at locations within immigrant neighborhoods, but many immigrant parents felt that the Reform curriculum had the effect of undermining traditional belief and practice. The Hebrew School created at Neighborhood House was careful to strike a balance between the various educational goals and approaches available. In part, this can be attributed to Loewenberg herself, who understood the importance of the program in fostering the connection between children, their parents, and their heritage. As she explained,

We have . . . encouraged to our utmost capacity the Hebrew School and the establishment of the children's service and cherishing the faith of great traditions of our past, that we can hope to solve the great problem that now confronts American Jewry, that of the chasm between the old and young generation, between fathers and sons, between mothers and daughters. No Jewish center can hope to be a factor in welfare work; there will always be something fundamentally lacking if we neglect the culture of Judaism and ignore our religion.[49]

After several less-formal arrangements, the Portland Hebrew School was incorporated in 1913 and began to meet at Neighborhood House in 1916.[50] Serving boys and girls of South Portland's Conservative and Orthodox congregations, the school's directors prided themselves on its modern approach and fostering of Americanization. With public school students receiving release time to attend Hebrew School by the early 1920s, and Orthodox Shaarie Torah's rabbi Fain urging his congregants to send their children to the school to help facilitate their

Portland Hebrew School students, c. 1923. Credit: Oregon Jewish Museum

Americanization,[51] Hebrew school attendance was one of the touch-stones of a South Portland Jewish childhood.

Critical to the school's success was the fact that, rather than being a program provided for immigrants by established Reform Jews, the Portland Hebrew School was financed by the establishment, but to a large degree was directed by early arriving, progressively oriented East European immigrants. According to community historian Steven Lowenstein, there was considerable support among South Portland residents for a modern Hebrew school as "many . . . were resistant to Old World teaching methods. They wanted to retain Jewish tradition and culture, but within a revitalized American context."[52] Both Temple Beth Israel members of German descent and well-established East Europeans served on the board. The program, led by Bert Treiger, a young educator, focused on "modern" techniques, emphasized the spoken Hebrew championed by Zionists, and conducted study of the Bible, Jewish history, Jewish law, and Jewish customs.[53] Students could receive high school language credit for the study of modern Hebrew undertaken at the school.

The degree of neighborhood support for the Hebrew School and for other Neighborhood House activities is an important indication that South Portland immigrants and their children embraced much of what the NCJW was offering.[54] Demand for English and citizenship classes was high—and the Hebrew School's popularity suggests a widespread rejection of Old World teaching methods, even by immigrant Orthodox leaders such as Rabbi Fain.[55] Yet while both patrons and clients may have embraced house programming, their visions of the settlement house were not indistinguishable. Patrons tended to see Neighborhood House as a piece of their broad civic involvement, but clients often viewed the institution as the lynchpin of their insular neighborhood.

In the oral histories conducted in the 1970s, the NCJW women and their daughters repeatedly stressed the broad vision of Neighborhood House and of the council. Often, this included a depiction of the settlement as one serving a diverse constituency, rather than a specifically Jewish one. For example, several made a point of noting that the first graduate of the Neighborhood House sewing school was an African

American girl, with Ida Loewenberg's niece, Gladys Trachtenberg, mentioning the girl by name and indicating that this was a point of pride: "Grace Duncan was the first Negro graduate of the sewing school at Neighborhood House and everybody was terribly proud of it and her name went down in history as the first Negro graduate."[56] Speaking more generally of Neighborhood House, where she worked for several stints as a social worker and served a brief term as director after her aunt's retirement, Trachtenberg emphasized the universal rather than the parochial aspects of the program, contrasting the "all Jewish" Jewish Community Center with Neighborhood House:

> Neighborhood House would admit to membership anyone, regardless of race, creed, color or ethnic background. It didn't matter. Anyone was welcome and we did have several black members. They were a little reticent at first to come in and use the pool because they knew the swimming coach was not fond of blacks. This was most unfortunate, but my aunt overcame it. It took a lot of work on her part and many hours of talking, but she was successful.[57]

This emphasis on the settlement's tradition of welcoming all is a common theme in house publications and histories, which consistently emphasize a mission to serve, inclusively, all the people of the neighborhood, rather than depicting the settlement program as ethnically focused. The 1928 annual Neighborhood House report, for example, emphasized that "Neighborhood House has never been exclusive; rather, it has endeavored to serve all elements in the community, Jewish as well as non-Jewish, believing it can best fulfill its function as a neighborhood center by disregarding differences in station, race and religion."[58] And a 1954 council history of the settlement emphasized that its mission had long been to serve the "people residing within the vicinity."[59]

Given this emphasis on the universal, the recollections of East European clients, also interviewed in the 1970s, provide a sharp contrast. The overwhelming majority of the East European women interviewed, whether first or second generation, participated in activities at Neighborhood House. Many mention that their parents attended English classes there, and participation in sewing classes appears to have been a must for girls growing up in South Portland. But in contrast to the official emphasis on broad service to a diverse neighborhood, in the eyes of the East Europeans, the athletic facilities, social activities, and parochial programs were far more central. While the Beth Israel women volunteers at Neighborhood House saw the institution as a reflection of their outward-looking civic involvement, many of those who used the facilities as clients cast the house as the social and educational center of an insular, ethnic, and religious community—the "heart" of Jewish Portland—and envisioned the neighborhood it served as exclusively Jewish. As Gertrude Feves, daughter of Russian immigrants who moved to Portland from Colorado explained, "The Neighborhood House was something to us, a wonder, because living in Pueblo, Colorado, we did not have anything like this and the marvelous thing about the Neighborhood House was that everybody there was Jewish . . . that was just something that was hard for me to believe, that everybody in this building was Jewish."[60]

Depictions of the settlement house as overwhelmingly (or even exclusively) Jewish are extensions of a vision of the surrounding neighborhood as similarly homogeneous. In her oral history, Frieda Cohn explained,

> At that time [in the teens] upper South Portland housed practically every Jewish person in the city. There were very few that lived any place else. It was really a teeming place for the Jews, and what an exciting place. They brought up their children, they educated them, they sent them to Hebrew School. They never had to go out of the neighborhood to do their shopping.[61]

Diane Holzman Nemer similarly recalled, "On the whole block there might have been two families that were not Jewish. . . . Everyone around there to me at that time was living the same kind of life that I was living."[62]

The richness of Jewish networks and the concentration on particular blocks often obscured the neighborhood's true diversity. As Frances Schnitzer Bricker explained, "Well, when I grew up, I was going to say, everybody was Jewish, but that wouldn't be true because we had Italian friends, but everybody lived such a Jewish life. We walked to shul and shul was a part of our upbringing and every holiday was important."[63] A similar pattern occurs in several interviews, as informants begin to paint a portrait of an all-Jewish neighborhood, but then remember the actual diversity. For example, Nettie Enkilis Olman recalled, "We were all Jews, we were all of the same class. No distinction, no difference, and we had the same holidays and that's how you grew up." Shortly thereafter, she added, "There were Italians that lived in the neighborhood and we had a few black neighbors, but not many."[64] And, although Augusta Kirshner Reinhardt described it as "a community of Jews or Italians. There were Negro people, and I can remember as a child in school that there were also Chinese people, so there were a mixture of people," she concluded that "most of the people were Jewish . . . . If there was a ghetto in Portland, South Portland would have been the ghetto. However, it was a self-imposed ghetto. They chose to live close to each other and it was a wonderful way to live, really, very much as we think of a shtetl."[65]

Despite the contradictions within these accounts, and between client and patron recollections, there is a basis for *both* visions of the settlement and its neighborhood. As official Neighborhood House histories and patron testimony suggest, the settlement had always served a population that was diverse (or at least not exclusively Jewish). From the earliest efforts of the NCJW in the neighborhood, prior to the construction of the house, the sewing and household school, served many non-Jews. In 1899, for example, of over one hundred children served, only about half were Jewish.[66] This reflected the demographics of the neighborhood, which, in addition to Jews, had a substantial Italian population, as well as smaller numbers of Germans, Irish, Scandinavians, and a handful of Asians and African Americans.[67] Although those who were not of Jewish background were clearly welcome, the council reports demonstrate that the percentage of Jewish clients was at least sporadically tracked and that maximizing Jewish attendance was a priority. Thus, in 1903, the tally at the sewing school led to a recommendation that "the attendance be closely watched and an effort be made to increase the number of Jewish children."[68] Several times during these early years, regret was expressed in these reports that the percentage of Jewish students was not higher. Despite efforts to increase Jewish attendance, such "deficits" in Jewish students continued, as in the case of a girls' gym class in 1906 in which only six or eight of twenty-six students were Jewish, or a 1909 night school in which only twenty of seventy students were Jews. These were contrasted with "successes," such as the 1909 cooking class in which sixteen of nineteen girls were Jewish. [69]

The demographics of Neighborhood House users during its first decade reflect the pattern of delayed migration to the West Coast—at that point, the neighborhood was not yet as heavily Jewish as it would later become. Although the mass migration of East European Jews to the United States is dated from 1880 and peaked just after the turn of the century, the impact in the West, as discussed earlier, was delayed. As late as 1912, Neighborhood House Board chairman, Blanche Blumauer, was still *anticipating* the influx. "The tide of immigration to the Pacific Coast is slowly but surely approaching," she warned. "Let us hope that these years of preparation have helped to show us the way that we may be a protection and guide to those who need protecting and guiding, a power for good in the upbuilding of our state."[70]

Over the next two decades, a steady stream arrived in the Rose City. Toll's analysis of Jewish residential patterns in 1920 demonstrates that, within the Failing School area immediately adjacent to Neighborhood House, one could find both diversity and pockets of heavily Jewish settlement. Although only 38 percent of Failing's students were Jewish, the percentage was higher in the upper grades (likely because Jewish students generally spent more years in school). Therefore, "young people would have from twelve to nineteen Jewish classmates in public school during the day, and many would attend Hebrew school, physical education classes, or social events at Neighborhood House perhaps as often as four or five afternoons and evenings a week."[71] The sense of insularity created was reinforced for many students by residential clustering within the larger neighborhood. Several blocks along Caruthers, Sheridan, Arthur, Meade, and First, Second, and Third Streets were very heavily Jewish—including groupings within these blocks of related families.

Along with the increased influx of immigrant Jews in the 1910s and 1920s, the opening in 1912 of a new Christian facility, the Manley Center, just a few blocks away, drew non-Jews who had previously attended Neighborhood House, leading to a more heavily Jewish profile at the house.[72] By the mid-1920s, headworker Ida Loewenberg was able to report that, "while Neighborhood House has always been non-sectarian, the percentage of Jewish attendance has largely increased, and that at the present time Jewish enrollment is the greatest in its history."[73] Yet even during this period, the house—and the established community more broadly—continued to emphasize its diverse appeal. As the *Scribe* reported in a 1926 editorial commending its successes, "The Neighborhood House has ignored barriers of faith and creed and offered its benefits generously to Jew and non-Jew in its neighborhood."[74] The settlement's 1928 annual report, after reminding readers of its historic diversity and emphasizing that it could "best fulfill its function as a neighborhood center by disregarding differences in station, race, and religion," was able to report that 57 percent of those using the recreational facilities and 62 percent of those enrolled in educational, cultural, and social groups were Jews.[75] And a few years later, a survey of gymnasium use indicated that most classes were overwhelmingly Jewish.[76] Likewise, an undated report from the mid- to late 1930s indicated that "the children of Neighborhood House up to and including the High School age of boys and girls are almost entirely Jewish and from the community."[77] Many oral histories reminiscing about an overwhelmingly Jewish atmosphere recall this period.[78]

At the same time that this influx was occurring, upwardly mobile members of the second generation were already beginning to move out of the area. Ida Loewenberg speculated in a 1921 editorial that if the influx of new immigration were to cease, "the Ghetto may be cleared out" if the "exodus" continued.[79] Roughly 20 percent of South Portland families present in 1920 had moved to the East Side by 1930, and a smaller number moved to the city's Northwest.[80] Despite Loewenberg's worries, it is clear that the majority of Portland's Jews continued to reside in South Portland through the 1920s, providing a Jewish constituency for Neighborhood House that included both newcomers and longer-term residents. And among those who did move, many relocated to the nearby Shattuck School area, still in Southwest Portland but closer to the B'nai B'rith Building.[81] In 1924, a survey of all Jewish children in the Portland public school system revealed that, of the total of 964, over a quarter (285) attended Failing School, the elementary school nearest Neighborhood House. Another 278 attended Shattuck School.[82]

Despite the arrival of newcomers in the 1920s, the Jewish population of the area became increasingly native born and middle class. Because the new national quota system cut off immigration in the early 1920s, those who arrived in Portland in subsequent years were secondary rather than direct migrants. These trends led to shifts in the types of demands made on the house. In 1928, correspondence from the settlement described it as "becoming more and more a community center, serving the needs and desires of its members, with no idea of rendering charity, but much rather of providing recreational, social, and cultural facilities for the normal, middle class families of the neighborhood."[83]

However, this trend was short-lived. In the 1930s and especially in the 1940s, there was a marked acceleration in neighborhood transition, as the area began to become both less Jewish and poorer. In part, this was a continuation of patterns that had begun in the 1920s as the American-born children of immigrants accessed educational and business opportunities that allowed them to move to more affluent parts of the city, or leave for other parts of the country.[84] In addition, the widening of Barbur Boulevard and the construction of the Ross Island Bridge in the mid-1940s displaced some residents. By the 1940s, the area's Jewish population was increasingly elderly, as children and grandchildren moving out of the area left their parents and grandparents behind.[85]

As neighborhood demographics changed, Neighborhood House worked closely with other Portland-area service agencies, both public and private, as it reassessed needs and rededicated itself to serving area residents. As we have seen, the women of the Portland NCJW section had taken part in Portland women's club activities and social service projects since its earliest days, although their responses to invitations to participate on joint efforts were somewhat inconsistent through the teens.[86] By the 1920s, however, integration into citywide social service initiatives became more pronounced. According to Michele Glazer's history of the Neighborhood House, this trend began in 1920 with the formation of the Neighborhood Community Club, which united the area's residents and community centers in fighting against a plan by the Multnomah Hospital to create an isolation hospital in the area. This focused effort led to cooperation on a number of neighborhood improvement initiatives that continued in subsequent decades.[87]

Activities at Neighborhood House in the 1940s increasingly emphasized intergroup work. Boys Club at Neighborhood House, 1948. Credit: Oregon Jewish Museum

Such cooperation was reinforced by the simultaneous integration of Neighborhood House into citywide fundraising networks. In its early years, Neighborhood House had been supported through direct donations, and an early decision was made to "accept, but not solicit, donations from non-Jews." However, 1920 saw a major shift in funding as both the Federation of Jewish Societies and the Portland Community Chest were founded. The federation (of which Neighborhood House was a constituent agency) quickly joined the Community Chest. While the federation was an autonomous organization, the common fundraising through the Community Chest reinforced programmatic efforts at cooperation and coordination.

By the early 1940s, Neighborhood House representatives were playing an active role on the newly founded Southwest Portland Neighborhood Council, part of a citywide initiative to build such associations. Neighborhood councils were charged with "cooperative planning for better living for the boys and girls in the neighborhood," and in Southwest Portland, Ida Loewenberg assumed the chairmanship of the group.[88] The Neighborhood Council provided increased opportunity for coordination with stakeholders in the area, as Neighborhood House continued its practice of expanding or contracting its services in coordination with other social agencies. For example, when the Manley Center decided to relocate to another part of the city in 1946, Neighborhood House was asked to "minister to the needs of the remaining community." "You can rest assured," replied a Neighborhood House representative, "that we will be glad to do everything possible to cooperate with you and to try to take care of the needs of the people in this community."[89]

The same year, the Council of Social Agencies suggested a study of "the needs of the neighborhood" and that Neighborhood House "redefine its function, analyzing its services" based on those needs and seek "to include in the membership of the board, staff and committees, persons of the major religious groups and racial groups of the neighborhood." The memo noted that the Jewish Community Center (formerly the B'nai B'rith Building) was sufficient to serve "the city-wide Jewish population," and that "Neighborhood House, being inter-racial and inter-cultural, and being necessary as a neighborhood settlement center, there is no over-lapping of work and that it should, therefore, continue to function." The Neighborhood House Board responded affirmatively to these recommendations, noting that their absorption of the Manley Center's functions demonstrated their willingness to meet current neighborhood needs.[90] Taking a concrete step toward a more inclusive government structure, the house revised its constitution to allow for greater neighborhood representation on the board, and chairman Flora Berkowitz (wife of Beth Israel rabbi Henry Berkowitz) sent letters inviting potential board members "who live in the immediate community and who participate in the agency's activities" to tea.[91]

As it shifted its program to include former Manley clients and make adjustments to changes in local demographics, Neighborhood House continued to provide many of the same services it had pioneered earlier to a changing clientele. An advertisement for a camp program in 1940 boasted, "It is a place where all elements of the community may meet on common ground, regardless of race, creed, or political belief."[92] The program of Americanization and citizenship classes continued in the 1940s, now serving a diverse population of mostly European immigrants.[93] A variety of clubs used house meeting space, including a theater group, the Girl Scouts, and even church groups. A tally of Neighborhood House users from 1946 to 1947 that broke down the population by age and "nationality" indicated that, for each group, with the exception of adult women, Jews were in the minority of users. Thus, of thirty-six kindergarteners, only seven were Jewish; among "juniors" (age six to fourteen), 53 of 316 users were Jewish; and among high school students only 22 of 166. Only a handful of Neighborhood House's clients were racial minorities ("Colored," Chinese, and Filipino), and "Anglo Saxons" were the overwhelming majority.[94] These figures are not surprising. Although Portland's African American population increased by nearly 500 percent between 1940 and 1950, they remained a tiny minority of under ten thousand (only 3 percent of the city's population) and were concentrated in the northeast section of the city, in Vanport (until 1948) and the Albina district.[95]

Given that Portland was still 96 percent white in 1950, it is interesting that so much of the discussion about the house and its changing clientele during the 1940s focused on the presence of racial minorities. This discussion was a reflection of both the growing liberalism of the Jewish community and the concerns of the broader citywide network of social service agencies to which Neighborhood House was connected.[96] Of the major West Coast cities, Portland had the smallest African American population and a long history of racism. De facto segregation in public facilities, restrictive covenants in housing, and discriminatory employment policies were widespread.

These practices were brought into sharp relief in the 1940s. Wartime hysteria led to the mass removal of the entire West Coast Japanese American population, which, in Portland, had been concentrated north of Burnside, just west of the Willamette River. In their place—and in far larger numbers—came workers, drawn by the newly opened shipyards. Portland's population, which hardly grew at all in the 1930s (increasing only from 301,815 to 305,394 between 1930 and 1940), jumped sharply, to 373,628 by 1950. During the war years, many of these newcomers—among them the first substantial number of African American migrants—were accommodated in housing constructed by the Kaiser Shipyards at Vanport, on reclaimed flood land. In 1948, when a flood erased Vanport in an instant, its residents were forced into a city that had inadequate housing stock and restricted much of the stock it had to whites. Not surprisingly, the growth of the African American community—and particularly the Vanport crisis—led to increasing concern among social service agencies about race relations in Portland.

Although the racial diversity of South Portland was limited, these broader citywide concerns made the issue of race increasingly prominent in Neighborhood House discussions and is an indication of how deeply engaged the house leadership was in the network of area social service providers. The language of "intergroup" work and race relations began to appear more in house publications, as in a report from the war era that emphasized house contributions "toward the development of intergroup understanding and cooperation in natural group situations."[97] The Portland Neighborhood Councils and the Council of Social Agencies (CSA) urged their constituent groups to reach out to minorities and push race relations to the top of their agendas. Neighborhood House participated actively in these discussions, repeatedly reaffirming its commitment to serve the changing population of the area. The Neighborhood House Board received inquiries, such as one in the fall of 1944 from the CSA about the settlement's policy "with regard to the Negro." "Miss Loewenberg," the minutes record, "was instructed to fill out questionnaire attached, stating that we had no policy against negroes."[98] Several months later, a CSA report urged groups to follow the example of "the forward looking inter-racial policy and program of the YWCA . . . [which] is doing much to relieve tensions in this period of the rapid increase of our Negro American population." It recommended that groups embark on a program of educating their boards and committees and that agencies "extend their service to Negro-American and other minority group."[99] Within months, the CSA sent a notice regarding "a referral center to include children of minority groups for group experiences in group work agencies." The Neighborhood House Board endorsed the project, deciding to appoint a committee to consider how to respond to possible staff objections to "working with a certain minority group." After further discussion the following month, the board agreed to send the CSA a letter indicating Neighborhood House's acceptance of "responsibility for referrals of minority groups."[100]

The NCJW matched local Portland social service agencies in encouraging Neighborhood House to move in this direction. Indeed, in

The focus on integrated activities is reflected in this South Parkway Club teen dance at Neighborhood House, 1948. Credit: Oregon Jewish Museum

communicating their commitment to meeting neighborhood needs in a diverse setting, the Portland section emphasized their national organization's endorsement of activities serving broad constituencies. On March 3, 1947, the Portland Section resolved,

> The Council believes that Neighborhood House is meeting an important intercultural need. This is in keeping with the national policy restated at the Triennial Convention in Dallas, Texas, November 1946 to the effect that "activity should not be restricted to Jewish interests and materials but should reflect the whole checkered pattern of American cultural life."
>
> Therefore, in accordance with this policy, and to sustain its essential services, both Jewish and non Jewish, the National Council of Jewish Women, Portland Section, will continue its operation of Neighborhood House as a valuable and essential social enterprise in this community.[101]

The selection of Arthur "Archie" Goldman as executive director of Neighborhood House in 1947 was clearly tied to the shift in focus toward a broader community perspective. A job advertisement for the position characterized the settlement program as "inter-sectarian" and mentioned the diversity of the neighborhood.[102] Goldman had a deep personal commitment to interracial work and clearly aimed to champion this direction as Neighborhood House director. Early in his tenure, he took a public stand against racism, writing a letter to the editor of the *Oregonian* in response to a short news piece about a local restaurant that had refused to serve African American singer Carol Brice. Goldman criticized this action at length, calling the incident "a shame."[103]

By 1948, Goldman was a key player on the CSA and had been appointed (along with a Catholic and a Protestant community leader) to the CSA's new Institute on Cultural Factors in Social Work. Goldman had, according to a CSA document, "considerable educational experience in the field of race relations."[104] During the same year, Goldman entertained the idea of opening a branch of Neighborhood House in Albina, a neighborhood with a rapidly growing black population.[105] Notably, in 1948, Goldman arranged for Neighborhood House to provide temporary shelter for sixty flood victims from Vanport, both black and white, placing each family in one of the house's meeting rooms. In addition, he and his wife opened their home to an African American family. As Goldman wrote to a social work colleague, "I'll make a bet that it's the first time that Negroes have lived in that area of our neighborhood." Goldman saw this activity not just as an act of charity, but also as a step that might encourage neighbors to rethink their racial views:

> From the point of view of the community at large, and our neighborhood specifically, this can be a positive experience. In the first wave of emotion, families volunteered to take in evacuees, and, so, suddenly, in nice, staid, respectable neighborhoods, Negroes moved in, and surprisingly enough "somehow" it didn't seem to make much change in neighborhood living. It is true that Negroes had a harder time to find a place because white families didn't wish to take them in, but I gather, that in the shelters and dormitories, etc., many Negroes and whites slept side by side and "somehow" nothing

seemed out of order. If the city fathers are alert a lot of good can happen out of this thing, and there you have the $64 question. [106]

Despite the house board's clear direction toward increasing interracial work in this period, this sort of transition was not without controversy, locally or nationally. During the postwar period, urban African American populations increased, and Jews became part of "white flight" to the suburbs. Many historically Jewish settlement houses and community centers facing the same issues of changing community demographics as Neighborhood House decided to move in the opposite direction. For example, the Sisterhoods of Personal Service in New York City, pioneers of the "personal service" model, moved away from social service work as early as the 1930s. In 1936, according to historian Felicia Herman, they terminated their programs, which were replaced by synagogue sisterhoods with focus "directed inward instead, toward the synagogue."[107] Although there were many factors that influenced this shift, it is interesting to note that the sisterhoods had, from their founding, been exclusively focused on serving disadvantaged *Jewish* populations.[108] This stands in contrast to the Portland case—although service to coreligionists was a primary aim of Neighborhood House, the Portland group had always been emphatic about serving the diverse residents of the area. In this sense, Neighborhood House was more similar to a Philadelphia Jewish settlement house known as the Neighborhood Center, which made a conscious decision to shift from exclusively Jewish work to neighborhood service in 1918. However, in the Philadelphia case, a shift back to specifically Jewish work came in the early 1940s. The reembrace of its ethnic origins, combined with changing neighborhood demographics, led it—like similar institutions in several cities in this period—to relocate to one of the new Jewish neighborhoods.[109]

The challenge posed to Jewish community centers and settlements by changing neighborhood demographics was such a widespread issue that it became the topic of national study and debate in the 1940s. The National Jewish Welfare Board, of which Neighborhood House was a member, issued a 1948 report addressing this situation. Known as the Janowsky Study, it asked whether Jewish community centers "should be Jewish" in focus, and came to the conclusion that Jewish purposes *should* be emphasized—a conclusion Neighborhood House's director rejected. In correspondence with Samuel Kohs, head of the Western States Section of the National Jewish Welfare Board, Archie Goldman explained that in Portland, "generally, the feeling is this: that as a neighborhood center program, we cannot go along with the Janowsky Study. That if the Janowsky report is accepted, we as a neighborhood center would probably have to leave the Jewish Welfare Board." Despite his strong wording, the Neighborhood House Board was, according to Goldman, divided on the question.[110] Eight months later, the Neighborhood House Board voted to join the National Federation of Settlements, resolving the issue in favor of the neighborhood, rather than the ethnic, model. Yet Goldman continued to wonder about the extent to which the board "emotionally accepted a settlement philosophy which to me means service to a neighborhood and trying to meet neighborhood needs," versus more specifically Jewish goals.[111]

Goldman's concerns were warranted. Although the board had endorsed the focus on neighborhood, it was clear that NCJW members were not as personally committed to the house as they had been in earlier decades. A special committee, assigned to revisit the question in 1954, recalled that council members had once had an "intense personal interest" that was fostered in part by the "common religious and national origin and background of the persons served, and a real desire to assist these immigrants in their adjustment to their new country and a sincere effort to help them in all the necessary steps in their assimilation." By the time of the report, however, there was little member interest in the workings of the house and few volunteered. At this point, continuing its services "without regard to race, color, or religion," the settlement's client population was only 3 percent Jewish. With a staff and volunteer base that was also largely non-Jewish, only the board remained Jewish, with fourteen members from the Portland NCJW section (including the section president and first vice president) serving on a twenty-five-member board. Although it pointed out that Neighborhood House's mission remained consistent with NCJW objectives despite these trends, the report concluded that the Portland section

does not have a continuing obligation with respect to Neighborhood House. It has made an outstanding contribution to the Portland

community and its demonstrations of an opportunity for social
service work of the sort performed by the Neighborhood House has
been full and complete.

There is reason to believe that the supervision of the activities of the
Neighborhood House and the character of the performance rendered
by it might be benefited if supervision were entrusted to a board
composed of people having more direct interest in and affiliation
with its activities and program.[112]

Given these findings, a change in relationship seemed inevitable. In
keeping with the recommendation of the report, the council retained
title to the property but transferred management of the facility to a
newly created social service entity. The new Neighborhood House
agency leased the building from the council for one dollar a year, and
the council turned over to the agency $14,000 in donations earmarked
for the settlement. Although still owned by the Portland section of
NCJW, Neighborhood House continued its recreational and social service activities under the new, community-run board.

The transfer of the house away from NCJW control signified the
end of an era. The special tie to South Portland that had been sparked
by the settlement of immigrant Jews in the area had dwindled, and
the women of the council shifted their focus toward new forms of
activism. No longer engaged in the day-to-day operation of the house,
they remained committed to service work and activities related to race
relations in Portland. Rather than direct involvement in the sort of
intergroup work that took place at the house, the council continued
its engagement primarily through advocacy work, by supporting state
level civil rights legislation, integration of public schools, and fair
employment measures.[113] In this, the women of the council continued
to prove themselves leaders both within the Jewish community and in
the broader Portland community. The public role that they had developed through their work at the house helped pave the way for their
continuing engagement in the second half of the twentieth century.

CHAPTER 4

A Jewish Vote?
Class, Ethnicity, and Politics

In 1916, several grocers, confectioners, and billiard proprietors in Portland were served warrants and arrested for violating the long-standing statewide Sunday closure law. Unless the law was repealed by the voters, Oregonians were warned, those who provided goods and amusement on Sundays would face "wholesale arrests."[1] Moving to prevent such an eventuality, Oregon's Independent Retailers Association launched a vigorous campaign for repeal—a campaign with strong "ethnic appeal" for both the established Reform Jewish community and newcomers in the immigrant neighborhood of South Portland.

Six years later, Oregon became one of the most active centers of Ku Klux Klan activity in the country. Klan-backed candidates stood poised to sweep state offices, and activists rallied to pass the infamous Oregon Schools Bill—an anti-Catholic measure aiming to abolish private schools. This election generated a particularly impassioned and unified response by the Jewish community. Despite a strong aversion to "ethnic voting," these examples demonstrate that some elections in early-twentieth-century Oregon did generate a clear Jewish response. In these cases, prominent leaders called on the community to take a stand, and the resulting vote in the most heavily Jewish precincts suggests distinctive patterns of Jewish voting.

Given both the emphasis on rapid integration and the relatively small concentrations of Jews in western states, historians have paid scant attention to the possibility of ethnic politics among Jews in Oregon (and in the West more broadly). Rather, the story of western Jewish engagement in politics has been told principally as a story of

individuals. From the mid-nineteenth century on, successful Jewish
Oregonians of the merchant class participated actively in state and
local politics. It was their early arrival in the newly settled region and
the pivotal economic roles they played that opened doors to civic and
political leadership. This was the explanation for the proliferation
of Jewish civic leadership in towns across Oregon—Albany, Astoria,
Burns, Eugene, Heppner, North Powder, and Pendleton all elected
Jewish mayors in the nineteenth century. All were towns where Jews,
though few in number, were among the early settlers. Even in Portland,
nineteenth-century Jewish officeholders such as Mayors Bernard
Goldsmith and Phillip Wasserman were elected based on their status as
successful business leaders and civic boosters; the Jewish community
was far too small to be considered a viable constituency.[2] By the end
of the century, Oregonians had elected Joseph Simon to the US Senate,
as well as several prominent Jews to the state legislature. This pattern
continued into the twentieth century, as demonstrated by Ben Selling's
leadership in both houses of the Oregon legislature in the 1910s, and
Julius Meier's election as governor in 1930, even as the state's Jewish
population remained small.[3]

Not only would appealing to a "Jewish vote" not be a viable path to
victory, but Jewish politicians prided themselves on being mainstream
leaders, taking positions that reflected their class status and regional
values and scorning the idea of ethnic politics.[4] Their careers, according to Toll, were based "on their mercantile prominence" and often
on fraternal ties through organizations such as the Masons.[5] In 1902,
prominent Jewish community and Republican Party leader David Solis-
Cohen explained, "Political organization founded upon racial or religious cohesiveness is sternly discountenanced by Jews generally, and
the effort by politicians to such an end is as far as possible prevented."[6]
Thirty years later, Governor Julius Meier expressed a similar sentiment:

> It is inconceivable to me that Jews should so betray their American
> citizenship as to organize into a Jewish political body. No religious
> group in this country can with impunity seek political aggrandize-
> ment upon such a basis. The Catholic citizens of our country have
> suffered much from the false accusation that they are bound together

for political ends. Does the Jew wish to open himself to this same accusation?

I believe the Jews of Oregon would not look with favor on any suggestion that they be organized for political purposes. And such an action taken in New York, the greatest center of Jewish population in the world, would be a menace to the citizenship of Jews throughout the country.

You have my permission to publish this statement, if it will carry any weight in dissuading those who are planning so un-American a project.[7]

But if the story of Jewish political activism in nineteenth-century Oregon was one of individual accomplishment, how did that change as a concentrated Jewish neighborhood emerged for the first time in the early twentieth century? How did immigrants in South Portland respond to—and impact—the well-established, native-born Jewish politicians? On what issues did the working-class sensibilities of the largely East European newcomers mesh with those of their better-situated coreligionists? To what extent did these groups unify in supporting Jewish candidates as well as issues?

The broad participation patterns of Jewish voters, including those from the South Portland immigrant neighborhood, are difficult to determine and have not previously been systematically examined.[8] While certain issues, including the Sunday closing law and the School Bill, mobilized the community, the class interests informing the traditional Jewish political elite were unlikely to excite their working-class coreligionists. Indeed, to the extent that immigrant Jews in Oregon shared the political affinities of their counterparts in other regions, one would expect to find a significant political gap between them and the political elite.[9]

Yet, beginning in the 1910s, there was a decided shift in Jewish political leadership that could potentially bridge this gap, fostered in part by the appearance of issues such as the School Bill, and in part by a shift from the patrician, class-based leadership toward an increasingly progressive political agenda. This helped mitigate the substantial economic and cultural gap between the affluent and acculturated community, which produced prominent politicians, and the working-class immigrant neighborhood of South Portland. This chapter explores the dynamics of these community politics, examining the elected, and generally elite, officeholders and the growing block of working-class Jewish voters. Despite the aversion to the notion of ethnic politics, a Jewish political sensibility emerged among Portland Jews during the interwar years, with Jewish politicians from the elite merchant class increasingly embracing a progressive agenda, as working-class South Portlanders navigated the sometimes competing pulls of class and ethnicity.

ETHNIC PULLS

In 1902, Oregon became one of the first states to adopt an initiative and referendum system. Within a decade, Oregonians were voting on dozens of measures in each election cycle. In 1915, the measure to repeal Sunday closing laws became one of the first ballot measures with an explicitly religious focus, one likely to generate a unified Jewish response. This vote came just at the time when a growing settlement of immigrant Jews, among them an increasing number of eligible voters, was emerging in South Portland. Although returns from these South Portland precincts reflect the voting behavior of the entire, rather heterogeneous, neighborhood, the area's concentrated Jewish population meant that precinct-level results were influenced by Jewish voting patterns, with that influence increasing during the 1910s and 1920s as the concentration grew.[10]

Sunday closing laws, enacted in Oregon in the mid-nineteenth century, were resented by many business owners for restraining trade, and by consumers who enjoyed the convenience of purchasing fresh goods and frequenting entertainment venues on Sundays. The laws had fallen into disuse by the 1910s, at least in major cities. In 1915, however, a group—described by the Independent Retailers Association of Portland as "self-inspired fanatics in ardent frenzied zeal"—set out to have them enforced, first in Eugene, and then in Portland.[11] In response, the retailers association used the initiative process to introduce a bill to abolish closing laws in the 1916 election.

Sunday closing laws had historically been particularly troublesome for Jews. Since a six-day workweek was typical at the time, Jews who observed their own Sabbath on Saturday and were forced into idleness on Sunday by blue laws were at an economic disadvantage. In

Portland, both the established community and the immigrant population were overwhelmingly concentrated in the business sector. In the
South Portland immigrant district, where shops generally closed on
Saturdays, being forced to close on Sundays as well represented a real
economic hardship for small shopkeepers and for their employees.[12]
Portland's *Jewish Tribune*, the community's sole Jewish newspaper, ran
a brief opinion piece on the Sunday closure laws several weeks before the
election, criticizing the "meddlers" who wanted to control what others
do.[13] The following week, a paid advertisement called on *Tribune* readers to "Help us repeal the Sunday closing law!"[14] And on November 3,
four days before the election, after noting that poor people are those
most hurt by Sunday laws, the *Tribune* editorialized, "The truth of the
matter is that the majority of clergymen do not give a broken penny for
all the poor people in the world: THEY LOOK ONLY FOR THEIR
OWN BENEFIT. The Sunday laws are un-American because their aim
is the UNITY OF CHURCH AND STATE . . . the people of Oregon
should vote for the repeal of the Sunday laws"[15] (emphasis in original).
The strength of feeling on this issue in the neighborhood was reflected
in the voting returns: while the repeal won 70 percent of the countywide vote, it was approved in the core South Portland Jewish precincts
by a margin of eighty-four to sixteen.[16]

Ethnic and religious sensibilities were again directly engaged in
the 1922 election, when voters decided on a compulsory public school
measure that was widely perceived as anti-Catholic and on a gubernatorial election that pitted Democrat Walter Pierce, a strong advocate
of the bill, against incumbent Republican Ben Olcott. Both the ballot
measure and Pierce were closely associated with the Oregon Ku Klux
Klan, which reached its greatest strength in this period, succeeding in
November in electing what became known as the "Klan legislature."
Pierce welcomed the Klan's endorsement and its money. In contrast,
Olcott denounced the group during the campaign, as he had earlier in
1922, in his "Proclamation Against the Ku Klux Klan," which began,
"Dangerous forces are insidiously gaining a foothold in Oregon. In the
guise of a secret society, parading under the name of the Ku Klux Klan,
these forces are endeavoring to usurp the reins of government, are stirring up fanaticism, race hatred, religious prejudice and all of those evil
influences which tend toward factional strife and civil terror."[17]

Although many advocates of the School Bill (including the Masons who were among its chief proponents) framed it as an Americanization policy aimed at equalizing and standardizing education, the role of the Klan in supporting the measure was widely known and was the focus of the opposition movement. Unlike the Sunday closing issue, in which supporters spoke in terms of business and consumer interests, the debate over the School Bill focused directly on issues of religious intolerance, and Jews were very visible in the campaign.

Established Portland Jews would likely have supported Olcott in any event, based on their long-standing Republican ties. Still, their strong efforts against the School Bill are particularly notable for several reasons. First, many in this leadership group had long been closely affiliated with the Masons (the bill's official sponsoring organization). Second, the School Bill directly affected relatively few in the Jewish community, as the overwhelming majority of the community attended—and supported—public schools. Finally, the Oregon Klan tended to avoid (and discourage among visiting Klan speakers) overt anti-Semitism.[18] Despite these potentially mitigating factors, community leaders and the Jewish press voiced frequent and strong condemnations of the organization, its endorsed candidates, and the bill.

The *Scribe*—by then the sole Jewish press outlet in the state, having succeeded the *Tribune*—published a number of strong statements against the bill and the Klan, blending its discussion of the School Bill with the broader issue of Klan-backed candidates such as Pierce. In doing so, the *Scribe* went well beyond the bill's anti-Catholic intent to emphasize the dangers in the Klan's broader prejudices. Klan involvement in politics could lead to the "permanent division of American life into bitter race and religious factions," the *Scribe* warned, emphasizing that "such a calamity must at all costs be avoided."[19] In its coverage, the *Scribe* made clear that not only Catholics but also Jews were specifically threatened by the Klan. For example, on May 12, 1922—the day before Olcott's anti-Klan proclamation and just before the primary election in which Klan candidates were prominent in a number of legislative races and in the gubernatorial primary—the *Scribe* published a full-page paid advertisement titled "A Public Statement" focusing on the dangers of the Klan:

There exists in this City and State a secret, oath-bound organization
which is fomenting suspicion, distrust and ill-feeling in civil, social
and commercial life. It is the Ku Klux Klan. Many of the principles
advertised by the KKK are found in most fraternal organizations.
But what the KKK is now best known for is its attempt to assume
the sole ownership of the title "American"; its policy of considering
Catholics, Jews, Negroes and all naturalized citizens as being incapable of loyalty to the Government and attempting to proscribe them
from public and civic offices. . . .

It is stirring up prejudices and enmities and is violating the constitution of the United States and the State of Oregon by attempting
to apply a religious test. . . .

If your family has been in the United States since the formation
of the thirteen colonies, you are not a good American if you are
a Jew or Catholic. If you are a naturalized citizen, no matter how
loyal you are, you are not considered a 100 per cent American by
the Klansmen. No colored man, native American though he be, can
expect to have his constitutional rights respected by the Ku Klux
Klan.[20]

By July, attention focused more closely on the School Bill, generating several strongly worded editorials, as well as the reprinting of
an exposé of the KKK that had appeared in the *Nation*.[21] In running
the piece, the *Scribe* was explicitly linking Oregon Klan activity to the
larger specter of Klan and national intolerance. In one August edition, for example, the paper printed three editorials, all relating to this
theme: one on Henry Ford's anti-Semitic *Dearborn Independent*, one
on religious restrictions at Harvard, and a third on a sheriff in Jackson
County who was able to defeat a Klan candidate.[22] The newspaper's
campaign culminated in a November 3 lead editorial titled "Vote No":

The time has come for every man and woman to defend Oregon
from an invasion of bigotry. No Attila sweeping across the plains of
Europe was more threatening than the sinister policy suggested in the
Compulsory Education Bill. To vote for it is to support reaction and
tyranny; not to vote at all is to stand idly by the destruction of one's
own house. There can be no alternative. Every man, with the love of

American institutions in his heart, should not only vote himself but see that every other man and woman votes and votes right.[23]

Although the *Scribe* editor, Beth Israel's rabbi Jonah Wise, clearly played a lead role, he was joined by a number of equally prominent Jewish Oregonians who publicly spoke out against the Klan measures and candidates, both within the Jewish community and in the broader arena of statewide politics. In the *Scribe*, full-page advertisements signed by the most prominent members of the community—men including Ben Selling, David Solis-Cohen, Roscoe Nelson, and Nathan Strauss, along with Rabbi Jonah Wise—called on Jews to vote *as Jews*: "The time has come for Jews to assert their patriotism in defense of fundamental American institutions and the absolutely unabridged right of liberty and conscience." They warned, "This weapon is not at present aimed at the Jews but we feel that all Jews are deeply concerned in the promotion of religious freedom and jealously interested in its promotion."[24]

Beyond the pages of the *Scribe*, Jewish leaders played a prominent role in the anti-Klan/anti-School Bill campaign. Ben Selling was a prominent member of the Protestant and Non-Sectarian Schools Committee that traveled the state speaking out against the bill.[25] His son, Lawrence, was one of several Jewish doctors who signed a full-page statement by "non-Catholic physicians" protesting against the bill in the public affairs journal *Oregon Voter*.[26] The Jewish League for the Preservation of American Ideals published a full-page ad in the *Portland Telegram*, and Rabbi Wise's sermon against the bill was quoted extensively in the *Oregonian*.[27]

Although opposition to a Klan-backed measure and gubernatorial candidate may seem a given for the Jewish community as a whole, the election was more complicated in the working-class South Portland neighborhood, because Pierce was more than just a Klan candidate. Rather, Pierce was known as a champion of Progressive politics, with a lifelong commitment to what Robert Johnston has called "democratic populism," of a type central to Portland's distinct "radical middle class" tradition in this period.[28] An early supporter of the democratization of politics through measures such as initiative, referendum, and direct election of senators, Pierce also worked to limit the influence of corporate power on the economy and the political process. He favored progressive tax policies, protections for unions, workman's compensation, and even a state-funded full-employment program.[29] Such positions, as we shall see, appealed to South Portland's Jewish community much as they did to their non-Jewish counterparts.

Despite the potential pull of such "radical middle class" positions, the anti-Klan, anti-compulsory school, anti-Pierce message clearly reached the immigrant and working-class Jewish voters in South Portland. Neighborhood House's newsletter the *Neighborhood*, helped the *Scribe* to get the word out, and election returns suggest that voters in the South Portland neighborhood responded strongly. Although Pierce won 55 percent of the countywide vote, helping him to his statewide win, Olcott dominated the South Portland precincts. In the core Jewish precincts, 69 percent voted for Olcott. Likewise, the School Bill, which passed statewide and won a 54 percent majority in the Portland's Multnomah County, was soundly defeated in South Portland. In the core Jewish area, the bill went down 32 percent to 68 percent.[30]

After the election, Ida Loewenberg used the pages of the *Neighborhood* to express her strong dismay. The recent election, she editorialized, threatened "to change Oregon's reputation as being one of the most progressive states to a reputation as being the most reactionary." Loewenberg singled out the School Bill as breeding "intolerance, religious rancor, and racial bitterness," and encouraging "the growth of secret organizations that appeal not to open and legitimate desires, but to selfish and perverted prejudices."[31] The same November

TABLE 1: 1922 School Bill and Gubernatorial Election

	YES	NO	PIERCE (D)	OLCOTT (R)
Precinct 89	37 (30%)	87 (70%)	31 (21%)	119 (79%)
Precinct 90	58 (37%)	97 (63%)	69 (44%)	89 (56%)
Precinct 91	54 (30%)	125 (70%)	57 (30%)	135 (70%)
Total:				
Core Jewish	149 (32%)	309 (68%)	157 (31%)	343 (69%)
South Portland	300 (33%)	621 (67%)	307 (31%)	587 (69%)
County-wide	41,424 (54%)	35,300 (46%)	43,771 (55%)	35,295 (45%)

edition of the *Neighborhood* announced a new program of public fora to discuss the issues of the day, indicating that the second session would focus on the question "Is the School Bill Constitutional?"[32]

Significantly, the election results in South Portland contrasted sharply with those in areas of the city with a similar socioeconomic—but not ethnic—profile. In fact, those were precisely the areas that gave the School Bill its greatest support. Historian Robert Johnston's analysis frames the School Bill in terms of its populist appeal to working people in its promise that "all American children would receive the same education in ethics and 'equality,' so that 'there shall be no classes.'" According to Johnston, "those living in mixed working-class and middle-class residential areas provid[ed] overwhelming support for the initiative."[33] For Jews in South Portland—an area with a similarly mixed population of workers and small-business owners—the School Bill clearly activated ethnic sensibilities that trumped class-based concerns.

Indeed, the 1922 election points out a key divide between the South Portland immigrant district and its class counterparts on the East Side in terms of response to the radical middle-class agenda in Oregon. This divide is based on a fissure in populist politics itself. As Robert McCoy explains in an article on the career of Walter Pierce, although Johnston's "radical democratic populism" represented one side—the Progressive side—of these politics in Oregon, the other side of the coin was "reactionary populism," which included strong attraction to nativist groups including the KKK.[34] As McCoy explains, Pierce and many of his supporters "sought ways to democratize politics and limit the negative impact of capitalism, but they also sought ways to limit who could participate in the political social and cultural life of the republic."[35] South Portland's Jews, who were, as workers and especially as small shopkeepers, attracted to the Progressive side of the coin, were understandably wary of the reactionary side.

Taken together, the 1916 and 1922 elections suggest that a cross-class Jewish vote could be activated in Oregon, particularly when the exclusionary side of the populist agenda came to the fore. Despite differences in economic interests among voting groups, blue laws, the School Bill, and the threat of Klan-supported candidates could bring together the wealthy, native-born segment of the community with immigrant workers and small shopkeepers. And despite their aversion to the very idea of an ethnic vote, established politicians could be moved to call on their coreligionists to vote Jewishly. The potential for bridging class differences within the community, however, extended beyond direct ethnic threats represented by the Sunday closing laws or Klan threats, as a generation of progressive Jewish politicians emerged in the early twentieth century. As political leaders such as Ben Selling and, later, Julius Meier moved away from a strictly pro-business agenda and toward more progressive stances, the "old" Jewish community came into closer alignment with the issues motivating the growing "new" community in South Portland. That alignment, however, did not always translate into ethnic unity.

JEWISH POLITICAL LEADERSHIP: FROM SIMON TO SELLING

In a state where Jews were a tiny minority and the political successes of individual Jewish candidates had long been based on class rather than ethnic ties, the rhetoric of the election of 1922 represented a break from the established norm. That norm had a history going back to the 1860s and 1870s, when the critical economic roles that Jews played in towns and cities across the state led to their early participation in local politics. Jewish merchants, bringing their families to isolated locales and building brick buildings that conveyed their confidence in these towns' futures, were rewarded with opportunities for civic leadership. Such men included Julius Durkheimer of Burns, who established a network of stores with his brothers and other relatives and was elected mayor. Similarly, Samson Friendly started in Eugene as a Wells Fargo clerk and later branched into retail and supply businesses, providing a vital service to farmers by extending credit and marketing their grain and hops. Soon, he was serving the city government, first as a councilman and then as mayor, as well as joining the board of trustees of the University of Oregon.[36]

A lawyer rather than a merchant, Joseph Simon represents the high mark of political influence for this generation of Jewish Oregonians. Simon, whose family emigrated from Germany when he was an infant and arrived in Oregon when he was six, would become the "most powerful individual in Oregon's politics" by the turn of the century.[37] As early as the mid-1870s, Simon, then in his early twenties, was elected to

Mayor Joseph Simon escorts President Taft during the president's visit to Portland, 1909. Credit: Oregon Jewish Museum

the Portland city council. He quickly emerged as one of the key power brokers in the Republican Party, first in Multnomah County and later in the statewide party committee. In 1881, he narrowly missed being elected mayor (after a tie vote, the city council decided the election in favor of his opponent). The defeat did not interrupt his eleven-year tenure in the state senate, which had begun in 1880. After he prevailed in the disputed election of 1896 and took his seat in the US Senate in 1898, he found that Washington, DC, did not live up to the political intrigue at home. Returning to Oregon after completing his partial term, he was elected mayor of Portland in 1909.[38]

Typical of nineteenth-century Jewish politicians in Oregon, Simon's political influence was built not on ethnic ties but on a firm business foundation. As a politician, he represented the same railroad interests as he had as a lawyer in the prominent firm, Dolph, Mallory and Simon. The connections that linked him with the business community also tied him to Republican elites—Joseph Dolph, his law partner, preceded him in both the Oregon and the US Senate. Operating as more of a "broker" than a "boss," according to Portland political historian E. Kimbark MacColl, Simon's long tenure as party leader was dominated by bitter competition between his own and the Senator John Mitchell faction of the Republican Party, both at the state level and in Portland city politics. Simon consistently championed private enterprise and promoted a good business climate, whether that meant preventing the City of Portland from asserting public ownership over the water system or ensuring that the police refrained from suppressing vice such as a bordello operated out of a Simon-owned property (a not-atypical arrangement for politicians in this era).[39] Indeed, during the 1896 legislative session, he and his cohorts used vice to prevent action favorable to his rival in the Oregon House, spending tens of thousands of dollars on "entertainment," including prostitutes and keeping the representatives "drunk, and intoxicated for days."[40]

Such shenanigans aside, Simon was long considered the consummate establishment politician, as was the case in his 1909 mayoral run against Progressive Harry Lane. Simon was backed by Portland business leaders as "someone who could be trusted and who was an integral part of the major corporate complex."[41] Although supporting civic improvements under the City Beautiful banner, Simon was primarily a "defender of private interests," who was averse to public debt and advocated that public projects be financed privately—a practice that enabled private interests to make "handsome profits from city bond issues."[42] In this way, Simon was the quintessential politician of the business community, representing—like many of his peers in this era— the interests of a class in which he was firmly entrenched.

Simon's career can be seen as the high point of what might be called "old school" Jewish political engagement in Oregon, characterized primarily by individual office holding based on class standing, participation in elite circles, and support for business interests. This was decidedly not a leadership style that called on ethnic interests, in contrast to the later campaign to block the School Bill. Although Simon was the most politically powerful Jewish Oregonian of his era, there is little evidence that he was supported by Jews who did not share his class background.[43] Indeed, although Simon's allies within the party did include several fellow members of Congregation Beth Israel and a few Jewish merchants benefited from his patronage, it would be difficult to make the argument that there was much religious/ethnic basis for these connections. [44] For example, Simon had ties to Solomon Hirsch, who had served in both houses of the state legislature and was serving as president of the state senate when Simon was elected to that body. Yet Simon's support for Hirsch for US Senate in 1885 was largely motivated by his desire to stymie the ambitions of his rival, Mitchell, for that office (Hirsch lost by one vote when he failed to vote for himself). [45] Ties between politicians such as Simon and Hirsch seem based not on religious or ethnic affinities, but on shared membership in the Republican, pro-business establishment.

Certainly, the broader Jewish community may have taken some pride in the achievements of Jewish political leaders, including Simon. Yet there was a substantial economic and cultural gap between these leaders and the workers and small shopkeepers in the emerging community in South Portland. The immigrant community may have found it affirming that Simon, as a Jew, could achieve high political office, but his patrician politics were unlikely to resonate with their priorities. Yet a new, more community-centered Jewish political model was beginning to emerge. This was not a new generation, for several of these "new" politicians were Simon's contemporaries, and even his friends and allies. Yet their closer ties to the Jewish community, broadly defined, set them apart from Simon. And those ties were likely an important factor in their increasing embrace of a Progressive agenda that was in tune with the growing community in South Portland.

David Solis-Cohen and Ben Selling are the outstanding examples of this group. Both had close political ties to Simon going back to the 1890s: Simon had selected Selling to be on the Republican slate of state senatorial candidates in 1896, and had Solis-Cohen appointed to the police commission, as well as endorsing his mayoral candidacy in 1896. [46] The *Morning Oregonian*, for example, called Solis-Cohen a "Simon man" and speculated in early 1902 that Simon and his friends would like to see Solis-Cohen nominated to fill the seat the senator was vacating. [47] Yet, while sharing Simon's business-oriented views and class background, Solis-Cohen and Selling were known for their activism *within* the Jewish community, both in established Reform circles and in immigrant South Portland, in a way that Simon decidedly was not. And both became increasingly linked to progressive causes, an association that further enhanced their connections with the growing population of working- and lower-middle-class families in the neighborhood.

David Solis-Cohen, of the Sephardic Philadelphia family, arrived in Oregon in 1877, working first as a merchant and later as a lawyer. Widely recognized as a Renaissance man, Solis-Cohen was known for his intellectual achievements, both secular and Jewish, and enjoyed writing plays and poetry, acting, chanting Torah, and speaking publicly on a wide variety of topics. His political career included service on the Police Board, the State Board of Charity and Corrections, and the State Board of Immigration. In the Jewish community, he held dual membership in congregations Beth Israel and Ahavai Sholom and was considered a pillar of both, serving as the essential orator at every important Jewish communal event for a period spanning over thirty years, from the 1890s until his death in 1928. A committed and enthusiastic Mason and member of B'nai B'rith, among other fraternal organizations, he played a critical role in the establishment of the B'nai B'rith Building.[48]

Given his status as an icon and moral leader of the Jewish community, perhaps it is not surprising that there is some conflict between portrayals of him in community and secular political histories, particularly as they relate to his connections with Joseph Simon. According to Oregon political historians such as MacColl, Solis-Cohen was an ally of Simon's, closely tied to his faction of the Republican Party. For example, MacColl characterizes Solis-Cohen as "Simon's regular Republican candidate" for Portland mayor in 1896.[49] Two years later, when a different candidate allied with Simon won the mayoralty, he appointed to the police commission "Simon men," including Solis-Cohen. In an era when many of Oregon's prominent politicians actively participated in or profited from gambling, prostitution, or both, there is no evidence that Solis-Cohen himself was tied to these activities. However, as "Joe Simon's close friend," he was willing to turn a blind eye to vice, according to MacColl.[50] He did so despite pressure from Rabbi Stephen Wise, who was "appalled to see members of his own congregation playing the slot machines," asking, "What's the use of preaching to stone walls? The rotten Golden West." Wise later wrote about Portland,

I came into closer touch with the things out of which grew lawless power of civic corruption. It was the union of gambling and liquor interests plus organized prostitution, which, in collusion with city officials and above all with the police department, poisoned and corroded the life of the city. The hold of these forces upon the city's life was fully known to the acquiescent and rather cynical population, which seemed to take it for granted that organized vice was entitled to no small part in managing the city and its affairs.[51]

In 1903, when a reforming mayor, George Williams, tried to move against police corruption relating to vice, MacColl notes, he replaced "Simon's protégé, David Solis-Cohen."[52]

In contrast with MacColl's depiction of Solis-Cohen as a cog in the Simon machine, historians of the Jewish community tend to portray Solis-Cohen not as Simon's ally, but as his critic. Steven Lowenstein states that Solis-Cohen "identified with liberal reform [and] strongly opposed the 'Simon machine.'" Indeed, Lowenstein claims that Solis-Cohen was a reformer during his service on the police commission, and that his views in favor of civil service reform, women's suffrage, and union rights challenged "entrenched Simon Republicans."[53] Likewise, William Toll casts Solis-Cohen as one of those who "identified with national reform interests rather than the local merchant class . . . [and] became outspoken opponents of the 'Simon machine.'"[54] Rather than turning a blind eye to vice during his tenure on the police commission, Solis-Cohen was, according to Toll, on the side of Rabbi Stephen Wise, expressing outrage at "the indifference of many Jewish merchants to the gambling and prostitution that flourished," and speaking out against evils including child labor.[55]

The discrepancy over Solis-Cohen can be attributed in part to the fact that his roles as Jewish community leader and statesman were of far more significance than his political career—and extended far longer. In contrast to Simon, who is remembered primarily as a politician rather than a Jewish community leader, Solis-Cohen has become the symbol of the civic virtue of the Jewish Portland, serving as community intellectual and moral exhorter. His speeches, according to Toll, provide the "clearest expression of the social ideology of the second-generation Jews"[56]—and the vision that he articulated, emphasizing the importance of reforming civil service, controlling special interests, and expanding democracy, was largely one that was the antithesis of Simon's. Practical inconsistencies, such as his tolerance of vice during his period as police commissioner, tend to be forgotten in light of his longer-term and better-known passionate advocacy for civic virtue. Ultimately, Solis-Cohen—whose political career was far more limited than Simon's and consisted primarily of service on boards and commissions—is remembered not for brief episodes of alleged cronyism, but for his articulation of the tie between Jewish values and civic virtue, his emphasis on universal values, and his moral leadership. Although playing a brief role in the Simon machine, Solis-Cohen's key role in Portland's Jewish community was to communicate a largely progressive vision.

Yet it was not Solis-Cohen, but his contemporary, Ben Selling, who translated this vision into practical politics. Like Solis-Cohen, Selling was widely recognized by both the Jewish and general populations as a model citizen; he was named Portland's first First Citizen in 1928. Steven Lowenstein, who profiles Selling, along with Rabbi Stephen Wise and Neighborhood House's Ida Loewenberg, as one of "three exceptional individuals," focuses on Selling's philanthropic—rather than political—career. Although a member of the merchant class and a man of considerable means, Lowenstein argues that he was "different from most other successful German Jewish businessmen," in terms of "his profound desire to help others."[57] Selling was recognized as one of the state's most active philanthropists, supporting a wide variety of causes, Jewish and secular, local, regional, and international. He served as president of the Hebrew Benevolent Society for two decades and opened a Working Men's Club that served 450,000 meals at a nickel apiece during periods of mass unemployment. Closely tied to the South Portland community, he personally supervised the settlement of East European Jews sent by the Industrial Removal Office and contributed generously to any number of community institutions, including Neighborhood House, where his wife served a term as president and taught sewing for decades.[58] Likewise, his detailed ledgers of charitable giving demonstrate his support for causes outside the community, ranging from Reed College to the Diocese of Oregon and the Seventh-Day Adventists. He also frequently gave to individuals in need, meticulously

Ben and Matilda Selling, c. 1925. Credit: Oregon Jewish Museum

recording donations such as ten dollars to a "little old lady" or twenty-five cents to a "stuttering girl."[59]

Like Solis-Cohen, Selling was a successful merchant, a Republican, and connected politically to Simon. Yet Selling's career was defined not by party loyalties, but by a long-standing commitment to democratic reforms that meshed well with his philanthropic and social commitments. Among these commitments was support for the Oregon Plan of initiative and referendum. As early as the 1896 state senate campaign—despite being the candidate selected by party chair Joseph Simon—Selling openly advocated for a direct primary. Once in the Oregon Senate, Selling continued to champion democratic reforms, including the direct primary and initiative and referendum, eventually joining the People's Power League, led by direct-democracy icon William U'Ren.[60] After two terms in the state senate, Selling returned to private life, but he was again elected to that body in 1910 and selected as its president in 1911. In 1912, after defeating incumbent Jonathan Bourne in the primary, Selling ran as the Republican candidate for the US Senate, facing both Bourne (now running as an independent) and Democrat Harry Lane, a former Portland mayor described by historian Robert Johnston as "the most powerful middle-class radical in

Progressive Era Portland."[61] The *Voters' Pamphlet* statement, supplied by the Republican State Central Committee, touted Selling's credentials as a reformer and a democrat, pointing to his long-standing support for the initiative, direct primaries, and election of senators, recall, judicial reform, and anticorruption measures. He was, Republican regulars claimed, the man who stood up against "machine politics," "thoroughly an Oregonian," and "an ideal representative of progressive Oregon."[62] A *New York Times* article predicting his primary victory over Bourne described Selling as "a Progressive . . . a strong advocate of the measures which have resulted in giving more direct power to the people."[63]

As the Republican Party's profile of Selling suggests, it is important to recognize that Selling's progressivism was part of a larger surge in national politics, and particularly in Oregon. As MacColl explains, as early as 1902, the use of direct democracy measures characteristic of national Progressivism had "lost its earlier Populist stigma" in Oregon.[64] Then, and throughout the next decade or so, establishment politicians including Simon found reasons, both practical and ideological, to support some of these reforms. Still, within this larger surge toward Progressivism, Selling stands out as a true believer, supporting measures aimed at curbing corporate corruption, creating state oversight, and establishing fair labor standards, along with his direct democracy efforts.[65] Selling was motivated, at least in part, on the labor issues by "humane and religious considerations. . . . [He] was known for his fair treatment of employees. A generous person, he was a champion of suffering humanity anywhere."[66]

In addition to being revered in the Jewish community for his philanthropic efforts, Selling's progressive political agenda had the potential to resonate with South Portland voters. Yet there is no evidence of a groundswell of Jewish support for Selling in the 1912 Senate election. In its November 1 issue, the *Jewish Tribune* ran no fewer than four advertisements admonishing readers to "Vote for Ben Selling," all of which were marked "Not a Paid Advertisement," yet the paper did not publish any news stories about his run or editorials endorsing him.[67] The election returns show a rather complicated race among six candidates who all claimed to be progressive. Bourne and Selling split the Republican vote, enabling Lane's victory. The South Portland vote was

TABLE 2: 1912 Senate Election, by Precinct

PRECINCT	BOURNE INDEP.	LANE DEM.	SELLING REP.	CLARK PROG.	PAGET PROHIB.	RAMP SOC.
32	89	67	65	24	6	13
33*	65	59	61	13	3	29
34	93	73	83	19	11	21
37*	43	55	34	12	3	23
38*	54	48	65	16	5	17
40	95	88	94	25	9	17
Total	439	390	402	109	37	120
Percent:						
Jewish Core	29%	26%	27%	7%	2%	8%
County	27%	29%	24%	9%	2%	6%
State	19%	30%	29%	8%	5%	8%

*Core Jewish districts

not dissimilar to the county or statewide returns, with Selling polling slightly higher than in the countywide totals, but slightly lower than he did statewide.

These results have to be read with care—1912 is an early date for assessing an ethnic vote in South Portland, as the concentration of Jewish voters was far less extensive than it would be later, and the percentage able to vote was still relatively low.[68] Still, despite Selling's association with Neighborhood House (both on his own and through his wife, Tillie) and his direct contact with working-class immigrant Jews through his philanthropic efforts, there is no clear evidence that they mobilized to support him in this election.

In the years that followed, the movement of Jewish candidates toward more democratic and labor-oriented platforms and away from traditional patrician politics continued apace. This increasing alignment of prominent, wealthy Jewish politicians and community leaders with a progressive agenda was reinforced by the community's influential Reform rabbis and by the local Jewish press. Thus, Selling's identification with progressive causes reflected a broader shift in the politics of the established community—a shift closely connected with the influential rabbis of Beth Israel congregation—the congregation to which Simon, Solis-Cohen, Selling, and Hirsch all belonged.[69] Rabbi Stephen Wise, who served Temple Beth Israel from 1900 to 1906, played a critical role in this political realignment. During his time in Oregon, Wise was a driving force behind the embrace of social activism by the Portland section of the National Council of Jewish Women (NCJW). Beyond the community, Wise was an active fighter for progressive causes and candidates—even when it meant railing against members of his own congregation, as on the vice issue. He was a key leader in the campaign for child labor laws in the state and closely tied to Harry Lane (who would later defeat Ben Selling in the US Senate race of 1912). Wise was a key part of Lane's successful mayoral campaign in 1905, and he was even invited to be part of Lane's cabinet.[70]

Stephen Wise's successor, Rabbi Jonah Wise, continued the tradition of championing progressive causes among his well-to-do business-owning congregants during his tenure from 1907 to 1926. Like his predecessor, his activism extended beyond the Jewish community—he served as a vice president of the Social Hygiene Society of Portland (a group largely dedicated to battling vice and venereal disease).[71] Within the Jewish community, Jonah Wise's position from 1919 to 1926 as editor of the *Scribe*, the sole Jewish paper serving the entire community, enabled him to broadcast his message well beyond his own congregation.

Through the pages of the *Scribe*, Jonah Wise and publisher David E. Cohen affirmed the linkage among morality, Jewish values, and public life that had been so central to the messages of politicians, including Solis-Cohen and Selling, and was an emerging theme in national Jewish discourse during the interwar years. Although it proclaimed itself open to all views, the *Scribe*, from its beginning in 1919, promoted an explicitly progressive agenda.[72] From 1920 until his departure for New York in 1926, Jonah Wise used his position as editor to emphasize the link between Judaism and a progressive social ethic. In the opening issue, for example, the paper proclaimed that America's ideas were a fulfillment of those of "Old Testament prophets crying for justice."[73] In a typical piece in April 1920, Wise traced "every outstanding effort for political and social justice" directly to the Old Testament: "Hebraism stands for Justice," he proclaimed.[74] Examination of the editorial page during these years provides a window into the kind of justice that Wise had in mind.

Wise used the editorial page to spotlight examples of charity, at times reprimanding those who were wealthy but stingy, claiming that they "save their money but they sacrifice the good will of their fellow men."[75] Yet his advocacy of social action went beyond the traditional giving of alms. For example—and not surprisingly, given the connection of Neighborhood House and the NCJW to Wise's congregation—his editorial page frequently supported the settlement work of Neighborhood House.[76] Education for all was clearly a priority, as the paper repeatedly endorsed public education initiatives and urged readers to support measures raising funds for both local schools and state educational institutions.[77] In addition, Wise's editorials denounced prejudice and linked tolerance to Jewish values. Most notably in this regard, Wise questioned the exclusion of Asian immigrants—an exclusion that was immensely popular in the West and that western Jewish papers scrupulously avoided discussing in this period.[78] In a 1923 editorial, the rabbi questioned the restriction, arguing that "there has never really been an attempt intelligently to study the problem to find out just where the menace lies," and arguing that any restrictions should be based on fact rather than prejudice.[79]

Given that Wise's own congregants were overwhelmingly business owners and managers, his advocacy for labor in the pages of the *Scribe* is particularly striking. In his editorials, Wise argued in favor of the right of workers to organize and bargain collectively, the eight-hour day, the regulation of child labor, compensation for industrial accidents, and other pro-labor positions. He often conveyed these positions through his reporting on and endorsement of the Central Conference of American Rabbis (CCAR) Committee on Social Justice, and, on several occasions, the *Scribe* printed in full the committee's resolutions.[80] In July 1920, Wise presented a full-page report on the CCAR convention, highlighting the Committee on Social Justice report as "of the utmost importance" and framing the social justice agenda as one tied to Jewish traditions and values. Wise noted its importance "especially for the Jewish employer to take that view in his dealings with labor." His column emphasized a series of social justice and pro-labor positions, including that "the right of labor to organize and the right of collective bargaining thru representatives of labor's own choosing are fundamental, as well as its right to share in the formation of conditions under which it shall work." The column further explained that "the welfare of the public is supreme over the interest of a class or classes."[81] Later, in June 1923, he published several editorials against the twelve-hour day, saying that workers were being treated "as a commodity just as pig iron or steel ingots," lauding the CCAR position, and arguing that Judaism teaches "the obligation of the group to the individual . . . it is the business of organized religion to continue to keep it in the minds of men."[82]

It is difficult to determine with any certainty what influence individuals such as Ben Selling or Jonah Wise, or a publication like the *Scribe,* may have had on the political views of Jewish Oregonians. That these pro-labor views were being espoused by the most prominent Jewish political and communal leaders, the sole community paper, and the rabbis of the leading Reform synagogue (a congregation to which most of the prominent community employers belonged) certainly helped to bridge the political gap between elites and the working class. Working-class Jews in South Portland, of course, did not look only—or even primarily—to Jewish community elites for political information. Internally, the immigrant community was developing its own leadership cadre during these years, with a new middle class emerging from within South Portland.[83]

COMPETING INTERESTS?

Influences on South Portland Jews were diverse but certainly included the voices of the labor movement, since there were, according to Toll's critical study, "many skilled craftsmen with *arbeiter ring* political connections."[84] These skilled and often unionized workers shared residential districts, as well as synagogues and immigrant traditions, with small businessmen (ranging from peddlers and junk dealers to proprietors of small shops). Together, they developed a common identity, reinforced because the line between workers and small-scale business owners was quite porous.[85] At the same time, Jews mixed in the neighborhood and at work with Italians as well as other diverse immigrants and native-born Americans. Through these personal relationships, and through the secular labor press, they became engaged in the broader class politics of the city.

South Portland Jews were attracted to some causes that appealed to their class interests and others that resonated with their ethnic/religious priorities. Yet there were times when ethnic or religious sensibilities conflicted with class affinities. One example is the case of the School Bill, when proponents' argument that the bill was an equalizing, anti-elite measure won over much of the working class but was overshadowed in South Portland by the bill's prejudicial overtones and its association with the Klan. We can explore these politics and gauge the degree to which they were influenced by class versus ethnic/religious factors by comparing the neighborhood's voting behavior to that of non-Jewish precincts with similar socioeconomic composition. *The Radical Middle Class*, Robert Johnston's widely acclaimed history of Progressive era Portland, provides an excellent comparative opportunity. Johnston examines a set of initiatives and candidates supported by a constituency made up of laborers and small-business owners. This coalition, Johnston's "radical middle class," sought, among other things, to expand "populist democracy, abolish most class distinctions, eliminate capitalist exploitation, bring women to full political power, [and] allow ordinary families to make decisions about their lives in an age of expert control."[86] In doing so, he argues, they provided a challenge to "the authority of economic, political and cultural elites."[87]

Johnston's analysis focuses on the nexus between class and politics among primarily native-born white workers and small-business owners on the East Side of Portland. Although he occasionally mentions West Side "ethnic" neighborhoods that were similar in economic composition and sometimes voted as did their East Side counterparts, he does not examine ethnicity or religion as a factor in his analysis. By drawing in the West Side immigrant Jewish community in South Portland, we can begin to explore the impact of religion and ethnicity on the political activities of a group that shared a very similar occupational and economic profile.[88]

Not surprisingly, on issues and in races that were perceived primarily in economic terms, the South Portland neighborhood tended to vote with its East Side counterparts. For example, in 1914, a single-tax measure championed by Populist reformer and long-time democracy advocate William U'Ren appeared on the ballot. A variation on Henry George's plan, the measure had great appeal among working people and did well in the working-class districts of the city, including South Portland.[89] Likewise, in 1917, the ethnic South Portland neighborhood joined its East Side counterparts in supporting the mayoral candidacy of Will Daly, termed by Johnston a "hero of labor." The area's strong support for Daly[90]—who was attacked by the Portland establishment as a socialist[91]—is an indication that the community was able to embrace a candidate who employed class-based rhetoric that was at odds with Jewish establishment sensibilities.

As these examples demonstrate, the South Portland–immigrant precincts tended to vote based on class interests when the issue was primarily economic, but voted differently from other working-class districts when there was a clear religious/ethnic issue—like Sunday closing or the School Bill—at stake. But many election questions were somewhat subtler. Close examination of a few key races can provide further insights into the way in which the immigrant Jewish community reflected the sensibilities of the broader Jewish community, but was also attracted to some aspects of the agenda of their non-Jewish class counterparts.

Suffrage is a good example. Oregon was the seventh state to grant women's suffrage, enacting it in 1912 on the sixth attempt. Portland Populists and suffragists supported each other's goals, with key radical middle-class politicians, including Daly and Harry Lane, actively campaigning for women's suffrage.[92] Indeed, Johnston emphasizes "just how readily the language of suffrage could flow into a populist language of class," as suffrage activists tied their cause to justice and equality, while painting their opponents as tools of "corporate power and capital."[93] Such appeals were critical, Johnston argues, in winning the "middling East Side" to the cause. Thus, in the 1912 victory—with suffrage winning a 51.8 percent majority statewide— the East Side provided over half of the total, voting 54.8 percent in favor (compared to 46.8 percent on the West Side). Support for suffrage was particularly strong in the "neighborhoods that were bastions of direct democracy," although working-class areas were less enthusiastic than middle-class ones.[94]

Despite similar occupational profiles, voters in the Jewish neighborhood of South Portland refrained from embracing this cause, consistently voting more heavily *against* suffrage than the county as a
whole or the state. For example, in the 1908 attempt, suffrage forces
lost countywide, 31 percent to 69 percent, while in the most heavily
Jewish precincts the measure went down 24 percent to 76 percent.[95]
Four years later, as the measure passed in both the county and the state,
it lost 46 percent to 54 percent in the heavily Jewish precincts—despite
evidence that Jewish immigrant communities nationally were generally
more supportive of suffrage than "either native born women or those
from other ethnic communities."[96] In 1917, for example, of the one
hundred districts in New York City that voted in favor of suffrage,
seventy-eight were heavily Jewish. In those districts, the vote in favor of
suffrage ranged from 76 to 93 percent,[97] a sharp contrast to the 1912
South Portland returns.

Locally, there is evidence of some Jewish support for the suffrage
campaign both in the South Portland immigrant neighborhood and
among the more affluent segments of the population. For example, a
group of "Jewish boys from South Portland," came together to form
the Oregon Junior Booster Club, sponsored by prominent suffragist
Dr. Marie Equi. The club's boys—and their girl mascot—planned to
"participate in street meetings and other demonstrations," forming a
musical group to perform at such events, according to a report in the
Oregonian.[98] Prominent Portland Jewish suffrage activists included

TABLE 3: Women's Suffrage, 1912

	YES	NO
Precinct 32	127 (55%)	105 (45%)
Precinct 33*	83 (39%)	127 (61%)
Precinct 34	146 (49%)	150 (51%)
Precinct 37*	68 (49%)	70 (51%)
Precinct 38*	95 (50%)	95 (50%)
Precinct 40	163 (52%)	150 (48%)
Core Jewish*	246 (46%)	292 (54%)
Countywide	19,288 (52%)	17,701 (48%)

*Core Jewish districts

Mrs. Julia Bauer, who joined the State Equal Suffrage Association in the 1870s and presented a speech about it at the organizing meeting of the Portland Council of Jewish Women. Her pro-suffrage position had been supported vocally by Rabbi Stephen Wise during his tenure in Portland; he attended the National American Woman Suffrage Convention held in Portland in 1905 and maintained a friendship with Abigail Scott Duniway, Oregon's most prominent suffragist, even after his relocation to New York.[99]

In the 1912 campaign, Josephine Mayer Hirsch, the widow of Solomon Hirsch, a leading Portland businessman and central figure in the Oregon Republican Party, emerged as a key leader.[100] Mrs. Hirsch, a major supporter of Neighborhood House, served as the chair of the Portland Equal Suffrage League. In January 1912, she hosted two hundred guests at the league's inaugural event, and she was credited with bringing in prominent women—including some of her former St. Mary's Academy classmates. According to a newspaper report, Mrs. Hirsch dedicated herself to the league's work, installing "a telephone plug in every room in [Hirsch's] mansion, so that a servant could get incoming suffrage calls to her, wherever she might be."[101] Tillie Selling also participated in pro-suffrage events, as did her husband. Ben Selling, then serving as president of the Oregon Senate, oversaw the passage of the bill in that body in February 1911.[102] That spring, he awarded seventeen American flags to the "Jewish lads" of the Oregon Junior Booster Club and hosted a lunch for them.[103] And when a Jewish suffrage activist, Miss Elizabeth Nickolls, visited Portland for a series of lectures, the *Jewish Tribune* profiled her favorably.[104]

Yet, it is clear that Mrs. Hirsch and Mrs. Selling's Jewish peers were divided on the issue. On November 1, just before the election, the *Tribune* ran two anti-suffrage messages from the Oregon State Association Opposed to the Extension of the Suffrage to Women as well as one pro-suffrage advertisement. One of the anti-suffrage pieces appeared on the editorial page. Titled "A Protest," the item began "We, American women, citizens of the State of Oregon, protest against the proposal to impose the obligation of suffrage upon the women of this State," and listed a series of arguments against the measure. A second similar message ran as a letter to the editor. Neither was a paid advertisement, and the former was specifically labeled "not a paid advertisement." In contrast, the "Women Should Vote" advertisement by the College Equal Suffrage League was marked "paid advertisement." [105]

The *Tribune*'s coverage leaned toward opposition; the Portland section of the National Council of Jewish Women was more ambivalent. When the Women's Club of Portland asked the section to endorse a prosuffrage resolution, they declined. Their explanation that such an issue was beyond their group's "philanthropic, religious, and educational" scope was, according to council historian Michele Glazer, "incongruous," given that suffrage "would have enhanced Council's leverage as women in a great many matters relating to the health, education, and welfare of women and children." [106] Certainly, the council later came to see suffrage in this way, admonishing members to "VOTE," in a 1924 bulletin article: "The voting right, which is so recent a thing for women and which was fought for so earnestly and strenuously, is a right, a privilege, and a duty that should be exercised by us and should never be neglected. . . . Let each Council member be a good citizen. Go to the polls. Vote and vote intelligently." [107]

The ambivalence of the council and the gap between South Portland voters and their East Side—and East Coast—counterparts reflected both national and local factors. Nationally, although it is clear that individual Jewish women played an important role in the suffrage campaign, Jewish women's groups were hesitant, with no major organization endorsing the movement until 1917. [108] Mainstream suffrage groups "found it puzzling that Jewish women's organizations were reluctant to endorse suffrage when they were otherwise known for being socially progressive." [109] Historians, too, have struggled to explain this reluctance, particularly in light of "widespread Jewish communal support." [110]

Locally, the occupational profile of the Jewish immigrant community may have hampered the movement. In eastern industrial cities, socialists and trade unionists were often among the most active Jewish suffrage supporters, [111] but, with a Jewish community concentrated in petty trade rather than industry, such groups were far less active in Portland than elsewhere. This was particularly so with regard to women, as the industry most associated with organized women workers, the garment industry, had little presence in the Rose City.

In addition, local voting on suffrage was influenced by opinions on a second perennial ballot issue from the same period: prohibition. As with suffrage, Oregon voters had considered prohibition repeatedly during the decade and a half before its eventual passage in 1914. Clearly, there was a tight connection between the two issues: prohibitionists consistently supported women's suffrage in the belief that once enfranchised, women would vote dry.[112] It is no coincidence, then, that Portland, one of the most emphatically wet cities in the state, was also one of the places where suffrage forces struggled most.

In the East Side "middling" neighborhoods that are Johnston's focus, there was strong support for prohibition. Much of the prohibition rhetoric tried to appeal to the middle class and to workers, citing it as a key measure to preserve and protect the home. In addition, the embrace of the prohibitionist cause by many Protestant churches likely resonated on the East Side in ways that it could not in South Portland. In the 1914 vote, prohibition was heavily supported on the East Side, although, as with suffrage, support was weaker in working-class than in middle-class districts.[113]

In contrast, there was little in the prohibitionist campaign to attract Jews, and most Jewish merchants had no compunctions about selling alcohol. The *Jewish Tribune* took an unusually strong position on the measure, publishing several anti-prohibition editorials in the week before the election. The first of these aimed generally at prohibition measures being considered in many localities across the country and was likely a piece reprinted from another press outlet. Arguing that self-control, rather than prohibition, was the way to curb indulgence, this piece proclaimed that prohibition would "rob people of their God given personal liberty," and asked, "How dare they seek to dictate to others . . . what these others may eat, drink, believe, wear and enjoy?" It then accused prohibitionists of being "un-American meddlers," who were "intoxicated with a terrible poison of religious and moral undoing."[114] This piece was paired with a second, by the *Tribune* editor David Mosessohn. Headlined "The Prohibition Craze," the editorial began, "Bigotted [*sic*] clergymen, narrow-minded laymen and hysterical women have taken up the cry of prohibition," and set out to refute the various claims of the pro-prohibition forces.[115] The lengthy piece concluded with the cry, "PEOPLE OF OREGON! BEWARE OF

THE PROHIBITIONISTS; ASSERT YOUR RIGHTS. DO NOT LET THEM ROB
YOU OF YOUR LIBERTY AND PROSPERITY AND YOUR CITIES AND TOWNS
OF HEALTHY GROWTH. VOTE DOWN PROHIBITION." The paper's own
economic fortunes were affected by the issue, as the *Tribune* in this era
regularly ran several beer advertisements.[116]

Although the *Tribune's* editorials may have influenced some, they
likely reflected preexisting anti-prohibitionist views in the community.
Since the campaign was often waged in specifically Christian terms,
culturally and religiously the prohibition issue had no resonance among
Jews. In addition, Jews were joined in South Portland by a substantial
community of Catholic immigrants, who also had little cultural affinity for prohibition. Not surprisingly, South Portland voted decisively
against prohibition. Countywide, prohibition lost in 1914 by a hair
(49.9 percent to 50.1 percent). Yet in the South Portland precincts,
the anti-prohibition vote ranged from 63 percent up to 83 percent,
with the total vote in the core Jewish precincts coming in at 73 percent
against.[117]

Notably, the prohibition campaign was also closely tied to the
single-tax movement that South Portland precincts favored that same
year. The idea of the single tax, popularized by Henry George in
Progress and Poverty (1879), was that only land should be taxed, and
not income and profits. Because a land tax would fall primarily on the
wealthy, this was considered a progressive measure. Despite the apparent distance between these two issues, they shared a common appeal to

TABLE 4: Prohibition, 1914

	YES	NO
Precinct 32	29 (17%)	142 (83%)
Precinct 33*	56 (32%)	119 (68%)
Precinct 34	113 (32%)	242 (68%)
Precinct 37*	81 (16%)	232 (74%)
Precinct 38*	35 (24%)	113 (76%)
Precinct 40	43 (37%)	72 (63%)
Core Jewish	172 (27%)	464 (73%)
Countywide	36,573 (49.9%)	36,668 (50.1%)

*Core Jewish districts

radical middle-class notions of "preservation of the home," and both tended to be supported with religious appeals.[118] In addition, the issues were linked by the independent gubernatorial candidacy of democracy activist William U'Ren, whose platform consisted of single tax, prohibition, and full employment.[119] U'Ren connected the single tax with temperance and other moral crusades as "part of a larger program to restore the dignity of labor and humanity."[120] Although this linkage apparently resonated in the East Side precincts, where those areas that supported the single-tax measure also voted in favor of prohibition, South Portland voters distinguished between the two measures, voting in favor of the tax measure but against prohibition.[121]

A similar discrepancy in voting came two years later, when the same constituencies again moved to protect their homes—in this case from the kind of "expert" control so often associated with the Progressive Movement. Although the 1916 anti–compulsory vaccine measure lost by a thin margin in the statewide election, it won in Portland. As a measure "that emphatically repudiated the authority of governmental and medical 'experts' to define personal and public health,"[122] the campaign appealed to preservation of the home, parental authority, and personal liberty.[123]

The measure's popularity in Portland was rooted in the "alliance of lower-middle-class and working-class citizens" central to Johnston's study.[124] While 55 percent of the city's voters cast their ballot in favor of the initiative (voting against compulsory vaccines) the majority on the East Side was 57 percent, with more than four-fifths of East Side precincts (84 percent) voting in favor. The tremendous class-based support for the measure, however, did not carry over to the South Portland immigrant district. On the West Side as a whole, the measure was voted down by a slim majority (49.7 to 50.3). In the South Portland immigrant district, the vote was somewhat mixed, but in the three most heavily Jewish precincts, the combined vote was 57 percent against the measure.[125]

Certainly, Jewish South Portlanders were exposed to the vigorous and emotional anti-vaccination campaign in the city, yet these campaigns competed with their ethnic sensibilities about "expert" opinion. Trusted local institutions such as Neighborhood House promoted faith in scientific expertise, particularly in matters of health. Through its

TABLE 5: Anti–Compulsory Vaccine, 1916

	YES	NO
Precinct 32	23 (52%)	21 (48%)
Precinct 33*	52 (43%)	69 (57%)
Precinct 34	74 (50%)	75 (50%)
Precinct 37*	83 (46%)	97 (54%)
Precinct 38*	53 (40%)	78 (60%)
Precinct 40	98 (53%)	86 (47%)
Core Jewish	188 (43%)	244 (57%)
Countywide	36,563 (55%)	29,898 (45%)

*Core Jewish districts

educational programs, including a series of lectures on social hygiene beginning in 1912,[126] and through its advocacy for various public health measures,[127] the house conveyed confidence in public health officials and scientific experts. Neighborhood House had served as a site for a medical clinic since 1912, was affiliated with the Visiting Nurses Association, and provided vaccinations to area residents, although it is not clear whether this had already occurred by 1916.[128] These attitudes were also reflected in the Jewish press—the *Scribe* did not yet exist in 1916, but it editorialized strongly in favor of compulsory vaccination when the issue arose again in 1920, writing, "While Americans find compulsions repulsive, for public health this is acceptable. Bitter experience has shown that epidemics can be successfully fought . . . by hygienic and health measures."[129] In addition, the Jewish community generally held professionals—particularly doctors—in high esteem, saw professional education as a worthy aspiration for its youth, and was already producing such professionals among second-generation immigrants. Toll's analysis demonstrates that the number of professionals in the Portland Jewish community in the 1910s and 1920s expanded significantly, particularly among the sons of East European immigrants. While many of them chose to live in more upscale neighborhoods, they were closely tied to South Portland, often continuing to attend synagogues in the area or visiting parents or other relatives who still resided there.[130] For all these reasons, it appears that Jewish South

Neighborhood House's Well Baby Clinic served the area and helped to inspire confidence in vaccination programs, c. 1921. Credit: Oregon Jewish Museum

Portlanders were more ready to trust public health experts than were other members of their class.

JEWISH POLITICS

Although the heavily Jewish South Portland precincts could be attracted to class-based issues and candidates, as is evident in the single tax or the Daly mayoral race, issues including suffrage, prohibition, compulsory vaccination, and the School Bill clearly activated ethnic sensibilities during the 1910s and 1920s. At the same time, prominent Jewish politicians, reflecting a shift in both Oregon politics and in national Jewish sensitivities,[131] moved away from a strictly pro-business posture and toward progressive positions more likely to attract their South Portland brethren. The gap between traditional elites and more recent arrivals was also eroded by the rise of an ethnic middle class and increasing contact and collaboration in Portland's Jewish community, symbolized most clearly by the merging of B'nai B'rith chapters in 1919.[132] The increasing unity was reinforced by growing concerns about local and national anti-Semitism during the 1920s. Ironically, at a time when the American Jewish community was torn by conflict over ways of responding to anti-Semitism at home and abroad, Portland's Jewish community was coalescing in powerful ways.[133] The impact of these trends can be seen in the election of Julius Meier as governor of Oregon in 1930. Although Meier was well known as one of the state's most prominent business executives and not particularly visible as a Jewish communal leader, precinct level returns suggest that he received very strong support in the South Portland neighborhood. [134]

Unlike Simon, Hirsch, and Selling, Meier was not a career politician. The youngest son of Meier and Frank founder Aaron Meier, Julius began his career as a lawyer in Joseph Simon's law firm but soon joined the family business, becoming general manager in 1910 and, with the death of his older brother, president. Although long active in civic affairs, Meier did not enter electoral politics until 1930. That year, his close friend, George Joseph, was running for the Republican gubernatorial nomination on a progressive platform focusing on public ownership of power. In the wake of Joseph's sudden death, "Old Guard" Republicans moved to nominate a conservative candidate who would protect the interests of private utilities. Meier, whose name recognition made up for his lack of political experience, quickly emerged as the popular favorite to take up Joseph's public power mantle. When the machine handed the nomination to conservative Phil Metschan Jr., the progressive wing rallied around Meier, who launched a campaign as an Independent.[135]

Meier's campaign made public power its signature issue. Endorsed by the State Federation of Labor, he spoke of the need to wrest government from the hands of "the interests" and to develop hydroelectric power to serve the people of the state rather than enriching the "power trust."[136] His profile in the *Voters' Pamphlet* promised that Meier would "liberate Oregon from the stifling domination of the power monopoly," by serving "the people" rather than the interests.[137] In his campaign's opening radio address, Meier warned listeners that the country was "in the clutches of the power octopus" whose "tentacles radiate from Wall Street into every section of the nation." He asked, "Which shall it be—private development for further enrichment of the coffers of the power trust or public development for the benefit of the State of Oregon and its people?"[138] Once elected, Meier supported federal assistance programs and resisted conservative pleas to call in the Oregon National Guard against striking longshoremen during the West Coast strike of 1934.[139]

Reflecting the increasing anti-Semitism of the 1920s and 1930s, Meier was attacked in ways that Selling and Simon had not been. The *Oregon Voter*, a prominent political weekly, was particularly pernicious, repeatedly depicting Meier as greedy, tightfisted, and self-serving. The publication ran a series of mocking caricatures on its cover in the weeks leading up to the election, as well as scathing profiles that played on anti-Semitic tropes. "Meier is selfish, smart, tricky, ruthless, vain. He wants the long end of every deal, the new toy to play with, the spotlight, and the special discount below what anyone else can buy," read one.[140] Although *Oregon Voter* criticized the idea of holding his Judaism against him, the journal's coverage revealed "latent anti-Semitic racial attitudes."[141]

The *Scribe* embraced Meier's candidacy from the time he entered the race, publishing a front-page photo and full-page endorsement in early August. Proclaiming that Meier "is holding aloft a banner that is the symbol of a new hope for the masses and a new period in the life of the Commonwealth," the *Scribe* expressed pride in "the esteem . . . shown toward one who has been so intimately associated with the Jewish community of Portland." This prominent endorsement ran counter to the paper's own policy. As the editors explained, "The policy of *The Scribe* has ever been to dissociate Jewish interests from political entanglements. It has urged its readers to vote, and think, politically, as citizens and not as Jews."[142] In that vein, during the fall campaign, the paper published a national opinion piece, "The Election Jew," which leveled criticism at a "certain type of Jewish politician who is trying to capitalize on his affiliations with Jewish organizations these days and make his Jewishness pay political dividends."[143] Clearly, the coverage implied, Meier was not that kind of Jewish politician. In their final endorsement, in the issue just before the election, Meier was praised for his dedication to Oregon's people, without any mention of his Jewish community connections. Noting his steadiness in the face of "exaggeration, distortion of facts, lies, and trickery" by his political

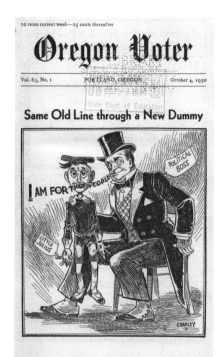

The *Oregon Voter* played on anti-Semitic themes as it campaigned against Julius Meier in his run for governor in 1930. Credit: *Oregon Voter*, October-November, 1930

enemies and the "defenders of vested interests," the *Scribe* lauded Meier as "a man of political vision and statesmanship" and expressed confidence in his chances.[144]

Although it is impossible to determine the precise impact of the *Scribe*'s endorsement, it seems likely that, along with the anti-Semitic flavor of attacks against Meier and his positioning of himself as the candidate who stood to defend the public against special interests, it contributed to strong support in the South Portland neighborhood. Winning the election with more votes statewide than his Democratic and Republican rivals combined, Meier ran particularly well in Multnomah County, where he polled nearly 72 percent of the vote. In the South Portland precincts, Meier's share of the vote was ten points higher than that.[145] In the Ninety-Sixth Precinct—the very heart of the neighborhood, where Neighborhood House was located[146]—Meier brought in 88 percent of the vote, leaving the other candidates in the single digits.

Interestingly, Meier expanded his leadership role within the Jewish community during his tenure as governor, serving as president of Portland's Federated Jewish Charities and assuming the presidency of Congregation Beth Israel in 1933. Meier's actions as governor and Jewish community leader attracted much attention in the Jewish community. The *Scribe* covered his activities with far more attention than it had given other political leaders, noting his comings and

TABLE 6: 1930 Gubernatorial Election, 1930

PRECINCT	BAILEY (D)	MEIER (I)	METSCHAN (R)	STREIFF (I/SOC)
84	18 (10.5%)	123 (72.3%)	14 (8.2%)	15 (8.8%)
85	7 (4.7%)	127 (85.2%)	10 (6.7%)	5 (3.3%)
86	6 (4.7%)	104 (82%)	14 (11%)	3 (2.4%)
95	7 (4.5%)	128 (82%)	14 (9%)	7 (4.5%)
96	11 (5.6%)	173 (88%)	12 (6.1%)	1 (0.5%)
97	13 (8.7%)	123 (82%)	12 (8.0%)	2 (1.3%)
Total Jewish	62 (6.5%)	778 (82%)	76 (8.0%)	33 (3.5%)
County	12,036 (12.7%)	68,121 (71.9%)	12,855 (13.6%)	1755 (1.8%)

Governor Julius Meier, 1935. Credit: Oregon Jewish Museum

goings and running frequent photos.[147] It also covered various policy initiatives outside of its normal purview, as when the paper ran the full text of Meier's radio address supporting the ill-fated Sales Tax Bill in 1933.[148] Naturally, the paper paid much attention to Meier's communal leadership, running notes, often accompanied by a picture, of his activities with the Federated Jewish Charities and in support of the B'nai B'rith camp at Devil's Lake.[149] In early 1934, it ran the full text of his report as president of Congregation Beth Israel, accompanied by a full-page portrait; later that year, Meier's New Year's greetings and picture appeared alongside those of President Roosevelt and Felix Warburg.[150] And at the close of his term, the *Scribe* published a full-page tribute, praising him for his service "to the State of Oregon and to the Jewish people," writing, "together with all classes of citizens of Oregon, the Jewish people share a sense of the pride and satisfaction in his courageous leadership."[151] Beyond the newspaper, both Ahavai Sholom and Neveh Zedek dedicated new Torahs in honor of the governor during his tenure in office.[152]

The communal support for Governor Meier evidenced in both the precinct-level voting returns and the positive press coverage suggest a level of ethnic connection that had not been evident during the political career of Joseph Simon, or even of Ben Selling. Although many in the Jewish community certainly felt pride in these earlier candidates, voters in the South Portland neighborhood were pulled by class-based concerns and may have been ambivalent about supporting candidates who, while coreligionists, were representatives of the business classes. At the same time, these politicians and the community press were reluctant to link Jewish candidates' political fortunes to the Jewish community, criticizing the very idea of Jewish political interests or an ethnic vote and avoiding direct endorsement.

By 1930, however, these sensibilities had shifted. Despite the fact that the interwar period is considered one of the most divisive in American Jewish history, in Portland, working-class Jews and elites drew closer together in communal organizations and in their politics during this period—and clearly voted in large numbers for Meier. The *Scribe* not only abandoned its policy of "disassociate[ing] Jewish interests from political entanglements," but read in the election of Meier an affirmation of the Jewish community:

> This victory is an indication that the people of Oregon would not
> stultify themselves by rejecting leadership of a high caliber on petty
> grounds of racial differences. This factor, most happily, was almost
> entirely absent from the campaign as an important factor. For this,
> the Jews of Oregon feel deeply grateful. There will be a warmer and
> deeper confidence in our fellow citizens as a result of this evidence
> of justice and impartiality. We join all friends and supporters of
> Mr. Meier in wishing him a happy and fruitful period of political
> leadership.[153]

Governor Meier, who warned of the dangers of ethnic politics, was a clear beneficiary of an increasingly unified Jewish political sensibility in Oregon.

CHAPTER 5

A Western Exception
Zionism and Anti-Zionism

Even as western Jewish historians began to break free of the East Coast dominance of American Jewish history, new generalizations emerged—now based on California, and particularly San Francisco, rather than New York.[1] One new refrain regards the significance of Zionism, and of its critics. John Livingston argued in the introduction to *Jews in the American West* that weakness in the Zionist movement was characteristic of the region.[2] Historians of both western Jewry and of Zionism have noted the relative strength of anti-Zionism among western Jews.[3] This chapter tests the validity of this generalization by evaluating the strength of Zionism and anti-Zionism in Portland, using the city as a case study for understanding factors shaping the responses to Zionism in the American West. This analysis demonstrates that, although the anti-Zionist movement (represented most prominently by the American Council for Judaism), gained a solid foothold in San Francisco in the early 1940s, the organization never became popular in Portland. Despite apparent similarities and close personal ties between the San Francisco and Portland Jewish communities, crucial differences, both in the composition of the Jewish population and in the attitudes of the leadership group, made the Portland Jewish community more receptive to Zionism. The anti-Zionist movement in the Rose City never rivaled that in San Francisco.

REFORM JEWS AND ZIONISM
The Reform movement's antipathy toward Jewish nationalism goes back to the mid-nineteenth century, when liberal American rabbis, influenced by their West European counterparts, began to rethink

Jewish identity. The self-definition of Jews as a people in exile was replaced by an embrace of the diaspora as part of a new, spiritual Jewish mission and a strong affirmation of the compatibility of Judaism with modern citizenship. The Pittsburgh Platform, adopted by the Union of American Hebrew Congregations in 1885 and considered the key foundational document of the American Reform movement, embraced a concept of Judaism as strictly a religion, without a national or political component, stating "We consider ourselves no longer a nation, but a religious community, and therefore expect neither a return to Palestine, nor a sacrificial worship under the sons of Aaron, nor the restoration of any of the laws concerning the Jewish state."[4] Twelve years later, the Reform movement's rabbinical organization, the Central Conference of American Rabbis (CCAR), was even more emphatic, approving a statement which began, "We totally disapprove of any attempt for the establishment of a Jewish state."[5] As Michael Meyer and Jonathan Sarna have pointed out, there were several prominent Reform rabbis who consistently dissented from this position, and others who, over time, defected from it. Some of these rabbis would ultimately devote themselves to the Zionist cause.[6] Still, in these and a number of other official documents—as well as in their liturgy—American Reform Jews repeatedly proclaimed that they had found their Promised Land in the United States, and that embracing their American identity required them to reject any notion of national or political connection—or even a wish for an eventual return—to an ancient homeland.[7]

This articulation of Reform Jewish identity coincided with and responded to the emergence of the Zionist movement, usually traced to the early 1880s when groups of East European Jews established colonies in Palestine. This migration was triggered by the same conditions that led to the much larger flow of East European Jews to the United States and, although the majority of migrants opted for the West rather than for Palestine, the movement had great emotional appeal. Still, even when the political Zionist movement emerged, inspired by Theodore Herzl's publication of *The Jewish State* (1895) and embodied in the First Zionist Congress in 1896, it gained relatively little traction in the American Jewish community. Among East European immigrants, despite the passion it inspired, the practical aspects of the Zionist movement did not resonate with those who "had already made their *aliyah* [migration to Palestine, literally "going up"] to the United States, where they lived free from the persecution they had known in the Old World and where opportunity awaited those with talent and the willingness to work hard."[8]

More broadly, in American Jewish communities still dominated in leadership if no longer in numbers by the Reform community, Zionism was philosophically problematic. Jewish nationalism was, at its core, a rejection of the commitment to the diasporic mission that was central to the Reform movement. Many believed that Zionism would call into question Jews' loyalty to their home countries. In short, "Zionism, especially political Zionism, raised the specter of 'dual loyalty.'"[9] Conversely, Zionists generally believed that their movement was incompatible with Reform Judaism because of the Reform commitment to assimilation.[10] Not only among the established Reform community, but even among newcomers, many American Jews felt that the call to embrace a Jewish national identity "conflicted with their allegiance to the United States," greatly limiting the growth of the movement.[11]

It was not until a new, American version of the movement emerged in the 1910s that Zionism was made palatable to the broader American Jewish community. Prominent attorney Louis D. Brandeis (who would be named to the Supreme Court in 1916) articulated a vision that blended patriotic American citizenship with Zionism, making the movement more acceptable to increasing numbers of acculturated Jewish Americans. Key to this shift was the recognition that although American Jews had found their promised land in this country, events in Europe made clear that Jews elsewhere needed a place of refuge—a refuge that American Jews could support through their financial contributions. In emphasizing practical work in support of the *Yishuv* (Jewish settlement in Palestine), Brandeis was joined by Henrietta Szold, president of the newly established women's organization, Hadassah, which inspired tens of thousands of American Jewish women to become personally involved in supporting health care in the Holy Land. By linking the Zionist movement to democracy, social justice, and even Jeffersonian agrarianism, Brandeis articulated his synthesis, that "to be good Americans, we must be better Jews, and to be better Jews, we must become Zionists."[12]

Despite this "Brandeisian synthesis," sharp divisions remained. Although East European immigrants to America were generally not interested in joining the Zionist migration to Palestine, their grounding in traditional Judaism meant that the movement spoke to them on spiritual, political, cultural, and messianic levels—appeals which resonated less with assimilated American leaders such as Brandeis. Even as ever-larger portions of the American Jewish community came to support some form of Zionism over the next several decades, there were deep divisions in the movement, with sharp ideological and leadership struggles fracturing American Zionism through the 1920s and 1930s.[13]

During this period, although the CCAR maintained its official opposition, increasing numbers of Reform Jews edged toward Zionism. The shift was, in part, a pragmatic response to international events. After the passage of tight restrictions on immigration to the United States in the early 1920s, it was obvious that America would not serve as a refuge for future migrants. Yet continued turmoil and hardship in Eastern Europe, coupled with the rise of Hitler in the 1930s, made it increasingly clear that some refuge was, in fact, necessary. By the late 1930s, the threatened destruction of European Jewry served to convince the majority of Reform Jews—and their rabbis—that the establishment of a Jewish state was essential.

For Reform leaders, the shift was also a response to demographic realities much closer to home. American Reform Judaism was facing a crisis. With East European immigrants and their children now making up a sizeable majority of the American Jewish community, Reform congregations needed to attract members from their ranks to stem the movement's declining numbers and influence. Given the emotional and spiritual appeal of Zionism among East Europeans, the Classical Reform position alienated potential congregants. Meanwhile those Reform rabbis who did embrace Zionism (most notably Stephen Wise) rose steadily in stature, generating a strong following both within the movement and in the American Jewish community more broadly. As increasing numbers of second-generation East Europeans entered Reform, not only as congregants but as rabbinical students, they brought with them a sensibility about ethnic identity and Zionism that fed the ideological evolution within the movement.

These factors led to a sea change in the Reform position on Zionism. Despite the movement's continued official antipathy toward political Zionism, prominent Zionists began to move into leadership positions, and it was clear that this was the wave of the future. By 1930, 90 percent of rabbinical students at Hebrew Union College in Cincinnati reported that they "either favored Zionism or were neutral on the subject; only 9 percent firmly opposed."[14] At the Jewish Institute of Religion, the nondenominational rabbinical seminary in New York City established by Stephen Wise in 1922, students came from different branches of Judaism and varied in their theologies, but all "identified with the three pillars that characterized Wise's own rabbinate: Zionism, social justice and the task of servicing *k'lal ysrael*, the Jewish people as a whole."[15] In 1935, Felix Levy became the first "avowed Zionist" elected president of the CCAR, and the conference shifted its official position from opposition to neutrality. Just two years later, the conference embraced the Columbus Platform, which, while not endorsing the political aims of the Zionist movement, did recognize the centrality of Palestine in Jewish life and endorsed the concept of a Jewish homeland there. Finally, in February 1942, the organization voted to support the formation of a Jewish army in Palestine, a move that many equated with an endorsement of political Zionism and that opponents feared "could create the impression that American Jews were a separate nationality."[16]

It was against this backdrop that the anti-Zionist American Council for Judaism (ACJ) emerged in the early 1940s. As they watched the shift toward Zionism, those rabbis who maintained the Classical Reform, anti-Zionist position felt increasingly isolated. Alarmed at what they saw as a nationalistic form of Judaism, they believed that Zionism threatened the Reform commitment to Jewish identity based solely on religion. In June 1942, these rabbis, calling themselves the Non-Zionist Reform Rabbis, met in Atlantic City. There, "Zionism was equated with everything that is antithetical to Classical Reform Judaism, including traditionalism, orthodoxy, particularism, and anti-Americanism. . . . [It] played the part of a phantom concept that represented their fears for the future and concretized the decline of Reform to which the rabbis were witness."[17] This gathering resulted in the creation of the ACJ.[18]

While initially expressing concerns rooted in Reform Judaism, the ACJ message became increasingly political in the years following 1942.[19] At the time of the council's formation, Reform rabbis held sway and articulated a position based on the sensibilities of the Pittsburgh Platform, arguing that embracing a Jewish identity based on nationalism would sap the religious basis of Reform Judaism. However, lay leaders who presented the ACJ position in political terms—arguing that Zionism was racist, undemocratic, and a threat to the political status of American Jews—quickly eclipsed the influence of the rabbis. American Council for Judaism president Lessing Rosenwald explained the organization's position in the June 28, 1943, issue of *Life* magazine, arguing that Zionism revived the obsolete conception that Jews were a racial or national group and in doing so "embrace(d) the very racist theories and nationalistic philosophies that have become so prevalent in recent years, that have caused untold suffering to the world and particularly to the Jews." He contended that

> the result must inevitably be that here in America, or for Jews elsewhere, the question of dual allegiances will be raised by men who, in critical times, lack discrimination and understanding. This would be particularly unfortunate in America, where the Jew has found a security greater than has ever been known in all the long history of Israel. The only sure way to avoid such a misunderstanding is to avoid the creation of a National Jewish State.[20]

As early as 1943, political anti-Zionists came to dominate the organization, and many of the Reform rabbis who had seen the council as a vehicle for reviving a Classical Reform religious outlook defected.

The failure of the ACJ nationally, however, was less attributable to this shift taking part within the organization than to the growing awareness of the plight of European Jewry. Although the ACJ was able to attract about fourteen thousand members between 1943 and 1948, its voice was drowned out by the mass embrace of Zionism in this same period.[21] As historian Thomas Kolsky writes, "The first Jewish organization created for the purpose of opposing the establishment of a Jewish state in Palestine began its struggle at precisely the moment that the Zionists succeeded in winning over to their cause the vast majority of Jewish organizations."[22]

Although the ACJ could not compete with Zionism nationally, it did have regional appeal in the South and West, where the vast majority of its members were located.[23] The message of the ACJ resonated better in these areas for several reasons. First, the proportion of Jews of East European background, who tended to be Zionism's most ardent supporters, was relatively small compared to the proportion in the Northeast and Midwest. In the South and West, the Reform community remained dominant for longer, and its formulations about Jewish identity were strongly embraced. Southern and western Jewish communities tended to be small and relatively assimilated, giving them a great stake in the Reform vision of Jewish life in the diaspora. Indeed, historian Kolsky argues that a community's level of ACJ support was inversely proportional to its numerical significance in the larger community—the lower the percentage of Jews in a city, the higher the percentage affiliated with the ACJ.[24]

San Francisco was somewhat exceptional in this regard, for the popularity of the ACJ there was stronger than might be expected based on population statistics.[25] In every other way, however, the San Francisco Jewish community possessed the traits characteristic of ACJ strongholds. As Fred Rosenbaum argues in his work on anti-Zionism in the city, San Francisco's Jewish community was dominated by the wealthy, the Reform, and the well assimilated. They were thoroughly committed to a Classical Reform identity and convinced of "the integration of the Jews into the host country as the natural order of things." This commitment to diaspora Jewry and to integration of Jews into their home country made the San Francisco Jewish leadership very responsive to the anti-Zionist claim that the creation of a Jewish state would undermine the status of American Jews and raise questions of dual loyalty. Thus, the Jewish elite of San Francisco "joined the Council almost to a man," their chapter provided nearly a third of the national ACJ budget, and their leading rabbi, Irving F. Reichert, made the fight against Zionism "the highest priority of his career." According to Rosenbaum, their experience of "virtually unprecedented freedom, toleration, and prosperity in the San Francisco Bay Area had rendered the leaders of that Jewish community incapable of adequately assessing the needs and desires of the rest of world Jewry."[26]

ANTI-ZIONISM IN PORTLAND

That many of the factors contributing to ACJ strength in San Francisco (the dominance of Reform Jews of German origin, the relatively low level of East European immigration at the turn of the century, the high degree of assimilation and integration) were typical of other western communities explains the general strength of the organization in the region and would lead one to expect the same pattern in Portland. Indeed, the low percentage of Jews in the total urban population should have led to *greater* penetration of the ACJ in the Rose City, according to the pattern identified by Kolsky. Jews in Portland represented approximately 3.5 percent of the city's population in 1940, and probably less than 2 percent of the total population of the Portland metropolitan area, in contrast to San Francisco, where Jews made up 6.7 percent of the population in 1948.[27] However, the Portland case demonstrates that caution must be used in applying the San Francisco model to other western Jewish communities.

As in San Francisco, wealthy Reform Jews of German descent and primarily of merchant background dominated Portland's Jewish community well into the early twentieth century. As we have seen, Jewish Oregonians had experienced a very high level of acceptance and inclusion, demonstrated in Jewish civic participation, including access to political office. Portland Jews involved in politics did not perceive themselves as an ethnic block, but instead identified with an almost unchallenged merchant class. At the turn of the century, Portland Jewish elites embraced the Reform vision of Judaism as a religion rather than as a culture. Therefore, they might have been expected, like many of their counterparts in San Francisco, to respond to Zionism as "the most serious theoretical challenge to the identity of Jews as American citizens upholding the social order through voluntary association."[28]

Indeed, during the first several decades of the twentieth century, the Portland Jewish leadership's efforts to minimize the ethnic component of Jewish identity led them to participate enthusiastically in Americanization efforts aimed at more recent arrivals. Such efforts were particularly strong during the xenophobic 1920s, when Oregon's Jews for the first time faced a significant, organized anti-Semitic movement. Beth Israel rabbi Jonah Wise "joined the patriotic fervor," speaking out against residential clustering and the Yiddish language, and leading an effort to consolidate the various ethnically based B'nai B'rith lodges in Portland into one unified lodge, in order to foster Americanization.[29] For Jonah Wise, these efforts were closely linked to his Classical Reform sensibilities. As Rabbi Julius Nodel explains in his congregational history, "the stress was on 'being American,' at least as much as 'being Jewish.' Since Jews were more and more recognized as equals with other American citizens, distinctive differences and conspicuous customs were toned down in order to make them more easily acceptable as good neighbors."[30] Jonah Wise saw Zionism as a threat to American identity. In 1942, eighteen years after his departure from Portland, he emerged as a "moderate" non-Zionist, attending the Atlantic City meeting and joining the ACJ.[31]

Some Portland Jews maintained similar attitudes in the years leading up to World War II, and a few became ACJ activists. Those who became involved—Kolsky lists eight Portland activists—were similar in many ways to their counterparts in San Francisco.[32] They were Americans of German descent and members of Temple Beth Israel.[33] They embraced Classical Reform and objected to both ethnic and national definitions of Jewish identity. Several of them seem to have been part of Rabbi Jonah Wise's close circle. For example, Max Hirsch, a former Meier and Frank executive and founder of the White Stag company, was an ACJ activist who had served as president of Beth Israel from 1924 to 1926, at the end of Rabbi Jonah Wise's tenure. In an oral history, his son, Harold Hirsch, emphasized his parents' patriotism and belief in Judaism strictly as a religion: "Both my father and my mother were religious in both the philosophical sense and the communal sense, but with them, as with me, being a Jew or a Jewess is strictly a religious matter and not an ethnic matter."[34] In a 1934 letter to his predecessor, Rabbi Henry Berkowitz identified the "Max Hirschs" as part of the "old Beth Israel crowd," who regarded Jonah Wise as "an oracle. . . . For them you can do no wrong."[35] Milton Kahn, probably the most consistently active of the Portland ACJ group, had also been involved in congregational leadership during Jonah Wise's tenure, and attorney Sidney Teiser was a close friend of the rabbi.[36] Among the other ACJ activists were such prominent figures as Aaron Frank, president of Meier & Frank; Harold Wendel, president of Lipman-Wolfe department stores; Herbert Sichel, a prominent clothier and nephew of Ben Selling; and Mrs. Julius Meier, widow of the governor.

In addition to their background and status, an interesting common thread among anti-Zionists in Portland was their involvement in another Portland Jewish organization, the Oregon Émigré Committee (OEC). The OEC, founded in 1936, worked to sponsor Jewish refugees and help them settle in Portland. It became one of the Portland federation's four standing committees in 1940. Of the eight Portland anti-Zionists named by Kolsky, all were connected with the OEC, including Max Hirsch, who served as longtime chair, and Sidney Teiser, who became vice chair in 1940.[37] This is not to say that the OEC was an anti-Zionist organization; indeed, many prominent Portland Zionists were also involved in the group. Yet it does indicate that the OEC's cause was something that anti-Zionists could support, and therefore can shed light on anti-Zionist sensibilities in Portland.

The OEC's mission likely resonated with the anti-Zionist belief in the viability of Jewish life in the diaspora. Helping settle and integrate new Jewish immigrants in the United States rather than in Palestine put such beliefs into action. The group provided a philanthropic outlet for anti-Zionist donors who wanted to support refugees without aiding the Zionist project. This was articulated quite clearly by the wife of an ACJ activist, Mrs. Bertram Friedman, when she told a meeting of the OEC in 1948 that "persons who had not contributed to the Welfare Fund because they objected to the money going to Israel might be induced to make their donations to the Oregon Émigré Committee for its work."[38] Her statement confirms the specific attraction of the OEC for anti-Zionists, and suggests that, even as late as 1948, some in Portland still held such strong views that they would avoid giving to the community's unified fundraising campaign lest their contribution aid Palestine.

In addition to sharing a desire to support settlement of Jewish refugees in the diaspora, the OEC and the anti-Zionists shared a concern over the dual-loyalty issue. As an organization working with German refugees, who were classified by the US government as "enemy aliens," the OEC and its sister organization, the Jewish Service Association, were active in informing their clients about alien registration requirements and restrictions. The dual-loyalty issue was an abstraction for most American Jews, but for German refugees it was a real concern. The restrictions on enemy aliens on the West Coast in the aftermath of Pearl Harbor, including travel restrictions and curfews, applied to German nationals as well as Japanese Americans. Thus, at Beth Israel, a congregation which, by 1942, included a number of German émigrés, Flora Berkowitz, the rabbi's wife, organized a "visiting committee which goes about in the evening paying calls on the 8 o'clock stay-at-homes," who were unable to attend congregational events, such as the community seder, which took place in the evening.[39] Nationally, there were even several cases of German Jews who were subjected to internment as enemy aliens.[40] In Portland, as in San Francisco, where the internment of the entire Japanese American population received tremendous attention in the local press, the dangers of dual-loyalty accusations were clear. Indeed, in San Francisco, the most prominent leaders of the ACJ, Rabbi Irving Reichert and University of California Provost and Vice President Monroe Deutsch, were also leaders in the Fair Play Committee, a Berkeley-based group that protested the mass removal and incarceration of Japanese Americans.[41]

While neither the OEC nor the local Jewish press publicly connected their concerns about dual loyalty with what was happening to their Japanese American neighbors, attention to the possibility of actions against German Jewish "enemy aliens" was high. In his first sermon after Pearl Harbor, Rabbi Berkowitz assured those congregants "who have escaped from the lands of our enemies and are now sojourning peacefully and happily among us," that "no question will be raised as to your loyalty to America. You are safe and secure."[42] As restrictions were announced, Jewish Service Association meetings heard reports on alien restrictions and raised concerns about the welfare burden that would result if Jewish "enemy aliens" lost their business licenses. At one meeting, the group was warned, "No partiality can be shown our people. There may be more evacuations (but) there may not be drastic action in cases where loyalty can be proven."[43] The Portland *Scribe* published a number of articles in early 1942 emphasizing the loyalty of German Jewish aliens, cautioning against "hysterical discriminations," and advising their readers that "democratic minded aliens are assured that they have nothing to fear from the American Government."[44] Clearly, concerns about the enemy-alien status of German Jewish refugees dovetailed with the anti-Zionist focus on the dual-loyalty argument.

Despite these public concerns about the dual-loyalty issue with respect to German Jewish refugees, the ACJ's focus on this issue as an argument against Zionism was, apparently, a less successful recruiting tool in Portland than it had been in San Francisco and several other western Jewish communities. No Portland rabbi ever joined the organization—although it was likely common knowledge that former Beth Israel rabbi Jonah Wise, by then serving in New York, attended the founding meeting in Atlantic City in 1942 and remained a member for about a year.[45] His successor in Portland, Henry J. Berkowitz, had opposed Zionism early in his career, but came to embrace the movement during the 1930s and was active in trying to convince his non-Zionist colleagues to refrain from attending the Atlantic City meeting.[46] Although Portland lay activist Milton Kahn and several others continued to support the ACJ into the late 1940s, and in some cases well into the 1950s, there is little evidence that ongoing anti-Zionist activity ever took place in Portland. Only one ACJ sponsored lecture was noted in the local Jewish press in this period, although several informants remember attending or being invited to a meeting and indicate that there was some enthusiasm for it among a group of "old families" at Beth Israel.[47] Mollie Blumenthal, who worked as a secretary for Kahn, recalled that while Kahn maintained an active correspondence with ACJ leader Elmer Berger, the organization "never really got going" in Portland.[48] Rather, enthusiasm for Zionism in the Rose City was widespread. Jewish organizations in Portland during the war including the *Scribe,* philanthropic organizations, the B'nai B'rith lodge, and numerous organizations with ties to the local synagogues, including Temple Beth Israel, demonstrated clearly their receptivity to Zionists and Zionism. Given all the factors making Portland a likely stronghold for the ACJ, why were the active anti-Zionists such a small minority?

Part of the answer lies in the growing integration of the Portland Jewish community. Turn-of-the-century Portland Jewry was German-dominated, but the city's East European Jewish population grew rapidly in the early decades of the twentieth century, and had clear, pro-Zionist sensibilities. Early arriving and more successful East Europeans, and particularly the second-generation professionals, integrated relatively quickly into the established Jewish community, fostered by such actions as the consolidation of the B'nai B'rith lodges. As Toll documents in his Portland study, despite the persistence of the immigrant district and its Yiddish culture, and some friction between the descendants of the early arriving German families and the children of East Europeans, by the 1920s, the latter were becoming part of the new middle class.[49] East European members of the middle class were a significant portion of the Jewish communal leadership by the early 1940s and clearly contributed to the coolness toward anti-Zionism in Portland.

Indeed, the relative ease with which this integration took place—in comparison, for example, to San Francisco, where the gap between Germans and East Europeans was far more persistent, and even bitter—helped Beth Israel avoid the demographic issues facing the Reform movement more broadly. Flagging numbers in the movement were a key factor leading to the founding of the ACJ—anti-Zionist rabbis saw revival of Classical Reform as a way to stem the decline of the movement.[50] Yet at Beth Israel, the congregation was experiencing not a decline but notable growth under the leadership of Rabbi Berkowitz. As Berkowitz wrote in a personal letter in the fall of 1941, "You will be glad to hear that my Congregation is in the most prosperous condition it has been in many years. We have had a substantial increase in membership, my salary has been adjusted upwards, and we just completed a marvelous Holyday season."[51]

Among the rising East European leaders, the veterans of attempts at Jewish agrarian settlement in the upper Midwest and West who arrived in Portland during the final decades of the nineteenth century were particularly prominent. This group included individuals such as Leon Swett, who migrated to Oregon in 1882 with a group of Russian Jewish idealists intending to establish a communal agrarian settlement. Swett came with the group as far as Portland and then remained, farming in the area, as the others set up their short-lived colony in Southern Oregon. His sons, Zachary and Isaac, both became professionals and Jewish community leaders, and well integrated in Beth Israel circles. Zachary was a prominent regional B'nai B'rith leader; Isaac's wife, Julia

Swett, was an officer in the OEC, and a leader in the National Council of Jewish Women, the Federated Jewish Society of Portland, and the Jewish Community Center—all organizations generally affiliated with the established Reform community.[52] Likewise, the interrelated Lauterstein, Nudelman, and Bromberg families came to Portland after several years on an agricultural colony in North Dakota and became leaders of a variety of Jewish institutions, including the unified Hebrew school. Members of this group were prominent at a wide range of synagogues, from the Orthodox Sherith Israel, where Joseph Nudelman was a founder, to the Reform Beth Israel, where Paula Heller Lauterstein—daughter of the rabbi of Conservative Neveh Zedek and wife of an East European former North Dakota colonist—became a "devout Reform Jew" and a Hadassah leader.[53] Veterans of Jewish agricultural settlements, by virtue of their early arrival and leadership experience, were among the most prominent community-wide leaders of East European background. Their family histories led them to embrace many of the same beliefs that motivated the settlers of kibbutzim in Palestine, and they felt tremendous affinity for the Zionist project.

Yet the particular role of these East Europeans within the Jewish community cannot alone explain anti-Zionism's failure to generate a sizeable following in Portland. It is equally important that, even among the German Jewish "old" elite, anti-Zionism was embraced with enthusiasm by only a few. In San Francisco and other ACJ strongholds, the dominance of a wealthy German American Reform synagogue and the influence of a committed anti-Zionist rabbi, such as Emanu-El's Irving Reichert, were key factors explaining ACJ's success. In Portland, the likely center for anti-Zionist activity was Beth Israel; it exuded the same wealth, prestige, and German heritage as Emanu-El in San Francisco. It was the synagogue of all known ACJ members. Yet anti-Zionism never prevailed at Beth Israel.

The lingering influence of Rabbi Stephen Wise was a key factor. Wise served as Beth Israel's rabbi only from 1900 to 1906, but his influence was long-lasting. Although his departure pre-dated the founding of the ACJ by more than three decades, the Zionist infrastructure that he helped establish and the commitment to the cause that he engendered in Portlanders had a decided impact.[54] Wise, a proto-Zionist from childhood, was a founder of the Federation of American Zionists

Rabbi Stephen Wise's brief tenure in Portland significantly shaped attitudes toward Zionism. Credit: Historic Oregon Newspapers, http:// oregonnews.uoregon.edu

in 1897, attended the Second Zionist Congress in Basel, Switzerland, in 1898, and would become one of the foremost American Zionist leaders.[55] He was serving as a Zionist emissary on a tour of the Pacific Northwest in 1899 when he spoke to "a very large Zionist meeting in Portland" that included "Jews and Christians in equal number, including two US Senators and a former Attorney General of President Grant's cabinet."[56] Greatly impressed with the young rabbi, and in the midst of an effort to recruit a successor to the retiring Rabbi Jacob Bloch, the board of trustees quickly extended Wise an offer.

The year after his installation as rabbi in September 1900, Wise became a founder of the Portland Zionist Society (PZS). His enthusiasm and personal stature led many of his congregants to join him in this endeavor. Despite the general antipathy toward Zionism among Reform Jews at the time, Wise "made the pulpit at Beth Israel the focal point for Zionist organization, and he carried with him many of the most influential Jews and non-Jews of the city."[57] Because of Wise's leadership, many of the most prominent Beth Israel leaders joined the society and attended its meetings at the temple. Indeed, the Portland Zionist Society's founding officers were all Beth Israel congregants, including founding president Otto Kraemer, a Portland attorney and judge, and founding vice president Julius Meier, future governor of the state and congregational president.[58] Clearly, Wise's leadership made

Beth Israel and its influential congregation a center of Zionist support, rather than its enemy. In addition, his prominence in Portland beyond the Jewish community and nationally, after leaving Portland, raised the stature of the congregation and encouraged continued identification with the causes he championed.

Indeed, Stephen Wise's short tenure in Portland belies the continuing influence of the Zionist foundation he helped create. Although Wise spent only six years in the Rose City, his leadership and outspokenness, both within the Jewish community and in Portland civic life, left a lasting impact. Beth Israel's 1959 congregational history devotes a full chapter to Wise, while *The Jews of Oregon*, published in 1987, singles him out as one of "three exceptional individuals" profiled for the 1890–1920 period.[59] When Rabbi Wise passed away, nearly half a century after his departure from Portland, the two secular Portland papers memorialized him as "a great American."[60] Although some Beth Israel leaders, including Wise's successor, Jonah Wise, firmly embraced Classical Reform attitudes toward Zionism, it is clear that the earlier Rabbi Wise's influence helped to tip the balance toward a Brandeisian understanding of the compatibility of Zionism with American Jewish life.[61]

Yet Wise was certainly not the only influential early twentieth-century Zionist in Portland. Solomon Hirsch, who had achieved prominence in Oregon politics and served as ambassador to the Ottoman Empire, was a passionate Zionist, instrumental in bringing Wise to Portland, first as a speaker and then as Beth Israel rabbi. David Solis-Cohen, one of the Portland Jewish community's most respected and influential leaders, was a founding member of the PZS and "the main spokesman for Zionism in Portland until his death in 1928."[62] Solis-Cohen was a Beth Israel congregant who moved comfortably in both Jewish and non-Jewish circles, holding public office and serving as a grand master of the Oregon Masons. He articulated a vision of Zionism compatible with the outlook of the Reform community. As historian Toll explains, David Solis-Cohen, Stephen Wise, and Isaac Swett "achieved intellectual consistency by equating Zionism with American democracy as dual agents for a more enlightened world order," while other Temple Beth Israel leaders such as philanthropist Ben Selling responded to the pragmatic, philanthropic aspect of Zionism.[63] Such formulations anticipated the Brandeisian synthesis and set a precedent for the continued prominence of Zionists among the leadership group of Beth Israel and B'nai B'rith. Indeed, the founding president and vice president of the Portland Zionist Society, Judge Otto Kraemer and Governor Julius Meier, both served terms as Beth Israel president during the 1930s.[64] Prominent Zionists Swett and Solis-Cohen served as local and regional B'nai B'rith leaders, and the Portland consolidated B'nai B'rith chapter often cosponsored Zionist events.[65]

It was likely a combination of respect for Stephen Wise, recognition of the reverence in which Beth Israel congregants held their former rabbi, and the prominence of other Beth Israel leaders in Zionist activities that led Rabbi Jonah Wise to take a conciliatory approach to the issue. Despite his embrace of Classical Reform and his opposition to the CCAR's move toward Zionism in the 1930s, he apparently did little to "reform" the Zionist tendencies within his Portland congregation during his tenure at Beth Israel from 1907 to 1926. However, he shared his candid views in private correspondence with his successor, Rabbi Henry Berkowitz, writing of his frustration when a 1934 Zionist campaign in Portland interfered with a fundraising drive by the Joint Distribution Committee:

> Now then, take the Zionist crowd. We have been trying very hard to deal with the Zionists, but my dear Henry, you can no more deal with a Zionist than you can with an Armenian. Even our local Zionists in Portland get slippery and slide out of our clutches when they get the word from New York. Agreements are just scraps of paper with these birds and I feel that nothing we do can alter their disposition. Their piling into Portland for a campaign while we were holding parlays for a Community Drive is just one of those things.[66]

Despite this assessment, Wise characteristically avoided confrontation, writing, "I note that you and Julius Meier gave it your sanction and I know that you must have done so after the most careful consideration."[67] Later, during the notorious acrimony that led up to the 1942 Atlantic City meeting, Jonah Wise was known as a moderate and tried to reconcile the two sides.

Despite Jonah Wise's assumption in his letter to Berkowitz that the latter shared his stance on Zionism, Berkowitz's position was transforming. As he explained in a 1940 letter to his friend Rabbi Edward Israel of Baltimore,

> I have been won over [to Zionism] slowly but surely through the years, and while all the ardent Zionists in Portland look upon me as an ally, they know that my conversion has been slow. Some day you and I must talk about this, so I can tell you how Mordechai Kaplan's book in 1934 started me in that direction, and how Abba Silver's paper at the Chicago Conference [in 1935] also helped.[68]

In separate correspondence a few years earlier with Rabbi Edward Sandrow of Portland's Conservative congregation, Ahavai Sholom, Berkowitz had shared his excitement over Silver's 1935 speech and its impact on the CCAR vote for neutrality. Berkowitz recounted Silver's electrifying words, his "impregnable" logic, and the discussions that followed it until the wee hours of the morning. He was convinced that "Silver's paper will become the classic statement on the subject of Jewish nationalism and Reform Judaism. I hope thousands of reprints will be distributed." Berkowitz then enthusiastically recounted the historic vote that took place the following day:

> The debate centered around the Zionist Resolution, the purpose of which was to remove the traditional anti-Zionist label from the Reform Rabbinate. The old stand-patters tried their best to shelve the Resolution. A parliamentary tangle arose in which there were two substitute motions and an amendment to the original motion. But after we stripped off the layers by a series of roll calls and finally took a vote whether we should vote on the Resolution as amended, the crucial roll call was taken and the historic Resolution passed amid such a tumult as I have rarely seen. The tension had been so great that in this final battle tempers were lost and dignity thrown to the winds. I have forgotten the exact count, but it was better than two to one.[69]

Rabbi Henry J. Berkowitz of Congregation
Beth Israel. Credit: Oregon Jewish Museum

Although Berkowitz had come to Beth Israel in 1928 as a non-Zion-ist, by 1935, he clearly counted himself—and was recognized by col-leagues—as a Zionist. Indeed, in the same letter to Sandrow, Berkowitz reported that he had been slated to join the CCAR executive board but was removed "because of my Zionist sympathies." In keeping with the neutrality vote, the conference was trying to balance the board, and, with Zionist Felix Levy taking office as president, a majority of the other board positions were filled with non-Zionists. After the meeting, Berkowitz wrote to Levy, "They certainly cluttered you up with non-Zionists on the board."[70]

In his private correspondence, Berkowitz was positively gleeful about the 1937 vote, in which the conference replaced the vener-able Pittsburgh Platform with the new "Guiding Principles of Reform Judaism," or the Columbus Platform, proclaiming that "Judaism is the soul of which Israel is the body" and underscoring "the obligation of all Jewry to aid in [Palestine's] upbuilding as a Jewish Homeland."[71] "The Conference proved to be historical and hysterical," recounted Berkowitz,

> the famous six hour debate on a revised platform for American
> Judaism provided some fireworks that would have made you lick
> your chops with glee. I have seen histrionics put on by my colleagues,

but nothing to compare to Schulman putting on his last great fight. The old buzzard had his back to the wall, and supported by the conservatives of the Philipson-Rosenau-Franklin-Wolsey crowd, lost a war of words that none of us will ever forget. When I tell you that Schulman was in a state of collapse and had to have restoratives, you will have some idea of the scene. When the final vote was taken Philipson, who was the only survivor of the Pittsburgh Conference of eighty-five, arose and was sportsman enough to move that the new platform be accepted unanimously. Thus Palestine has been written into the platform of the Conference.[72]

Five years later, when the opponents of the proposal to form a Jewish army in Palestine began planning their meeting in Atlantic City in 1942, Berkowitz wrote to several of his colleagues—including his nephew Malcolm Stern, a recent Hebrew Union College graduate—"begging" them not to participate. Berkowitz had been "deeply disturbed" by news of the proposed conference and felt a "sense of tragedy that our colleagues should take such an action."[73] When Stern sent him an account of the meeting in June, Berkowitz shared his nephew's missive with Rabbi Heller, president of the CCAR, and ridiculed it, writing, "It sounds like something I would have written twenty years ago. Some of the statements are so obviously absurd that I have decided not to enter into a controversy with the boy because it will not do any good."[74]

Although Berkowitz participated in this national debate, he did so largely through these personal letters. At home, he wanted to preserve the peace in a congregation that had a long history of Zionist activity but also included a few active anti-Zionists who remained closely tied to former Rabbi Jonah Wise. Not unlike the national scene, where Berkowitz had close friends, colleagues, and relatives (including his better known uncle, Henry Berkowitz of Philadelphia as well as his nephew) who came down on the opposite side of the Zionist question, among his congregants, on his board, and in various other organizations in which he served, there were activists on both sides. For example, Berkowitz served on the OEC, which included all the local anti-Zionists as well as many vocal Zionists. Perhaps because of this, Berkowitz is remembered in community histories more as a peacemaker than as a partisan. As Nodel writes in his congregational history, "the

Rabbi's personal leanings were toward Zionism; but being by nature more a conciliator than a polemicist, he tried to keep both factions working together on the common task."[75] Berkowitz explained to a friend and colleague who asked him to "lend his name" to the cause of Labor Zionism for a Histadrut drive in 1940, "My own Zionism is not strong enough to rate this particular assignment. . . . Theoretically I am completely convinced—I'm just not on fire like you. Perhaps that will come too."[76] Perhaps Berkowitz felt better suited to a quieter approach, as when he explained to a representative from the United Palestine Appeal in 1937 that the Portland Federation's leaders "are not as warmly interested in Palestine as they should be, and at present there is considerable murmuring because our Welfare budget already includes U.P.A., Hadassah, Histadruth [sic], Youth Aliya, and Hebrew University. These many calls from Palestine make it difficult to propose still another one. I have a plan, however, for next year, which I trust will be workable."[77]

As this comment suggests, although he eschewed such roles as spokesman, Berkowitz's increasingly Zionist proclivities did affect his tenure as rabbi. Certainly, it was no coincidence that the Hebrew language, which had not been taught in the Beth Israel religious school for two decades, was reintroduced by Berkowitz in the fall of 1935, shortly after his "conversion." He addressed this move, which was met with resistance "by a group of assimilated members who organized a vociferous protest," in a sermon. In an exchange with critical congregants afterward, he explained, "You say you would be doing your grandchildren a service if you worked for their complete assimilation. That is what they thought in Germany. If the Arayan [sic] rule were adopted in this country, your Unitarian grandchildren would catch it just the same," and went on to emphasize that it was not just theology that mattered, but "the whole rounded picture of language, *land*, culture, folks-ways, etc."[78] (emphasis added).

By 1941 and 1942, Berkowitz was increasingly direct and open. That fall, after the justice's death, he delivered a sermon titled "Louis D. Brandeis—A Great American," in which he held up Brandeis as "a man who loved America and loved Palestine, served both with his whole soul, and yet was never compromised by his double loyalty." He concluded, "Let me close with the words that I believe to be the summary of his highest thought with regard to Americanism and Judaism: 'There is no inconsistency between loyalty to America and loyalty to Jewry.'"[79] And in 1942, just after the CCAR army vote, he explained his support to his congregation:

> Some American Jews may desire to disclaim their adherence to the nationhood idea, and they may do so with sincerity and conviction. Millions of European Jews desire to proclaim *their* Jewish nationality. It is all they have left to proclaim. The world has taken everything else, but their Jewish nationhood, so they want to fight to hold that last possession.
>
> I said to the committee, "This reminds me of the America First isolationist debates while the Japs were creeping up on Pearl Harbor. If we start any more such discussions there won't be any America to talk about."
>
> The same holds true for Palestine and for the Jews. While we argue what Jews really are—a nation, a religion—the Jews are being sucked into the maelstrom of destruction. Now is the time to fight not argue. Give those eager and willing thousands their weapons and let them enter the struggle in the one way that suits them best. Millions of Jews are in a battle for their existence. We Americans are in the same grim battle. All lovers of freedom are companions-in-arms now. To me, the idea of a Jewish army has a powerful appeal, and that is why I voted for this resolution which was passed by the rabbis of America.[80]

During the 1930s and 1940s, the lack of an anti-Zionist rabbi in Portland clearly differentiates the Rose City from ACJ strongholds in the West. In 1941, on the eve of the formation of the ACJ, rabbis from Portland's two main Conservative synagogues, Neveh Zedek and Ahavai Sholom, as well as Rabbi Berkowitz of Beth Israel, were serving on the board of the Portland Zionist Society. Rabbi Berkowitz's efforts to foster cooperation between pro- and anti-Zionists at Beth Israel seem to have been largely successful. Although there were prominent members of Temple Beth Israel, including temple trustees, on both sides of the debate, there was apparently little acrimony. Zionists and anti-Zionists cooperated on community projects such as the OEC and maintained friendships and even marriages that crossed these lines. For example, while former Governor Julius Meier served as the first vice president of the Portland Zionist Society early in the century, his widow is listed by Kolsky as one of the eight Portland ACJ activists.[81]

Following the example of their rabbinic leadership, most of the Portland Jewish elite came to accept Zionism as a philanthropic enterprise to aid Jews not fortunate enough to reside in an environment like their own. Their secure position in Portland allowed them to support Zionism without succumbing to the fears of dual loyalty that anti-Zionists tried to spread.[82] Such philanthropic Zionism is most clear in the Oregon Jewish Welfare Fund, the primary philanthropic organization in the community, which gave consistent and generous support to Zionist organizations including the United Palestine Appeal, Hadassah, Histadrut, and Mizrachi.[83]

The Zionist bent of Portland's leadership was also reflected in the *Scribe*, which presented a consistently Zionist viewpoint after the departure of its founding editor, Rabbi Jonah Wise, in 1926. [84] By the late 1930s and early 1940s, the *Scribe,* with the rabbis of the major congregations on the editorial board, was providing regular and enthusiastic coverage of Palestine and of Zionist activities locally and nationally. The weekly column of Rabbi Louis Newman of New York featured vitriolic coverage of anti-Zionist activity in the early 1940s.[85] Newman's column scathingly criticized the formation of the ACJ, calling the anti-Zionist rabbis "out of touch with the Jewish people and thoroughly unsympathetic to Jewish aspirations," "stubborn intransigent die hards," "quislings," and a "reckless minority," and ridiculing them as "presiding over institutions which are virtual tombs."[86] Such columns were reinforced by the *Scribe*'s extensive coverage of the destruction of European Jewry, the plight of Jewish refugees, and the news from Palestine. In particular, the *Scribe* reported sympathetically on the efforts of Jews in Palestine to form an army and on the CCAR's vote to support establishment of that army.[87] As awareness of the destruction of European Jewry heightened, and as the *Scribe*'s unrelenting attacks on anti-Zionism continued, membership in the ACJ became less and less acceptable—so much so that even decades later, oral history informants were often reluctant to provide names of anti-Zionists.[88]

In the Portland Jewish community, the mood was clearly Zionist.
A vivid example comes in the educational policy of the community-
wide Hebrew School. The consolidated Hebrew School, serving the
entire community, emphasized instruction in Hebrew language,
Jewish culture, history, and *nationalism*. While most members of the
Jewish Education Association overseeing the school were of Reform
background, in 1942 they went well beyond philanthropic Zionism
by passing a resolution pledging to "help Hebraize our cultural life
in the Diaspora," due to the need "to train the rising generation to
speak Hebrew and to be prepared to live in Palestine or to share its
living culture."[89] Such language went well beyond philanthropic duty
to embrace Zionism as central to the identity being cultivated in the
community's children.

Throughout the decades leading up to World War II, both the
Scribe and organizational records provide ample evidence of extensive
Zionist activity, ranging from mass meetings to speakers and fundraising events.[90] Not surprisingly, given the early embrace of Zionism by
the Conservative movement,[91] congregations Neveh Zedek and Ahavai
Sholom played a central role. Neveh Zedek's congregation, for example, enrolled en masse in the Portland Zionist roll call in 1929, while
Ahavai Sholom sponsored a series of talks on Zionism in the 1930s,
culminating with a lecture by Golda Meyerson (the future Israeli prime
minister, Golda Meir). The Zionist youth group Halutzim met weekly
after Sunday school at Ahavai Sholom.[92] Neveh Zedek's rabbi Phillip
Kleinman, who came to Portland in 1937, quickly assumed the presidency of the Zionist Society and expanded its operations in this period.
Like Hadassah and the unified Hebrew school, the Zionist Society
reached across class and synagogue boundaries, enlisting members and
receiving financial support from all sectors of the Portland Jewish community. Even organizations that were not explicitly Zionist embraced
the cause. For example, the South Portland Hebrew Sick Benefit Society
was focused on the needs of community members. Occasionally, it
made donations to the Orthodox synagogues. Aside from these local
concerns, its only other donations were to Zionist organizations.[93]
Similarly, the unified B'nai B'rith lodge frequently sponsored Zionist
speakers, and pro-Zionist resolutions were endorsed by the lodge.[94] In

sum, according to Deborah Goldberg, chronicler of Zionism in the city, "Portland was a nurturing center for Zionism."[95]

While a small group of wealthy and prominent Portland Jews committed themselves to the ACJ's anti-Zionist position, they remained a distinct minority, even among their social circle. In Portland, the majority of Jews, Reform as well as Conservative, German-American as well as East European, embraced Zionism. The rejection of anti-Zionism by the Portland Jewish community is evidence of a clear deviation from the San Francisco model. It demonstrates the significance of demographics and strong leadership in determining a community's response to Zionism, and suggests that the California experience may not be an appropriate model for western Jewish community development more generally.

CHAPTER 6

The Color of Community

The place of Jews in the American ethnic landscape has been much debated. Both societal attitudes toward Jews and Jewish attitudes toward other racial, ethnic, and religious minority groups have varied over time and place. For example, although it became common in the early twentieth century for northern Jews to publicly express support for African Americans, and for East European Jews in particular to view them as "fellow minorities," it was difficult for Jewish southerners to do so.[1] And despite the truism that Jewish prominence in the mid-twentieth-century Civil Rights Movement grew out of their own experience of discrimination and struggle to become fully accepted, it is clear that Jewish communities in some instances hesitated to identify too closely with African Americans, fearing such an alliance might put their own racial status in question.

In recent decades, scholars have framed shifting racial/ethnic alliances in terms of the relationship of Jewish Americans to "whiteness," arguing that Jews were not fully accepted as "white" until the mid-twentieth century. Their earlier status as "not quite white" was a key factor feeding an agenda of fighting prejudice in all forms.[2] However, this discussion has been largely based on the eastern and midwestern experiences, where, in the early twentieth century, reformers cast Jews and other southern and eastern European immigrants as a racial threat to the purity of white society, leading to the enactment of quota laws that severely limited their entry.

In the West, Jews were operating in a different, more diverse, racial context. Their early arrival in the region and the key economic roles that they played, along with the West's racial landscape, were factors that fostered early Jewish acceptance, mitigated anti-Semitism, and shaped Jewish Oregonians' identities into the twentieth century. In a region where first Native Americans and later Asian immigrants (and Latinos in California) were viewed as the primary racial threats, Jews and other diverse Europeans were readily accepted as whites. This acceptance, and the Jewish community's strong embrace of their identity as Oregonians, meant that many of them developed racial sensibilities—and prejudices—similar to those of other white Oregonians. If, as American Jewish historians have often argued, Jews had a special sensitivity to minority rights because of their personal and historical experience of discrimination, then, in a context where they were well accepted as part of the majority white culture, Jews were more apt to share the racial attitudes of other whites.

Despite this historic acceptance, after the turn of the century, and especially during the interwar years, Jewish Oregonians increasingly began to feel the sting of anti-Semitism. Residential, occupational, and social restrictions became more common. Overt anti-Semitism entered the public arena in a way that it had not before—as evidenced by the election of 1930. Julius Meier won the governorship in a landslide, but there were also unprecedented anti-Semitic attacks on him in a leading statewide publication. Not surprisingly, as Oregon's Jews became more concerned about anti-Semitism, they publicly endorsed the anti-prejudice agenda that was gaining strength among Jews nationally at this time. Yet, despite vocal expressions of support for this agenda, only a small group of Portland Jewish activists became part of the emerging coalition fighting local racism. It was not until after World War II that the community more fully and publicly embraced an anti-prejudice agenda that spoke to the plight of local racial minorities, and even then, continued to speak more confidently on national issues than on divisive local ones.

This chapter explores the interplay between the acceptance of Jews in Oregon and the attitudes of Jewish Oregonians toward other ethnic/racial minority groups, placing these in a broader national context.[3] What were the limits of Jewish acceptance and inclusion, and how did these change over time? How did Jewish Oregonians respond to restrictions on other minorities? When did they identify with the white majority and when did they choose to ally themselves with minority groups?

How were these identities affected by the influx of new groups, including Japanese Americans early in the century and African Americans during and after World War II?

WHITE PIONEERS AND RACIAL OTHERS

The high level of acceptance experienced by Jewish pioneers and those arriving in the first decades after statehood had a profound effect on their identities and their views of other racial/ethnic groups in the region. Arriving during the period of settlement, with a skill set that fostered the growth of new towns, early Jewish settlers were fully accepted as part of the white citizenry. Participating actively in associations ranging from chambers of commerce to fraternal organizations, many emerged as civic and political leaders and made their mark on the landscape with the brick structures they built that served to anchor new towns. Jewish settlers were included in organizations such as the Native Sons and Daughters of Oregon, which honored a shared pioneer past and marked the boundaries of white citizenship. Historians have noted evidence of extensive social interaction between Jews and non-Jews in this period, particularly among elites, who participated in mixed cultural, social, and fraternal organizations, and sent their children to the same private academies. Only at the "very pinnacle of polite male society," Portland's exclusive Arlington Club (founded 1867), were Jews excluded. About a decade later, the elite Jewish Concordia Club—which in turn refused to admit East Europeans—emerged as an alternative for German Jews.[4] While historians note a few prominent examples of anti-Semitism in Oregon in this period, they are portrayed as exceptions to the general trend of acceptance and inclusion.[5]

This experience stands in contrast to trends in the East and Midwest, where the arrival of diverse groups of Europeans led to more widespread anti-Semitism in the late nineteenth century. Although southern, central, and east European immigrants, including Jews, were able to naturalize and become full citizens, they were increasingly stigmatized during the final quarter of the nineteenth century, regarded as "not quite white."[6] In the West, however, the presence of Native Americans, and later Asian immigrants, made the racial landscape more complicated. These non-European groups were cast as both fundamentally alien and as a major threat to white settlement. The focus on countering these racial threats led to a broad, pan-European definition of whiteness, by which people of diverse origins were counted among the settler population as part of the white citizenry. As western historian Patricia Limerick explains, "In race relations, the West could make turn-of-the-century Northeastern urban confrontation between European immigrants and American nativists look like a family reunion."[7]

Thus, a racialization process took place in the West in which diverse European immigrants banded together as the "white citizenry," particularly at moments when the perceived threat of racial others was felt most strongly. For example, in San Francisco, Irish immigrants, often cast as despised others in an eastern context, were central to the movement that called on "white labor" to rid the West of Chinese competitors.[8] In Clifton, Arizona, Italians, Jews, and other diverse Europeans became part of an "Anglo" mob in a conflict with Mexican Americans.[9] Historian Tomas Almaguer argues that, in California, "race and the racialization process . . . became the central organizing principle of group life."[10] Frank Van Nuys characterizes the West as a place where a "racial frontier" led to a "categorization of immigrants and minorities as either unassailably white and thus possessed of proper citizenship qualities, or decidedly nonwhite and therefore undesirable as possible citizens."[11]

As this literature suggests, it was not only their economic roles and ability to contribute to town building, but also the larger racial context that fostered Jewish acceptance and inclusion. If that acceptance and inclusion was, in part, based on racial context, the same context informed Jewish settlers' identities and attitudes toward regional "others" who were not among the accepted and included. At the same time, historians have often noted that Jews carried a special sensitivity about discrimination, a minority consciousness, based on their personal and historic group experience. Analysis of the disposition of Jewish Oregonians toward nineteenth-century racial minorities including Native Americans and Chinese immigrants can shed light on how they negotiated the sometimes conflicting pulls of Jewish identity and regional prejudices, and how these informed their understanding of their own place in the ethnic landscape.

As discussed in Chapter One, several Jewish pioneers participated in Oregon's Indian Wars, including future Portland mayor Bernard Goldsmith, who served as an officer in the militia during the Rogue Indian War and as a mediator between Native Americans and government officials. Although this account—dating from shortly after Goldsmith's arrival in Oregon—clearly places Goldsmith with the white Indian fighters, his role as mediator suggests a relatively sympathetic posture toward the tribe.[12]

More often, these accounts suggest Jews likely held more typical white pioneer views of Indians as threatening "others," as when Henry Heppner's packing operation was captured by "hostile Malheur Indians" who "ran the mules off into a Blue Mountain meadow where the grass was knee-high, and in one moon had them hog fat and shot and turned into dried elk meat." Not long after, another of his packtrains was "ambushed by Snake Indians," and years later, he provided supplies to build a fort in Heppner when "Indian hostilities" threatened the town.[13] According to family lore, merchant Moses Fried often dealt with Native Americans at his store in the Willamette Valley in the late 1860s, but he suffered extensive losses when, finding the store closed for Rosh Hashanah, they helped themselves. Fried subsequently relocated to a site "nearer to more white patronage and lesser Indian trading."[14] And, as noted earlier, Moses's daughter, Delia Fried Durkheimer, experienced the terror of hiding in a cave when conflict between whites and Paiute Indians in the Canyon City area appeared imminent.[15] The fullest description of Jewish involvement in conflicts with Native Americans comes in the account of Samuel Rothchild, who fought in an encounter between settlers and the Bannock and Paiute tribes in the Pendleton area in 1878. Rothchild's description of the episode appeared in *Reminiscences of Oregon Pioneers*, first published in Pendleton in 1937, detailing several skirmishes in which he saw comrades killed and he suffered serious wounds.[16]

Involvement in Indian conflicts was one of the marks of a true pioneer, and was noted with reverence in biographies of prominent settlers. Such encounters elevated the status of individuals such as Goldsmith, Heppner, and Rothchild and marked them as authentic Oregonians. No doubt, the experience of anticipating an Indian attack, working with one's neighbors to build defense fortifications, or actually fighting in an Indian war, shaped these Jews' racial identities as white Oregonians and their understandings of the Native American other. With no Jewish newspaper from this era and relatively few firsthand accounts, it is difficult to determine whether their attitudes toward Native Americans were nuanced by their identities as Jews. Yet it is clear that, as economic boosters and businessmen, Jewish merchants and politicians generally took the same pro-growth positions as their non-Jewish counterparts, positions that often trampled on Native rights. For example, as a US senator, Joseph Simon, who had made his legal career by representing the railroad interests, "presided over the federal appropriation of Indian tribal lands and the expansion of the railways into the Pacific Northwest," including gaining extensive rights-of-way through tribal lands. "The net result," according to historian Mark Raider, "was the realization of decades of efforts by the US government, the railroad industry, and various business and legal interests to disenfranchise the region's Native American population and complete the area's transportation system."[17]

Although conflicts with Native Americans took place in Eastern Oregon as late as the 1870s, by that decade, Chinese immigrants had become the state's most visible racial minority.[18] With work on the transcontinental railroad complete, increasing numbers of Chinese immigrants—principally men—relocated to western cities, including Portland. Stigmatized as utterly alien and accused of a range of offenses from undercutting white wages to smoking opium, and endangering public health by carrying diseases and practicing poor sanitation, Chinese immigrants became the target of vigorous xenophobic campaigns that led to violence against their communities, passage of an array of local occupational and residential restrictions, and, ultimately, the federal Chinese Exclusion Act in 1882.

In Portland, anti-Chinese measures were enacted as early as 1863, when the city imposed a tax on Chinese laundries. Although this ordinance was overturned by the courts, and a second, in 1865, was vetoed by the mayor, enthusiasm for such measures did not wane. By 1868, the state legislature had enacted a tax on Chinese workers and barred them from employment on public projects—a measure vetoed by the governor.[19] Although Chinese brothels and other alleged vice generated much concern in Portland, Jewish mayors Bernard Goldsmith and Philip Wasserman, who served consecutive two-year terms beginning in 1869, showed little interest in cracking down on such establishments. In addition, Wasserman vetoed an ordinance that would have barred Chinese workers from city construction projects because he believed it was in conflict with federal law.[20] Over a decade later, in 1884, Goldsmith played a key role in opposing a measure to restrict Chinese residents to certain parts of the city. And in 1886, when anti-Chinese agitation reached its peak in Portland and mass meetings called for the forcible expulsion of the group from the city, Wasserman, Goldsmith, and Jewish community lay leader Ben Selling were deputized as part of a special police force charged with protecting the Chinese from the mob.[21]

Local Jewish histories cite such activity in defense of the Chinese community as evidence of minority consciousness and empathy among Portland's leading Jews. William Toll argues that, with regard to the Chinese, "Wasserman and Goldsmith showed a more liberal view than most of their colleagues, a view which seemed to reflect their own background as the offspring of a stigmatized people."[22] Elaine Friedman frames Selling's service on the special police force as part of a commitment to fighting prejudice by linking it to his efforts to counter anti-Semitism.[23] Despite these accounts, close examination suggests that their motives may have been more reflective of their class position and interests than of Jewish exceptionalism.

First, the records of these men on the Chinese issue are more mixed than the oft-cited examples suggest. Although Wasserman did veto the measure aimed at barring the employment of Chinese on city contracts, this came just two days after he approved a cubic space ordinance targeting the crowded housing practices of the Chinese, part of the standard arsenal of anti-Chinese activists.[24] Second, singling out these individuals as Jews who opposed anti-Chinese restrictions ignores the larger context. Noting only Wasserman's veto of the anti-Chinese ordinance, without mentioning that similar restrictions were reversed by the courts, by a prior mayor, and by the governor, incorrectly implies that the Jewish mayor was exceptional in his opposition, presumably because of his Jewish sensibilities. [25] Finally, although the two mayors and Ben Selling are frequently mentioned as defenders of the Chinese, their actions were not exceptional *for members of their class*. In 1886, Mayor Gates deputized between two hundred and three hundred individuals, many of them, according to Selling, from "the better class of citizens." Although there is no question that Selling, Wasserman, and Goldsmith took active roles in opposing the anti-Chinese agitation of the mid-1880s, Jews in general do not appear to have been overrepresented in these activities once class is taken into consideration. Moreover, Portland had a record of relative tolerance toward Chinese—especially in comparison to Seattle and Tacoma, cities that drove out their Chinese populations in the mid-1880s.[26] In addition, some Jewish shopkeepers joined in the boycott of Chinese labor.[27] Although he did not play a leading role, Senator Joseph Simon was part of the Pacific Coast delegation that joined together to craft the long-term extension of Chinese Exclusion in 1902.[28] Even those who tried to prevent violence against Chinese were often motivated by concern for public order and not necessarily opposed to race-based restrictions.

Examination of both those agitating against the Chinese and their "defenders" makes clear that class motives were critical. Anti-Chinese activity—both legislative and more direct—found its greatest support among the working classes. Despite the focus on alleged Chinese vice, this was primarily a conflict over labor: workers feared that the Chinese would undercut white wages. Thus, the Knights of Labor was a primary player in the anti-Chinese agitation in Portland and elsewhere in the Pacific Northwest in the mid-1880s, and politicians endorsing strong support for Chinese restrictions were seen as "champions of labor."[29] Portland's Jews, concentrated overwhelmingly in the trade sector, were not well represented among the working classes, although some small shopkeepers did identify with labor. On the other hand, Jews were well represented among the merchants and business owners who became Chinese "defenders." These men shared a strong concern about civic order, and their enterprises, like the city itself, often benefited from cheap Chinese labor.[30] Prominent city leaders including *Oregonian* editor Harvey Scott—hardly a champion of progressive attitudes—editorialized against the mob action, likening it to the 1863 Draft Riots in New York City.[31] When the emerging anti-Chinese agitator Sylvester Pennoyer advocated new restrictions on the Chinese, Bernard Goldsmith and his close friend, prominent Judge Matthew Deady, led the opposition. The two of them won "unanimous endorsement of their position [on the Board of Trade, a forerunner of the Chamber of Commerce] with the exception of Pennoyer, who became the state's most outspoken opponent of Chinese residency."[32] Clearly, individuals such as Goldsmith, Wasserman, and Selling were in good company among their Christian fellow businessmen. Although the anti-Chinese movement was popular among the working classes, the position taken by these successful merchants and civic leaders was reflective of their class, which, according to Toll "saw their defense of the Chinese as an assertion of their right to uphold civic order rather than as the expression of any special regard for an ethnic minority."[33] Such activity provided an opportunity for Jewish merchants to publicly display their role as civic leaders.

It is possible that the Jewish members of this merchant class, as Toll further suggests, were also motivated by "sympathy for the Chinese as a stereotyped and ghettoized minority."[34] Yet, with no local Jewish paper available in Portland until the final decade of the century and very few primary accounts, it is difficult to discern community attitudes on this question. Here, the record in San Francisco may be instructive. Despite increasing difference between the two communities in the early twentieth century,[35] the Portland Jewish community was closely linked to that in San Francisco: many Portland Jews had lived or sojourned there prior to coming north, merchants traveled there regularly for business, and many had family ties or found their brides in that city. In addition, some Jewish newspapers out of San Francisco covered—and presumed to speak for—the entire West. A study of the San Francisco Jewish press and of pieces by correspondents in that city posted to eastern Jewish papers shows increasing anti-Chinese rhetoric in the 1870s and 1880s, similar to that in the secular press.[36] For example, Isidor Choynski, who served under the pen name Maftir as western correspondent for the Cincinnati-based *American Israelite* from 1874 to 1893, repeatedly attacked Chinese immigrants in dispatches that made clear that he embraced local prejudices.[37] In response to such reports, eastern Jewish papers attacked the "unseemly biases" of their West Coast counterparts. Westerners responded with "lurid descriptions of

Chinatowns' dirty streets, strange odors, opium dens, prostitutes, joss houses, noise and confusion."[38] San Francisco's three leading rabbis took part in the anti-Chinese agitation, joining other local clergymen in signing a telegram urging President Hayes to support immigration restrictions on Chinese. The rabbis' action generated criticism from Jewish newspapers back East, and as far away as Paris.[39]

Portland, of course, was not San Francisco. Although anti-Chinese vitriol was common up and down the West Coast, it was more muted in Portland, in part due to the actions of the "leading citizens," as we have seen. In addition, Portland was the home to a vocal regional Jewish critic of the anti-Chinese prejudice of his western brethren, David Solis-Cohen. Solis-Cohen wrote to his hometown paper, the Philadelphia *Jewish Record*, in 1879 criticizing the San Francisco rabbis' intolerance.[40] Yet Solis-Cohen was a newcomer in 1879, having arrived just two years before. His views more clearly reflected the sensibilities of his home community than those of his adopted city; according to a study of the Jewish press on the issue, "nowhere else in the country was there the persistent defense of the Chinese shown as in Philadelphia's Jewish press."[41] Given the close business, fraternal, and familial ties between Jewish leaders in Portland and San Francisco at the time, it seems more likely that Jewish Portlanders shared the anti-Chinese views of their Bay Area counterparts than those of the Philadelphians.

EMERGING MINORITY CONSCIOUSNESS: NATIONAL TRENDS AND LOCAL SENSIBILITIES

The pages of Portland's Jewish newspaper, the *Scribe*, provide evidence of the increasingly national Jewish identity of the community by the 1920s. The central issues were reflective of those engaged by Jews across the country: Zionism, the threat of anti-Semitism at home and abroad, and, increasingly, concern for worker and minority rights. Indeed, much of this coverage originated in the East and was supplied to the Portland paper via Jewish wire services. Early in the century, the American Jewish community focused much of its attention internally, on the needs of the large numbers of impoverished and unacculturated immigrant Jews. However, by the 1920s and 1930s, the national Jewish social justice agenda had expanded to include the plight of workers and minorities more broadly. Historians attribute this shift

to the increasing influence of East European Jews, who disproportion-
ately toiled as industrial workers, engaged in the labor movement, and
embraced its sensibilities.[42]

Beyond their immediate experience in the labor movement, the
historic and recent persecution of East European Jews inspired their
deep identification with other oppressed groups. Thus, nationally,
the Yiddish press frequently empathized with the plight of African
Americans, comparing anti-black riots and lynch mob actions to
pogroms.[43] By the interwar years, East Europeans, whose numbers had
long since eclipsed those of established eastern and midwestern communities, were becoming increasingly acculturated, and the American-
born generation was moving into positions of influence. Both within
communal institutions and in local and regional politics, they became
a force to be reckoned with.

Shifting demographics also influenced national Jewish communal agendas in a less direct way. The arrival of large numbers of East
Europeans in the early twentieth century triggered increased anti-
Semitism, reflecting a growing, more general, anti-immigrant sentiment. This heightened the sense of minority status for the entire Jewish
community and created greater potential for alliances with other
downtrodden groups.[44] In addition, contact between "uptown" and
"downtown" Jews encouraged by Reform leaders who embraced a
vision of Judaism in which "moral conduct and social justice, rather
than faith, laws, and ritual practices, formed the essence of Judaism,"
led to an increasing concern about issues such as child labor and exploitation of workers.[45] The shift also reflected a broader societal—and
clerical—embrace of Progressivism. Even in the most well-established
Reform synagogues, where many of the congregants were employers, a
social justice agenda was cultivated. In 1918, the Reform movement's
Central Conference of American Rabbis (CCAR) adopted a social justice platform.

It is interesting to see these issues playing out in Oregon, since the
community was, in many ways, at the margins of these changes. Jewish
immigrants and migrants arriving in the Northwest in the early twentieth century tended to enter the trade sector, as had their nineteenth-
century predecessors. Indeed, Portland was an unlikely destination for
industrial workers; though it was, by far, the largest city in the state

and home to the vast majority of Jewish Oregonians, its manufacturing sector was not well developed. Politically, despite the activities of
what Robert Johnston has called the "radical middle class" during the
Progressive Era, Oregon was a conservative stronghold through World
War II—with influential factions of both "Old Guard" Republicans and
conservative Democrats who were hostile to labor and, in the 1930s,
to the New Deal.[46] Within the Jewish community, the relatively small
and gradual flow of immigrants meant that the older pioneer families
and their institutions continued to dominate well into the twentieth
century. The established community, long accepted as white, was somewhat sheltered from the harsh anti-immigration-based anti-Semitism
of the East. In addition, their business orientation meant that, like
their counterparts in San Francisco, this segment of Portland's Jewish
community remained solidly Republican in this period. Yet, despite all
these potentially mitigating factors, the emerging national social justice
agenda was clearly reflected locally.

The message of economic social justice can be seen from the earliest
issues of the *Scribe* in 1920, clearly driven by its editor, Congregation
Beth Israel's rabbi Jonah Wise, who strongly embraced the platform
articulated by the CCAR's Committee on Social Justice. During his tenure as editor (1920–1926), Wise communicated this agenda in lengthy
pieces that recounted the committee's program in detail. For example,
his account of "The Rabbinical Convention" in July 1920 included
a detailed description of the committee's report, with its "appeal to
all Jews to view the social struggle from the traditional standpoint of
the Jew as a lover of his fellow man, and especially for the Jewish
employer to take that view in his dealings with labor." The report specifically endorsed labor's right to organize and bargain collectively.[47]
Several weeks later, the *Scribe* printed the full Social Justice Program,
which focused on labor issues—including endorsing a minimum wage,
an eight-hour day, a six-day workweek, safety measures, abolition of
child labor, universal workman's health insurance, unemployment and
old age coverage, public employment bureaus, the right to organize
and bargain, proper housing, mothers' pensions, and "a more equi-
table distribution of the profits of industry"—as well as opposition
to lynching.[48] In the same issue, Wise called for an investigation of
the problems of steel workers, advocating community involvement in

"social reform" and a "whole-hearted effort" to help the poor: "It is the duty of lay readers to demand a participation of religion in the problems of justice."[49] When the CCAR announced its opposition to the twelve-hour workday in 1923, the *Scribe* published two favorable editorials on the subject.[50]

The practice of conveying and endorsing the committee's social justice agenda through articles, reprinting of its programs, and editorial affirmations continued in the following years.[51] Wise's successor at Beth Israel, Rabbi Henry Berkowitz (1928–1949)—who served on the *Scribe*'s now expanded editorial board—shared Wise's social justice sensibilities. In one of his first sermons after assuming Beth Israel's pulpit in 1928, Berkowitz preached on social justice, explaining, "It refers to the awakened conscience of mankind to the necessity of recognizing human rights." He continued,

> social justice deals with the relationship between employer and employee, capital and labor, freedom of speech and right of assembly. It includes the question of religious equality, the problem of the negro, the question of child labor, the settlement of strikes, the separation of church and state, and all the other problems that are connected with modern complicated society.[52]

Such messages resonated with a congregation that had earlier been inspired by the examples of Rabbi Stephen Wise and philanthropist/politician Ben Selling. The local chapter of the National Council of Jewish Women, whose signature initiative was Neighborhood House and whose membership was largely from Beth Israel, was likewise emphatic about its inclusiveness and mission to serve the entire community, regardless of race or religion.

Through the 1930s, the *Scribe*'s strong embrace of this Reform social justice program continued, often mentioned by San Francisco rabbi Louis I. Newman, a contributing editor with a weekly column, and by Rabbi Berkowitz. The rabbis frequently referenced the committee's work to frame their agenda, sometimes quoting at length from their statements on social justice in their columns in the *Scribe* and in other venues.[53] In 1933, despite the Republican bent of his congregation, Rabbi Berkowitz embraced the emerging New Deal in his Yom

Kippur sermon, explaining that it was replacing "the old worn-out system of laissez faire individualism" with "enforced recognition of human rights." Berkowitz saw the New Deal as the embodiment of an agenda that resonated with Jewish values: "I have chosen to speak about it tonight because it is the one time when we are all together, and as American citizens profoundly interested in the welfare of our country and as members of a religious group who are proud of their heritage of social righteousness, it becomes a duty to direct our thoughts to this vital problem."[54]

Along with economic justice, racial justice emerged as a theme in this era, as suggested by the 1920 condemnation of lynching in the Social Justice program and Berkowitz's mention of "the problem of the negro" in his 1928 sermon. As early as 1920, the *Neighborhood*, newsletter of Neighborhood House, ran an editorial urging acceptance of the "several Negro families [who] have moved into our neighborhood." The editorial continued,

> Undoubtedly, the attitude that we should take on this problem is one of tolerance toward our colored neighbors and intolerance toward those who raise malicious protests for no valid reasons. . . . The Negro families that are here are all well-behaved, good natured and orderly people. They are industrious and their family life is far above the average notion that one gets of the Negro family life. . . .
>
> If we, white neighbors, could educate ourselves to let our Negro neighbor use our 'phone, or hose, or lawn mower, do some shopping for them when we are downtown, take care of the children if the mother is sick, we would then reach a magnanimity of character which is the aim of American ideals.[55]

The Portland NCJW members responsible for the settlement house had attitudes informed by speakers such as NAACP leader, W. E. B. DuBois, invited to lecture on racial minorities at Temple Beth Israel by Rabbi Jonah Wise in 1923.[56] As national Jewish organizations including the CCAR and NCJW increasingly linked social justice with an anti-prejudice, pro–civil rights agenda, this was reflected in the *Scribe*. For example, the paper ran Jewish wire stories on the topic, such as a 1925 piece highlighting Charles Evan Hughes's speech denouncing

"racial and religious bigotry." The item quoted Hughes's proclamation that "true Americanism is of the spirit, not of any race or strain.
The bigoted citizen, however boastful of long American descent, who
would deny political privilege to his fellow citizen because of his race
or creed is exhibiting not his Americanism but his lack of it."[57]

General statements against prejudice were reinforced locally by
the Jewish community's vocal opposition to Klan activity in Oregon.
Jewish denunciations of the Klan, whether in the *Scribe* or in other
public fora, routinely referred to KKK attacks on Jews as one of several targeted groups, implicitly linking Jews with other minorities.
For example, articles in the spring of 1922 referenced KKK attacks
on "Catholics, Jews, Negroes, and all naturalized citizens," and predicted that the Klan would create "a division of American life into bitter race and religious factions."[58] Certainly, the KKK's prominence in
Oregon was one of the factors that contributed to the 1920s expansion
of the Anti-Defamation League's activities in Portland. A committee
was founded in 1915, and in 1925 attorney David Robinson became
its director (and the western representative of ADL). By the 1930s,
Robinson, too, had joined the *Scribe*'s editorial board.

Although anti-Semitism became a major focus in the *Scribe* during
the interwar years, relatively little attention was focused on local incidents. Even in the face of the vitriolic attacks on Julius Meier during
the 1930 gubernatorial campaign, the *Scribe* had little to say about
local anti-Semitism.[59] Instead, much of its coverage focused on national
and international developments. The *Scribe* gave ample coverage to the
anti-Semitic campaign of Henry Ford and his *Dearborn Independent*,
for example, often through wire service stories. International anti-
Semitism also received extensive attention from the earliest *Scribe*
issues and expanded further in the 1930s with the rise of Nazism in
Germany.[60] By the mid-1930s, the paper was saturated with items
related to Nazism. For example, in the January 1934 issue, eight of
the nine front-page stories touched on Nazism and the fate of Europe's
Jews.[61] In 1936, the paper ran a three-part exposé by a Jewish former
Portlander who had infiltrated the Silver Shirts in Seattle.[62] As was
the case nationally, coverage of anti-Semitism and Nazism was often
framed as part of a broader discussion of intolerance and race prejudice: just as Nazism and fascism were un-American, so were all forms

of racial and religious intolerance. Thus, in 1938, on a front page featuring a picture of George Washington with the quote "to bigotry no sanction" alongside several stories referencing German refugees, the paper published the Brotherhood Day "Ten Commandments of Good Will," promoted by ADL leader David Robinson. Among the ten were commandments to "honor all men and women regardless of their race or religion," to "protect and defend my neighbor and my neighbor's children against the ravages of racial or religious bigotry," to "challenge the philosophy of racial superiority," and to "protest against every manifestation of racial or religious prejudice."[63]

Certainly, the emphasis on social justice in the *Scribe* was heavily influenced by Reform leaders Wise and Berkowitz, who served on its editorial board. Yet such sensibilities also clearly resonated with the expanding East European communities in South Portland. As second-generation immigrants began to move into leadership positions in the community during the interwar years, they reinforced the trend. Indeed, it was during this period that the *Scribe* broadened its leadership base, establishing an editorial board that included the rabbis of *all* of Portland's major congregations, including the Orthodox congregations of South Portland. Perhaps even more critical were the voices of the rising second generation, who were beginning to enter the professions and associate with sons of the Jewish establishment in the B'nai B'rith and other fraternal organizations.[64] These sons and daughters of the South Portland immigrants, coming of age in the teens, 1920s, and 1930s with a growing expectation of social mobility, experienced a degree of anti-Semitism that had been unknown in the pioneer generation. In interviews years later, many noted social discrimination in high school, and those who attended the University of Oregon—as at many universities across the country—found themselves excluded from fraternities and sororities.[65] Like their counterparts in eastern cities, many developed strong identities as members of a minority group and sensitivities to prejudice more broadly—including to local race relations. For example, Gus Solomon, who would become a leading civil liberties lawyer and later a federal judge, was "sharply cut" by anti-Semitism as he grew up in Portland, and linked that directly to his emerging political sensibilities. Barbs from other children taught him that "I was different. I was a Christ killer," and, as he matured, he was aware

Judge Gus Solomon, c. 1950.
Credit: Oregon Jewish Museum

of the impact of discrimination in "education, job opportunities and social activities." Years later, he still felt "the hurt that I experienced as a young man being discriminated against because I was a Jew."

For Solomon, the personal encounter with anti-Semitism and identification as a minority was closely linked to his interest in progressive issues and his founding role in the Portland ACLU. As he explained, "Largely as a result of these experiences, and the emphasis on social justice in the Jewish tradition, I became active as a young lawyer in the problems of the poor." His civil rights activities were "not for the Jews alone—but for everyone."⁶⁶ Solomon had first encountered the ACLU as a law student in New York in 1927, when he heard its national director, Roger Baldwin, speak on the Sacco and Vanzetti case. The meeting, he later recounted, "opened up new horizons for me, and had a great impact on my life."⁶⁷ Home in Oregon that summer, Solomon volunteered in David Robinson's law firm to gain experience. Robinson had earlier served as Oregon's first public defender.⁶⁸

Solomon was one of a cadre of civil liberties activists who shared backgrounds as second-generation immigrants who had come of age in South Portland.[69] Another member of this group, Solomon's future colleague and friend Leo Levinson, similarly linked his civil rights work to his Jewish identity: "As a Jew I have always believed in freedom because I've studied the background of Jewish people and it's only in the last century . . . that we have received freedom from different countries." Levinson, who moved to Portland from Boston in 1910 at age seven, began to experience discrimination while in high school: "I was not invited to the parties, like a lot of my classmates were, and it never dawned on me the reason for it. And of course, since I have grown up, I realize that there was sort of a gentlemen's agreement in those days that separated Jews from Gentiles."[70]

In an earlier generation, Joseph Simon had become a partner at Mitchell and Dolph, one of Portland's most prestigious law firms, and was able to return to the firm after his political career, practicing there until the 1930s.[71] By the 1920s, however, such avenues were no longer open to the rising generation of Jewish lawyers. That Solomon and Levinson began their legal careers sharing an office and taking on civil liberties cases was a reflection not only of their minority identification and political sensibilities, but also of the professional discrimination rampant in Portland at this time. After completing law school in 1929, Solomon interviewed at many Portland firms before beginning a solo practice, "not because I wanted to, but because I couldn't get a job."[72] Levinson invited him to share office space and soon both began to collaborate with Irvin Goodman, an International Labor Defense (ILD, the legal arm of the Communist Party) lawyer and "Oregon's leading radical lawyer." According to Harry Stein, Solomon's biographer, Levinson and Solomon did not share Goodman's radicalism but were eager to work on civil liberties cases.[73]

Although the civil liberties and civil rights cases that these second-generation lawyers took on were, in many ways, in sync with the social agenda articulated in the *Scribe*, there was a significant disjuncture between the practical, local activities of the former and the more national, theoretical public agenda of the latter. This gap between broad principles of social justice or civil rights and their application to local affairs can be seen in responses—or lack of responses—to

Notice for a civil rights meeting featuring Irving Goodman, 1950. Credit: Oregon Jewish Museum

several prominent local episodes, beginning with the so-called Oregon Scottsboro case.

The case was that of Theodore Jordan, an African American who moved to Klamath Falls in Southern Oregon in 1932 and was convicted by an all-white jury in the murder of a white railroad worker after making a coerced confession. As in the Scottsboro Boys' case in Alabama, a mob surrounded the courthouse threatening to lynch Jordan, only dispersing after he was sentenced to death. After the sentencing, the NAACP hired Charles Robison, a local Jewish lawyer, to file an appeal. However, in another parallel to the Scottsboro case, when Jordan accepted the support of the ILD, the NAACP pulled out. As the Portland ILD lawyer, Goodman became the lead attorney in the case, and he drafted Solomon to prepare the appeal brief. Although unsuccessful in their legal appeal, their efforts—along with an extensive campaign of letter writing, petitions, and mass meetings organized by the ILD—led Governor Julius Meier to commute Jordan's death sentence in 1934. Nearly two decades later, Jordan would finally be paroled.[74]

Both nationally and locally, the Jewish response to the better-known Alabama Scottsboro case was vigorous, clearly reflecting the "increasing tendency among Jews to see anti-black racism and anti-Semitism as emanating from the same sources," according to historian Eric Goldstein. Although the marked increase in identification with blacks was tempered by a fear of "being placed in the same category with blacks as racial outsider," the Alabama case generated tremendous attention. Support for the nine Scottsboro boys "flowed from every segment of the Jewish community, from radical to conservative, Yiddish speaking to Americanized."[75] Hasia Diner, who studied the Yiddish press response to Scottsboro, claims that "from 1915 to 1935, no single episode received as much attention." The case resonated not only because of the community's identification with a persecuted minority, but also because of the involvement of Jewish attorneys in the case and "because the trial coincided with the earliest Jewish-American awareness of the threat developing in Germany." [76]

Like its counterparts nationally, the *Scribe* weighed in on southern racism in general, and covered the Alabama Scottsboro case specifically, often through the use of wire service stories that noted specific Jewish resonances. For example, in April 1933, under the headline "Anti-Semitic Issue Muddles Scottsboro Case," the *Scribe* ran a front-page story reporting that locals in Alabama were using the Jewish identities of the lawyers to criticize the case. In the same issue, the editors addressed the subject in an editorial titled, "Alabama Hitlerism."[77] Two weeks later, another editorial, headlined "A Crime," criticized the removal of an Alabama rabbi from his post after he expressed solidarity with the Scottsboro Boys at a protest meeting, proclaiming that "as a member of a persecuted race, I feel it is my bounden duty to champion the cause of any minority discriminated against." The *Scribe* castigated the congregation's board of trustees, proclaiming, "We need rabbis like Rabbi Goldstein."[78] Appearing on the same page was yet another editorial titled "Jewish Social Justice," praising the increasing efforts of synagogues and churches to work for social change.

Given the strong embrace of a social justice agenda in the *Scribe* and at major institutions including Neighborhood House and Temple Beth Israel, and the involvement of several Portland Jewish lawyers and Governor Meier, who, at the time of the commutation of Jordan's death sentence was also serving as the president of Temple Beth Israel, one might expect treatment of the "Oregon Scottsboro case" to echo, or even eclipse, coverage of the Alabama case. Yet the paper failed to report on the matter, and there is no evidence that local Jewish organizations joined in the efforts to exonerate Jordan. Among the dozens of petitions and statements of support in Jordan's appeal for a pardon are many from organized groups, beginning with phrases such as "We, the workers of Berkeley" or "We, the Finnish workers of San Francisco," many in the form of resolutions passed at mass meetings including the West Coast Anti-Lynch Conference in San Jose. Petitions and resolutions came mostly from ILD chapters and labor organizations, but others were sent by groups ranging from a Women's Christian Temperance Union chapter to farmers' groups. The leftist Jewish farming settlement of Petaluma, California, sent a statement in the name of "100 people of Petaluma," signed by Chairman Weitzman. Yet no petitions or statements were submitted by Oregon Jewish organizations.[79] Even when Irvin Goodman was one of two featured speakers at a "Jordan-Scottsboro Mass Meeting" in Albina Hall in Portland, the *Scribe* did not cover the meeting.[80] And although Rabbi Berkowitz delivered a powerful anti-lynching sermon in late 1933, arguing that "the Jew should be the greatest opponent of mob violence," there is no evidence that he mentioned the near-lynching of Jordan in Oregon the year before, despite the explicit linking of Jordan's case to the anti-lynching cause in public protest meetings and ILD literature.[81]

The same disconnect between national and local was evident in the community's response—or lack of response—to the strong anti-Nikkei (Japanese American) movement during the interwar years and after Pearl Harbor. Despite the growing emphasis on equality regardless of "race or creed," and proclamations about the importance of fighting prejudice in general, the community tended to ignore the vitriolic anti-Nikkei campaign in this period.

In many ways, the anti-Nikkei campaign took up where the anti-Chinese campaign left off. With Chinese immigration restricted severely in the early 1880s by the exclusion act, Japanese immigrants were quickly drawn to the West by the continued demand for labor. Soon, many of the same groups that had earlier organized against the Chinese came to see Japanese immigrants as a critical threat. Although efforts were made to completely eliminate further immigration early in the century, Japan's status as an international power allowed it to moderate this thrust. The result was that, although the immigration of Japanese workers was curtailed in the 1907 Gentlemen's Agreement between the two countries, those Nikkei already present in the United States were able to bring over wives, often as picture brides, until 1924, when all Asian immigration was cut off. Locally, groups organized to support restrictions on the Japanese immigrants, who, like their Chinese counterparts, were aliens ineligible for citizenship under federal law. Local governments, including Portland's, passed restrictions on business licenses, and the state legislature banned intermarriage and landowning by aliens ineligible for citizenship. The perception that Japanese immigrants and their growing families were a threat was most acute in the early 1920s, when the so-called Klan legislature passed Oregon's alien land law, and again in the months immediately following Pearl Harbor.

Despite the attention that these issues garnered in the popular press, as with the Oregon Scottsboro case, the Jewish community rarely went on record about the local/regional controversy over the Nikkei, even as it broadcast the national, largely African American–focused, anti-prejudice agenda. There were exceptions—as when the *Neighborhood* urged its readers toward empathy with Japanese immigrants, pointing out the hypocrisy of anti-Nikkei prejudice: "that industry, that frugality, that courtesy which we praised so highly as virtues in Japan become vices once they are transported here. Their industry becomes a bleeding of the soil; their frugality becomes miserliness; their superb courtesy becomes scheming intrigue."[82] More often, however, the community remained silent on the volatile issue. Thus, the *Scribe* denounced the anti-Catholic public-school initiative championed by the Klan and the

Masons in 1922, and organized groups and prominent Jewish individuals spoke out publicly against the initiative, but there was no similar Jewish response to the Alien Land Law, passed by the Oregon legislature in February 1923.[83] On issues of anti-Asian prejudice, the pattern echoed that in the Oregon Scottsboro case—there was a willingness to take a position against prejudice *in the abstract* or at a distance, yet similar, volatile *local* issues were not publicly engaged. Thus, shortly after the passage of the Oregon Alien Land Law went unmentioned in the paper, the *Scribe* published an editorial that addressed anti-Asian prejudice but said not a word about the Oregon law. Focusing instead on a 1923 Supreme Court decision on a Washington case that "even Hindus cannot be citizens," the editors called it "a shock" and then turned to the "Oriental question on the Pacific Slope" more broadly. The piece cited the need to study the "problem," noting that much of the discussion is "so obviously biased that it can lead to no opinion, merely prejudice," and that "good Americans are just as much put out mentally over doing an injustice to a dark-skinned fellow-being as over being threatened in their rights and liberties."[84]

This pattern of energetically speaking out against prejudice in general terms—or as it occurred in other parts of the country—while refraining from commenting on explosive local issues, is clearest in the community's engagement (or lack of engagement) in the 1942 debate over the removal and incarceration of Japanese Americans. As public officials, the leading newspapers, and an array of community, business, and patriotic organizations mobilized to support the emerging policy of removing all Japanese Americans (including the two-thirds of the community who were American citizens by birth) from the Pacific Coast states and incarcerating them in inland camps, the Jewish community remained silent. Even when making pleas against prejudice or in situations where the plight of Japanese American was the obvious context, Jewish voices in Portland avoided the issue. For example, the very week that President Roosevelt issued the executive order that would lead to Japanese American incarceration, the *Scribe* published editorials advocating for the rights of German aliens, criticizing those who would judge others by their national origins and condemning the idea of creating "concentration camps," even for anti-Semitic leaders, but avoiding specific mention of Japanese Americans.[85] Likewise, just weeks after congressional committee hearings on the issue in Portland and days before Japanese Americans in the city were subjected to a curfew, Rabbi Berkowitz delivered a sermon titled "Liberty and Justice for all—Except Negroes," focusing on the tragedy of discrimination against African Americans, without mentioning the Nikkei. "Cleanse yourself of prejudice," he urged his congregation, "Jews, above all, should be in the very forefront of the battle for the negroes' rights. A Jew who harbors race predjudice [sic] in any form violates a fundamental canon of simple justice and is unworthy of his heritage."[86]

This silence was not unique to the Portland community. Both regionally and nationally, American Jews seemed caught between two conflicting impulses: to support *all* aspects of the war effort (both as a patriotic act and in the hope of saving Europe's Jews) and to fight *all* forms of prejudice. That Jewish organizations and the Jewish press did not join in the chorus of western voices urging immediate mass removal of Japanese Americans suggests that they were hesitant to embrace a policy based on race; and analysis of the words around that silence suggest discomfort with the policy.[87]

Additionally, in contrast to Seattle and San Francisco, where opponents of the anti-Nikkei policy organized quickly and strongly criticized the race-based policy, there was no organized opposition in Oregon. This made it difficult for individuals to speak out. Thus, Gus Solomon, despite strong misgivings, did not protest—something he later bitterly regretted: "I am sorry to say that I was not involved in the beginning, when the Japanese-Americans were moved into concentration camps. I knew about it; I didn't like it; but I didn't protest."[88] Solomon tried, unsuccessfully, to get the ACLU to participate in the defense of Minoru Yasui, an Oregon native and fellow attorney who got himself arrested violating the curfew laws so that he could test their constitutionality.[89] Solomon also urged the local American Jewish Congress to speak out against the incarceration policy, arguing that "they have got to speak up against the treatment of the Japanese because today it's the Japanese and tomorrow it's the Jews." He found, however, that he "was the only Jew in Portland willing to stand up."[90] Later in the war, in 1944, Solomon became part of an interfaith group that urged the Exclusion Order be lifted and worked to pave the way for the Nikkei community's return.[91]

It is difficult to explain a silence—individuals and organizations rarely provide an explanation for *not* responding to an issue. Yet examination of the context of this silence suggests that the same insecurities that led Portland Jews to embrace the national civil rights/civil liberties agenda likely shaped their hesitancy on the local level. Increasing local, national, and international anti-Semitism, as we have seen, had shifted the national Jewish conversation toward a broad anti-prejudice agenda. At the same time, the very minority identification that increased anti-Semitism also heightened insecurity. While it was relatively easy for Jewish Oregonians to join the many voices condemning racial injustice in Alabama, it was far more risky to stand against well-established local prejudices and discriminatory practices. To stick one's neck out on such issues could result in the opposite effect, and actually increase local anti-Semitism.

The danger of retribution was real, as Gus Solomon experienced on more than one occasion. For example, Solomon played a leading role in the successful US Supreme Court appeal in 1936 of the conviction of Communist Dirk DeJonge for "participating in a meeting conducted by a political party that taught and advocated the violent and unlawful overthrow of the government,"[92] a violation of Oregon's anti-syndicalism laws. The case led to a boycott of Solomon, who was accused by the Portland Red Squad of belonging to a Communist organization—the ACLU.[93] Nearly a decade later, when Solomon was quoted in the *Oregonian* as supporting the lifting of the exclusion order and the gradual return of Japanese Americans to the state, he was threatened and called a "Communist, anarchist, and traitor."[94] Even Solomon's mother was concerned about his many "anti-establishment" cases. "Why can't you represent nice people?" he recalled her asking. He explained, "Her attitude and that of her friends represented the attitude of many Jewish people, particularly those who had made money and who had achieved some prominence. They did not want me, as a fellow Jew, to 'rock the boat.' They wanted to identify with the wealthy and the well-born and with the people 'who counted.'"[95]

The conflicting impulses—to support an anti-prejudice, liberal agenda that would open American society to all minorities (including Jews) or to retreat from causes that were unpopular and had the potential to create personal or communal backlash—were not unique to Oregon. As historian Eric Goldstein has demonstrated, despite the growing embrace of a pro–civil rights philosophy among Jews during the interwar years, "only a small minority of American Jews felt free enough from the daunting social pressures of white America to engage in consistent high-profile advocacy of black causes."[96] In those areas where racial conflicts were most heated—as in the American South—Jewish communities were particularly reticent to publicly flaunt or criticize local standards. More broadly, Marc Dollinger, in his study of Jews and liberalism, argues that liberalism was embraced as a "strategy of choice" that "offered a vision of pluralist democracy that demanded social and political inclusion." He continues,

> Yet at historical moments when Jewish social mobility clashed with a liberal political orientation, American Jews dissented from the dominant left-leaning trend. Faced with a choice between liberal politics and their own acculturation, Jews almost always chose the latter. The politics of acculturation, the process by which Jews advocated liberal political change in order to ease their adaptation to American life, cut like a double-edged sword. While it strengthened American Jews, giving them the drive to champion unpopular causes and establish themselves as the guardians of liberal America, the politics of acculturation also erected strict barriers to liberal success.[97]

The backlash experienced by Solomon helps to explain why, even as the community leaders from both the established Reform community and the emerging group of second-generation professionals embraced a progressive, anti-prejudice agenda during the interwar years, there was a gap between their rhetoric on the general issue and actual application of that emerging ethos to the most volatile local cases. Just as southern Jews agreed that "the preservation of Jewish social status relied on their conformity to southern racial standards," but "abstained from promoting the harshest forms of southern racism,"[98] Jewish Oregonians opted to remain silent in the face of the vitriolic anti-Nikkei sentiment that was so widespread in their region during the 1920s and early 1940s. Though activists such as Solomon were able to see and sometimes to counter local manifestations of racial injustice, community organs such as the *Scribe* were much more likely to speak to the broad principles or to injustices in other regions than to confront local issues.

POST-WORLD WAR II: MINORITY CONSCIOUSNESS?

American Jewish historians have often pointed to World War II as a turning point in terms of engagement of the community with the Civil Rights Movement. Speaking out against Nazism fostered the development of an anti-prejudice agenda, which could be expressed through the emerging wartime discourse that "condemned all forms of racism and bigotry as 'un-American.'"[99] During the postwar period, American Jews embraced a liberal ethos that included an "increasing commitment to end privilege based on race, religion, and national origin."[100] Although still facing professional and residential restrictions and other forms of social anti-Semitism, a new confidence and optimism propelled an increased civil rights activism. As Hasia Diner explains,

> while Jews had participated in the freedom struggle of African Americans since the beginning of the twentieth century . . . only in the aftermath of World War II did the organized Jewish community—synagogues, synagogal bodies, defense organizations and the like—become actively engaged in the movement. Notably, previous anxiety over their own status in America had prevented them as a community from risking the opprobrium of the non-Jewish majority.[101]

There were, however, exceptions to the trend—especially in the South, where, as Diner noted, "the outspoken support of national and northern Jewish organizations for civil rights . . . put Jewish southerners in a complicated and uncomfortable position."[102] In Portland, a liberal, pro–civil rights, interfaith coalition, in which individual Jews played a prominent role, gained strength after the war but faced off against what historians have called Oregon's historically "southern" attitude toward race, exacerbated by a dramatic change in Portland's racial landscape. Although Jewish Oregonians had a history of expressing support for civil rights in the abstract, negotiating local issues—especially as they felt the sting of social exclusions—continued to present challenges.

Japanese Americans, who, before the war, had been the most visible minority and the target of vitriolic racial prejudice, had been removed from the community in 1942. When they began to return in 1945, they faced much hostility—including campaigns in several towns to discourage resettlement. Activists worked through inter-religious organizations such as the Committee to Aid Relocation "to make the transition easier for Japanese Americans who were coming home from concentration camps."[103] Fanny Kenin Friedman, who had worked as a social worker at the Tule Lake Camp, was part of the War Relocation Authority's resettlement program, speaking on the topic to groups that included the Portland section of the Council of Jewish Women.[104] Likewise, Solomon "spoke at churches about the desirability of treating the Japanese Americans like human beings."[105] The committee's efforts included helping returning Nikkei reclaim lost property, breaking a boycott of Nikkei produce, and working to repeal the state's Alien Land Law.[106]

Despite these efforts, the postwar Nikkei community shrank considerably. Only about half of the city's Nikkei returned to Portland, and an even smaller percentage to Hood River, where the anti-Japanese movement was particularly venomous.[107] Since the overall population in Oregon—and particularly in Portland—boomed during the 1940s, the Nikkei community diminished even more in percentage terms. Wartime employment opportunities, particularly in the shipyards, led to an influx of workers, including a substantial number of African Americans. Long a tiny minority in Oregon and in Portland, African Americans quickly became the largest nonwhite group in the region and the primary focus of the civil rights efforts that increasingly became known as "intercultural work."

The *Scribe* had a long history of speaking out in support of African American civil rights, as did several Portland Jewish organizations and individual leaders, but such statements had nearly always been focused on either the national issue in general or on specific incidents in distant parts of the country. Now, increasingly, African American civil rights was an important *local* issue—and a volatile one. Western progressive Carey McWilliams claimed in 1945 that Portland was "the major area of racial tension on the West Coast today," and Portland Urban League leader Edwin Berry characterized Portland as "a 'northern city' with a 'southern exposure.'"[108] And, as before the war, any discussion of civil rights for African Americans in Portland played out in the Jewish community against a context of social insecurity, as professional and social exclusions continued to be a major concern to the rising second generation.

Acknowledging the shifting demographics as early as the fall of 1942, Rabbi Berkowitz urged his congregation to support "negro rights," even as he acknowledged the fears that restrained many of them from speaking out:

> I have always believed Jews should be in the thick of the fight for negro rights. Some Jews have been afraid. They were unwilling to admit the similarity of problems among all minority groups. I do not share that feeling. Our problems are identical in some aspects. At the present moment in our own community there has been agitation along these lines. The increased negro population and the seething war activity has pointed up the problem. All the colored folk ask is that they be not judged by their worst elements, that the entire group be not condemned for the actions of a few. That certainly sounds like us. Also we read statements to the effect that the negros who live here are alright. It is only the ones who have recently come that cause the trouble. That sounds strangely like Nazi Germany of 1933–34 when it was said that the Jews who had been born in Germany were safe and desirable. Only those who poured in from eastern Europe—they were the ones that caused the predjudice [*sic*]. It ended up by the destruction of all of them—both old and new. We must beware of repeating such mistakes in America in dealing with our great racial question. And we Jews must be careful to see that we are on the right side of this vital issue. Let us not be misguidedly moved to race predjudice [*sic*]. We must remember that our enemies across the seas would love to have America hate its Jews. It has tried to create that condition. We must also remember that our enemies would love to have America hate its negroes, especially during war time, when the seeds of revolution and civil strife are in the situation.[109]

As Berkowitz's words suggest, allying with African Americans locally stirred Jewish insecurities. While he and others urged Jews to note the similarities between anti-Semitism and anti-black prejudice with an aim toward forging alliances and fighting prejudice in all its forms, some feared drawing the parallels too tightly, both because speaking out in support of African Americans could trigger direct backlash and because such comparisons could lead to a questioning of Jews' status as whites.

Rabbi Berkowitz was succeeded after his long illness and untimely death by Rabbi Julius Nodel, who was installed in time for Rosh Hashanah in 1950. He made it an early and consistent priority during his tenure to address local racial issues. Earlier in 1950, the Portland City Council had passed an ordinance barring discrimination in public accommodations. That November, the ordinance was submitted to Portland voters for approval. In anticipation of the vote, Rabbi Nodel focused his sermon for October 10, 1950, on the film *No Way Out*, starring Sidney Poitier. The newly established *Temple Bulletin* explained, "Rabbi Nodel will discuss the deeply moving film on anti-Negro prejudice now being shown in Portland and its relationship to the Civil Rights Ordinance which will appear on the November 7 ballot."[110] Just a few weeks earlier, the rabbi had been "one of the speakers at the Civil Rights Rally held in Library Hall," and the following March, he was invited by the NAACP to speak at the Williams Avenue YWCA.[111] A few years later, in the spring of 1954, Rabbi Nodel included in the *Bulletin* "Ten Commandments of Good Will," from a New Jersey congregation. Nearly all the commandments spoke to an anti-prejudice agenda, including "I. I will respect all men and women regardless of race and religion," and "II. I will protect and defend my neighbor and my neighbor's children against the ravages of racial or religious bigotry."[112] Likewise, the *Bulletin* ran the CCAR's "Message for Race Relations" in full in early 1958.[113]

It is not surprising that Rabbis Berkowitz and Nodel of Congregation Beth Israel were among those Portland Jews in the 1940s and 1950s who were most openly supportive of civil rights. Going back to the pre-war years, historian Eric Goldstein has demonstrated that, nationally, rabbis were "among the leading Jewish advocates of African American rights."[114] This was particularly true of Reform rabbis, whose rabbinical association, the CCAR, had taken a strong pro–civil rights position as early as 1918. In addition, Beth Israel's members' wealth, prominence, and connections fit the profile of American Jews sufficiently secure in their economic and professional circumstances to speak out.[115] By the postwar period, with the emerging consensus nationally and in Portland linking liberalism and the fight against discrimination, to work together with other prominent Oregonians on such measures was to continue the temple's tradition of engagement in the broader community.

Yet at least as many, including siblings Harry and Fannie Kenin, shared backgrounds like Gus Solomon's, as children of East European immigrants who moved into the professions and, as early as the 1930s, were beginning to take on leadership roles in the community. And these two groups would be bolstered in their civil rights activism by newcomers, as Portland attracted a small but growing group of professionals from other parts of the country, including several—such as Jewish Community Center director William Gordon and Neighborhood House director Archie Goldman—who came to Portland with strong civil rights experience. Gordon, who would arrive in 1953, had prior experience in other parts of the country, including the South, where he developed a strong sense of the unity of prejudice: "I am pretty sure that you would generally find that where there is one form of prejudice, there is bound to be a combination."[116]

The arrival of these professionals at this time was no coincidence. For example, as Neighborhood House, still governed by the Portland Section of the National Council of Jewish Women, shifted its mission away from sectarian Jewish interests and toward the broader community in the mid-1940s, it began to function as part of a Portland coalition of social service agencies.[117] This led directly to the recruitment of Archie Goldman to lead the reorientation of Neighborhood House activities to better serve the changing neighborhood with recreational and other activities for diverse youth. In addition to his activities at the house, Goldman became deeply involved in efforts to address housing and employment discrimination against African Americans in Portland—including his decision to shelter African American families at Neighborhood House and in his own home in the wake of the 1948 Vanport Flood. Explaining his organization's support for Oregon's fair employment practices bill that same year, he wrote, "Particularly since we are an interracial inter-cultural agency, since our staff and membership are mixed, we feel quite definitely that any law aimed at discrimination in jobs would be a step forward in Oregon."[118]

Although it is clear that far fewer Portland NCJW members were directly involved in day-to-day Neighborhood House activities in the postwar period than had been the case earlier, the local section did regular advocacy work, endorsing pro-civil rights positions taken by the NCJW and also addressing local and state issues in the *Bulletin*, the Portland section's newsletter. For example, in a March 1953 article on state-level legislation, Mrs. Seymour Coblens endorsed the civil rights legislation under consideration in the state legislature, writing,

> Each morning during the school year, our children turn to the American flag to give their pledge of allegiance—"one nation, indivisible, with liberty and justice for all."
>
> But some of these children later learn that ideals and practices do not always correspond. Some, with dark skin or Oriental features, may find restaurants and hotels open to "white trade only." Negro children who participate in the program at Neighborhood House have discovered that clubs in which they are members, were refused admittance to amusement parks in the area.

After explaining the bill under consideration, Coblens concluded with a call to action based, in part, on Jews' shared vulnerability as a minority group,

> It therefore behooves every one of us to inform our legislators of our stand on this significant bill.
>
> Let us remember that what we deny certain groups today may be denied to us tomorrow. It is possible that if we tolerate discrimination, we may some day find ourselves discriminated against because of religion, political beliefs or some other factor. When rights and privileges in our democracy are extended to everyone in equal measure, then can our children recite with conviction . . . "one nation, indivisible, with liberty and justice for all."[119]

Perhaps it was due to the passage of state civil rights legislation that the Portland NCJW's Legislation Committee seems to have become less active in civil rights work in subsequent years. Instead, attention shifted in the late 1950s to a new project focusing on juvenile justice—a project that continued for several decades and did raise concerns about the impact of race in the system.[120] Still, national reports continued to update members on civil rights issues. For example, in 1955, the *Neighborhood* reprinted a NCJW resolution calling for public school integration[121] and reported in 1963 on NCJW participation in a White House civil rights meeting with President Kennedy. The latter article emphatically urged readers to write to their senator in support of the Civil Rights Amendment: "We urge your immediate action for the passage of the Civil Rights Act of 1963." In the same issue, members were urged to ask "soul searching questions in regard to our personal responsibilities," and admonished that "no one with a genuine concern for social justice can ignore the necessity for personal commitment and personal action." [122]

Despite the continued involvement of the Council of Jewish Women and the fact that activists, both newcomers and longtime Oregonians, occupied prominent positions in the Jewish community, the bulk of the civil rights work in the postwar era was conducted not through Jewish groups, but through interracial organizations as part of a new liberal coalition that emerged and became increasingly vocal in the postwar period. Portland City Club's 1945 report, "The Negro in Portland," which historian Stuart McElderry describes as "Portland's version of *An American Dilemma*," was critical to shaping and spurring the conversation. The report was framed by an "assimilationist orientation," emphasizing the need to educate the public on the issue of race prejudice, work cooperatively through community organizations to effect legislative change in areas such as public accommodations, and break down barriers to equal employment, housing, and schooling.[123] The new coalition embraced "racial liberalism"—an assimilationist-oriented movement, focusing on addressing discrimination through education and work through interracial committees—embodied in the Urban League. As McElderry explains, the Urban League "reflected the tenor of the times. . . . Predominantly a white-run organization made up of moderate-to-liberal professionals and businessmen . . . [the League] used its political and business connections to position itself as the city's leading race relations agency."[124]

Thus, while maintaining his position as director of the Anti-Defamation League of Portland, David Robinson conducted much of his civil rights activity through and in cooperation with groups outside the Jewish community. He was a founding member of the Portland Urban League and served as a leader in city- and state-level civic affairs groups tackling these issues, including terms as the founding chair of the Mayor's Commission on Human Rights, as president of the City Club of Portland, and as chair of the Civil Rights Division of the Oregon Labor Bureau.[125] Such coalition building was emblematic of the kind of interethnic cooperation embraced by a variety of minority groups in this period; as historian Cheryl Greenberg explains, it spoke to both an idealistic universalism and to practical concerns. To illustrate, she cites Robinson's story of his work with an interfaith, interracial group led by Portland priest Thomas Tobin:

> When a black member observed that his community had been the primary beneficiary of the committee's efforts, Tobin demurred. As Robinson paraphrased it, Tobin replied, "Don't be too sure that the sole benefits will come to you colored folks. It happens that every person present here this evening is either a Catholic, a Negro, or a Jew. After this war we expect lots of trouble. A scapegoat will be sought. Whenever they start looking for scapegoats invariably they pick on Catholics, Negroes and Jews." As Robinson mused, "There are some 25 million Catholics . . . and about 13 million colored people and we constitute 5 or 6 million. Well integrated, such a group can do something."[126]

Such intergroup cooperation would play a key role in a neighborhood controversy involving Congregation Tifereth Israel in 1952. An Orthodox congregation founded by the small immigrant community in Northeast Portland in 1911, Tifereth Israel was housed in a small building just north of the Albina district, which would emerge in mid-century as the rapidly growing center of Portland's African American community. In 1952, the congregation, looking to move to a larger facility, bought a church a few blocks away and agreed to sell their original building to the Mount Sinai Church, an African American congregation. Soon, neighbors fearing the further expansion of the black community to their south and the impact of the black church on property values began to agitate against the sale. Ninety residents, citing concerns about neighborhood congestion and parking, signed petitions opposing the sale. Activating the city's civil rights coalition in support of the church, the Urban League sponsored a meeting at the YWCA, at which fifty organizations voted unanimously to support the sale and condemned the efforts to block it as racist. At an October meeting, the congregation voted unanimously to move forward, issuing a statement that "we believe we are morally obligated to go ahead with the sale." David Robinson commended Tifereth Israel president Hyman Balk for his conduct of the meeting, calling him "a good president, a good American, and a good Jew." The incident demonstrates the degree to which the civil rights ideology was embraced well beyond elite circles in the Jewish community. Although neighborhood pressure must have caused some angst for the congregation (most of whom resided in the neighborhood), they embraced their decision as a point of pride. A decade later, a congregational account of the incident, titled "Portland 1952: One Ethnic Group Supporting Another," recalled that they had "helped turn the tide historically for Portland, Oregon and a return to the biblical concept toward respecting our neighbor."[127]

As they had in the Tifereth Israel incident, the civil rights coalition mobilized support for boycotts against restaurants and other establishments that refused service to African Americans and supported a 1949 city public accommodations law, after efforts on the state level failed. The ordinance, authored by Irvin Goodman, gained the support of a coalition of fifty-two civic groups.[128] Goodman was one of four featured speakers at a rally to "Help Us End JIM CROW in Portland," a few weeks before the city council approved the measure unanimously in February 1950.[129] Soon after, the ordinance was overturned by a 10 percent margin in a popular referendum.[130] As the city negotiated these waters, it established a new group, the Portland Intergroup Relations Committee, to "advise the city council on civil rights and race relations and settle disputes over these matters." Robinson was one of two Urban League leaders named to this eleven-member committee.[131]

As the 1950 general election rejection of the city's public accommodations ordinance made clear, despite the presence of a strong, interracial, interreligious coalition supporting liberal reform, Portland's traditionally "southern" attitude on racial issues persisted. In the wake of the defeat, liberals redoubled their efforts. For example, a group of women from the American Association of University Women and the League of Women Voters, led by Maurine Neuberger, staged "high style sit ins" at upscale restaurants to pressure them to serve African Americans.[132] Ultimately, the Oregon Civil Rights Act of 1953 desegregated public accommodations statewide.

In the meantime, the same coalition took on the issues of employment and housing, again focusing on a combination of legislation, education, and persuasion as the keys to effecting change. For example, after national efforts to make permanent the fair employment standards of World War II, state senator Richard Neuberger led the campaign to pass a similar bill at the state level, succeeding in 1949.[133] Convinced that positive experiences with carefully selected and screened African American employees or home buyers could change minds, civil rights organizations attempted to place individuals in workplaces and neighborhoods that had been all white. The Urban League, for example, worked on "uplift" efforts, to prepare black workers for employment, focusing on so-called black behavior and emphasizing to candidates that they would be judged as representatives of their race.[134] Thus, ironically, at the same time that these coalitions attempted to debunk stereotypes through education of whites, their "uplift" programs aimed at African Americans sometimes reinforced such images.

For Jewish Portlanders, both those working as civil rights advocates and those being pushed to reexamine their employment policies, these efforts produced poignant moments. For example, when Aaron Frank was approached in the late 1940s by a coalition activist about the possibility of hiring an African American in a customer service position at Meier and Frank, he balked, fearing the reaction of white patrons. Activist Susannah Malarkey recalled in an oral history that Frank "put his head in his hands and wept, saying 'I can't do it yet. I can't do it. I know what it is like to be discriminated against. I am a Jew.'"[135]

Because of Jewish prominence as owners and managers of department stores, community connections were used to apply pressure.

Such tactics are vivid in the account of Harry Gevurtz, a business-man and longtime member of Congregation Beth Israel. Gevurtz was approached by fellow congregant David Robinson to get involved in fair employment efforts, working with Catholic leader, Father Tobin. Gevurtz recalls,

> We started out by attempting to contact department stores and ask them to put some employee in sales work, because heretofore they only had a few janitors. Meier & Frank Co. refused to discuss the matter with us at the time, and so we went to Lipman, Wolfe, whose leader and president was Harold Wendel, well known in Portland Jewish circles. Mr. Wendel was not completely negative, but very uncertain as to the possibility of doing this and said that if we put one black person to work there, he was pretty sure there would be a large number of employees who would want to quit working near this employee. To my astonishment, Father Tobin replied to Mr. Wendel that Father Tobin and Harry Gevurtz would see to it that any person who might want to quit under the circumstances would be interviewed by us and would be convinced not to quit work. This took me quite by surprise as I certainly did not feel that I was equipped, not being a man of the cloth, such as Father Tobin, but the statement was made and under those circumstances, and further dif-ficult meetings and conversations, we managed to get the first negro man employed in Lipman, Wolfe on the first floor where he could be seen by everybody that came in, whether to his department or not. I held my breath, since I felt sure I would be called upon to use persua-sion, but the argument that Father Tobin had given was evidently legitimate because we didn't have this problem, and we felt it a great victory.
>
> We then proceeded by several means of attack to let Meier and Frank's know that there was a negro working in Lipman Wolfe's. We surreptitiously informed them that we felt the negro people would certainly be more interested in doing business in such a store. Therefore, shortly afterwards, Meier and Frank's called Father Tobin and I and asked us to recommend a negro for employment in their store. We did so, and this was the beginning for employment of negroes in the retail establishments in Portland and from this small

beginning many negroes got employment in various capacities, some of them reaching as far as assistant managers of departments, and at last the problem that seemed insurmountable was accomplished in this manner.[136]

In the meantime, similar efforts in manufacturing led White Stag, another Jewish-owned firm, to hire forty African American workers for its plant in 1946; significantly, they would work alongside whites and share facilities including restrooms and cafeterias. Despite a threatened walkout by white employees, company president Max Hirsch stood firm and urged his employees to "give the qualified Negro a chance."[137] In the end, all the white workers remained on the job.

For activists including Solomon and Robinson, such efforts must have had particular resonance. The businesses targeted for African American employment were in sectors that employed Jews at every level, or were even Jewish owned, as in the case of Meier and Frank and White Stag. Yet as these campaigns for African Americans were waged, a parallel effort was taking place at the professional level, to open employment opportunities to Jews. Remembering his own inability to get hired as an attorney, Gus Solomon made it his personal mission to place a Jewish lawyer at each of the major Portland firms. As a federal judge beginning in 1950, Solomon made "friendly calls" to senior partners, applying, in his own words, "a considerable amount of heat to a number of offices to hire Jewish lawyers." [138] For example, Meyer Eisenberg, a young lawyer who had come from New York to clerk for Oregon Supreme Court chief justice William McAllister in 1958, was pulled into Solomon's efforts to break "the wall of discrimination, firm by firm," despite the fact that Eisenberg had no intention of staying in Oregon. He recalled,

A few months after I had arrived in Salem, Judge Solomon made a point of inviting us . . . to his son Richard's bar mitzvah. Solomon was the Chief Judge (and at the time the only federal judge in the State). Every major, and many not so major, Portland law firm partner was at the reception and he made a point of taking me around to introduce me to as many of the senior partners of these firms that he could find. . . . Subtle, he was not: "This is Mike Eisenberg, he's Bill

McAllister's law clerk, from Columbia and we thought you should meet him. . . ."

Shortly thereafter, Judge McAllister called me into his office and directed me to go up to Portland and see Judge Solomon—and to bring a resume. . . . I went to Portland . . . and he called the managing partner of a large Portland firm that had never hired a Jewish associate.

"Hello, Gus Solomon here."

"Yes, Judge what can I do for you?"

"Well, I've got Bill McAllister's law clerk here and I'd like to send him over to see you—we think he'd make a fine associate in your firm."

"Yes Judge, when can we see him?"

"In 15 minutes . . . he'll be right over. . . ."

I was carefully instructed that I need not take their offer, but if I wanted to turn it down to wait a few days. . . . I went for the interview. Three partners interviewed me in less than five minutes. They never asked for a resume. . . . I later turned down the offer, with thanks for their consideration.

Judge Solomon's message was sent. The next associate the firm hired was Jewish.[139]

Professional employment restrictions such as those at the law firms were reinforced through Portland's exclusive clubs. By the early twentieth century, the long-exclusive Arlington Club had been joined by a variety of business, social, and athletic clubs that excluded Jews—the University Club (1898), the Multnomah Athletic Club (1891), and the Waverly Country Club (1896).[140] This discrimination persisted through the mid-twentieth century and presented a major hindrance to Jewish businessmen and professionals. As Solomon explained, "There was a correlation between social acceptability and job opportunities or economic opportunities. . . . Many of the real business transactions occur not in offices but in the social clubs."[141] Thus, Solomon embarked on an effort to integrate the private clubs, quietly using his connections to influence members to overturn restrictions and encouraging organizations and individuals to refuse to sponsor or attend events held at these facilities. Although Solomon himself was recruited to the

Multnomah Athletic Club in 1958, the problem persisted. In 1962, the *Jewish Review* reported that ADL's National Civil Rights Director and General Counsel, Arnold Forster, was coming to Portland to meet with the regional ADL board on the issue of club discrimination in the city.[142] It was not until 1966 that attorney Moe Tonkin was admitted to the University Club; Arlington followed in 1967 and Waverly, finally, in 1972.[143]

Although Solomon made a point of challenging restrictions, he found that many in the community "were indifferent or hostile to his appeals because they feared controversy or dreaded challenging the status quo." Some felt that public campaigns to address this discrimination exposed "social disabilities" that many found embarrassing.[144] Rather than drawing attention to local manifestations of anti-Semitism, community profiles emphasized the long history of Jewish inclusion in Oregon. For example, *The Ties Between*, a congregational history of Beth Israel published in 1959 and authored by Rabbi Nodel, paints a portrait of a region untouched by prejudice and, particularly, by anti-Semitism in the twentieth century:

> The Jews of the city have marched along with the rest of the community in amiable partnership. Visitors marvel at the lack of visible discrimination against religion or national minorities. Many Jewish youngsters raised on the Willamette River never knew of artificial lines drawn between members of the different faiths until they visited certain parts of America's Eastern Seaboard.[145]

Notwithstanding Nodel's claim, consciousness of local prejudice did shape the community and inhibit their embrace of the local civil rights movement. As had been the case nationally before the war, in Portland the bulk of the local civil rights work performed by Jewish leaders came through coalitions and groups including the Urban League, rather than directly through Jewish organizations. Likewise, despite the prominence of community leaders, including Rabbis Berkowitz and Nodel, and Beth Israel presidents Robinson and Gevurtz, who publicly condemned prejudice and were prominent in city and state civil rights efforts, their activities were rarely highlighted in the *Scribe* and its successor, the *Jewish Review* (the rabbis did share their passion through

Beth Israel's weekly *Bulletin*). Both papers tended to avoid uncomfortable issues, particularly local ones, during the 1950s. For example, the *Scribe*, by this time publishing only quarterly, did not cover the Oregon Public Accommodations law in 1953. Its focus in the 1950s was more inward on Jewish affairs than had been the case decades earlier. Issues and events outside the Jewish community were referenced only in occasional reports, such as the article in the July-August 1959 issue explaining the American Hebrew Congregations' opposition to capital punishment, and, like that story, tended to be national rather than local in focus.[146] In the nine issues published during the *Review's* first year (1959), no stories or editorials focusing on African Americans, discrimination, or civil rights appeared. The reluctance to engage in these issues was still palpable in 1960, even at Beth Israel, where there was a long tradition of rabbinical outspokenness. When Rabbi Emanuel Rose arrived, he recalled hearing from congregants who took issue with his candor: "I was very strong on social action and I think maybe a little stronger at that stage than they had expected."[147]

The ebb and flow of communal engagement in local civil rights efforts says much about both the increasing national consciousness of Jewish Oregonians and the continued influence of place. In joining as individuals in broad liberal coalitions that took action on local issues, Portland Jews echoed national trends, just as the local Jewish press echoed broader American Jewish sentiments—often verbatim, by running wire stories and pieces from the eastern press in their pages. Yet in a community that had long prided itself on its acceptance and prominence, the battles that the community waged in the mid-twentieth century clearly left their mark. Ironically, a community whose pioneers and native sons had been so exceptionally secure in the nineteenth century was notably insecure about speaking out in the 1940s and 1950s. Although the professional and social exclusions that shaped community consciousness in Portland were not unlike those in other parts of the country, the volatility of the race issue in Oregon created a context that, in some ways, echoed that in the South.

Jewish Oregonians in the postwar period embraced the liberal agenda of the broader American Jewish community and played a prominent role on the local stage. Yet, in contrast to their early experience, when they identified fully with and were accepted as pioneers, their mid-twentieth-century experience was more mixed. The sting of prejudice and exclusions heightened their sensitivity to the plight of more disadvantaged groups in the state but also made them reluctant to speak out in ways that drew attention to the community. Gradually, they would become more publicly engaged both as individuals and as a community in local civil rights activities, but far more than their nineteenth-century predecessors, they did so while looking over their shoulders.

Afterword

As professional and social exclusions dissolved, the baby boom generation came of age, newcomers arrived in Oregon, and attitudes in the
state began to shift more generally, the insecurities of the immediate
postwar period began to fall away. As the final professional and social
barriers to Jews fell, they became far more willing to speak out, not
just as individuals or through secular associations, but as an organized
Jewish community. Thus, in the 1960s, Portland Jewish organizations,
including the major congregations, the federation, local B'nai B'rith
and Council of Jewish Women chapters, as well as other Jewish enti-
ties, would weigh in on volatile local issues like the desegregation of the
Portland public schools.

The ability of Jewish organizations to take a stand on such local
issues reflects the confidence of a community that had overcome past
insecurities. Indeed, as the community moved into the final decades of
the twentieth century, full acceptance into middle-class life began to
present new challenges. If Jews had access to the Multnomah Athletic
Club and various other clubs, would there continue to be a need for
a Jewish Community Center and for Jewish social and fraternal organizations? In an era when prohibitions against interracial dating and
marriage gradually fell away, how would identity be maintained? And
as the community swelled through the arrival of young and largely
unaffiliated Jews, attracted to Portland and Oregon as a progressive
and hip center, how could they be drawn into community? In the
1970s and beyond, attention of community leaders increasingly turned
inward to questions like these.

This turn inward also reflected national trends, as American Jews
became increasingly concerned with questions of identity.[1] Although
Jews remained committed to the goals of fighting prejudice and achieving
equality, with the major legislative goals of the Civil Rights Movement

accomplished, there was less consensus on key issues. In addition, there were breaches in the civil rights coalition on issues ranging from affirmative action and black nationalism to the Six-Day War and Palestinian aspirations.[2] Nationally and locally, Jewish communal attention shifted to internal Jewish affairs, from affiliation patterns and demographic concerns to Israel and the prospects for peace in the Middle East.

In both the increasing civil rights coverage in the early 1960s and the shift toward identity politics later in the decade, the gaps that had been evident earlier between local and national Jewish sensibilities seemed to erode. To be sure, Jewish Oregonians had concerns that were local in nature—chief among them, the displacement of the South Portland neighborhood and its institutions first by urban renewal and then by highway construction. Yet even this particular local circumstance helped to reinforce a national trend in Jewish communities—a shift to the suburbs, in this case to Southwest Portland. The convergence with national trends would become even more evident in the final decades of the twentieth century, as Oregon's Jewish population—long relatively stable in numbers—grew dramatically through the in-migration of Jews from other parts of the country, particularly to Portland.[3]

Yet even as newcomers began to flood in, the convergence was not complete. Jewish Oregonians would continue in the late twentieth and early twenty-first century to reflect not only their roots but their context. For example, like other western Jews—and members of other faith communities in a region characterized by scholars of religion as the "unchurched belt"—Jewish Oregonians were less apt to join a congregation or marry a Jewish partner than were their counterparts in eastern communities. And, as Oregon emerged in the 1990s and the early twenty-first century as a magnet for all things hip and environmental, Jewish versions of *Portlandia* emerged, reflecting both local sensibilities and self-selection among those choosing to join the community.

Since pioneering days, Jewish Oregonians (whether natives or newcomers) were shaped by a combination of local and national influences, by their communal and familial roots, and by their current environment. Despite troubled periods, when the community struggled with exclusions at elite levels, Jewish Oregonians have generally embraced both their identities as American Jews and the particular local context, which they continue to celebrate and embrace.

Notes

INTRODUCTION

1   Hasia Diner, "American West, New York Jewish" in Jewish Life in the American West, Ava F. Kahn, ed. (Seattle and Los Angeles: University of Washington Press and Autry Museum of Western Heritage, 2002), 33.

2   Ibid., 34–37.

3   The New Western History, which emerged in the 1980s, shifted the main focus of western history toward issues of class, gender, race, and environment.

4   See Elliot Barkan, From All Points: America's Immigrant West, 1870s–1952 (Bloomington: Indiana University Press, 2007), 1–2.

5   Steven Lowenstein, The Jews of Oregon, 1850–1950 (Portland: Jewish Historical Society of Oregon, 1987), 100.

6   "Sixth Annual Report of the Hebrew Sheltering and immigrant Aid Society of America," The Jewish Immigration Bulletin 5, no. 3 (March 1915): 49.

7   John Livingston, "Introduction," in Jews of the American West, eds. John Livingston and Moses Rischin (Detroit: Wayne State University Press, 1991), 20–22.

8   Mark K. Bauman, The Southerner as American: Jewish Style (Cincinnati: American Jewish Archives, 1996), 30.

9   Marci Cohen Ferris and Mark I. Greenberg, eds., "Introduction," in Jewish Roots in Southern Soil: A New History (Hanover, NH: University Press of New England/Brandeis University Press, 2006), 2.

10 Ellen Eisenberg, Ava F. Kahn, William Toll, Jews of the Pacific Coast: Reinventing Community on America's Edge (Seattle: University of US Press, 2009), 4–5.

11 This chapter draws together and builds on several of my earlier published works, including: "Western Reality: Jewish Diversity during the 'German' Period," American Jewish History 92, no. 4 (December 2004); "Transplanted to the Rose City: The Creation of East European Jewish Communities in Portland," Journal of American Ethnic History 19, no. 3 (Spring, 2000); and Jews of the Pacific Coast, co-authored with Ava Kahn and William Toll, chap. 3.

12 This chapter builds on a previously unpublished conference paper, "Immigrants, Ethnics, and Natives: Jewish Women in Portland, 1910–1940," presented at the Western Jewish Studies Association annual meeting, March 1999.

13 This chapter builds on an essay previously published as "Beyond San Francisco: The Failure of Anti-Zionism in Portland, Oregon" American Jewish History 86, no. 3 (September 1998).

14   This discussion builds on analysis presented in The First to Cry Down Injustice? Western Jews and Japanese Removal during WWII (Lanham, MD: Lexington Books/Rowman & Littlefield, 2008), chap. 1.

CHAPTER 1

1   *Daily Capital Journal* (Salem, March 26, 1896), 1. Unless otherwise noted, all references to Oregon newspapers in this chapter come from the Historic Oregon Newspapers database, University of Oregon.

2   The Brooks precinct, which included the towns of Brooks and Gervais, had a population of just over 1,400 in the 1900 census. US Federal Census, 1900.

3   Gervais was not incorporated until later. In the 1860 census, the Mitchell family is recorded as residing in the Fairfield District. In the 1860 and 1870 censuses, he is listed as "Michael Mitchell." By 1880, he is recorded as McKinley Mitchell.

4   The Bancroft dictation indicates that McKinley's father, Isaac, arrived in Oregon in 1850. However, Isaac's death notice lists 1849 as the arrival year. "Dictation from McKinley Mitchell," Gervais. Notes by J.A. Moore, 1885. Bancroft Collection. Death notice, *Willamette Farmer* (Salem, March 24, 1882), 5.

5   *City of Gervais Centennial Commemorative Book*, 1878–1978, written & compiled by Mrs. Carl Prantl (1978). In the notes drawn from the city council ledger, Mitchell is listed as a member of city council in 1881 and again in 1897. The *Salem and Marion County Directory* of 1893 lists him as an alderman, 144.

6   "Republican State Convention," *Daily Astorian*, (May 1, 1884).

7   Mitchell is listed as a general merchandiser in the 1881 minutes cited in the *City of Gervais Centennial* book, as a grain dealer in the 1893 directory, and as the owner of a grain and hops warehouse in the 1905, 1909, and 1911 county directories. By the time of these latter entries, Mitchell had moved to Portland, but he continued to operate his business in Gervais. Mitchell is referred to as the editor of the *French Prairie Gazette* of Gervais in the *Evening Capital Journal* (Salem, November 7, 1888).

8   Mitchell is listed as a delegate to the Northwest Insurance Association in 1895. "No Ratecutting Now: Insurance Men Organize Northwest Association," *Portland Morning Oregonian* (July 11, 1895), 8. (Mitchell file, Willamette Heritage Center).

9   Mitchell appears in Gervais in the 1860, 1870, 1880, and 1900 censuses. In 1910, 1920 and 1930, he is listed in Portland. US Census Collection, accessed on Ancestry.com. On the Yamhill property, see "Many Societies to Get Bequests: Will of McKinley Mitchell filed for Probate," *Oregonian*, February 2, 1936. (Mitchell file, Willamette Heritage Center).

10   *The Dalles Daily Chronicle* (The Dalles, OR), May 20, 1896, 3.

11   "Big Man Than All Oregon," *Daily Capital Journal* (Salem, February 16, 1897), 1; "Mitchell is Losing Ground," *Daily Capital Journal* (Salem, February 22, 1897), 1.

12   E. Kimbark MacColl, *Merchants, Money, & Power: The Portland Establishment, 1843–1913* (Portland: Georgian Press, 1988), 325–27.

13   "Hon. McKinley Mitchell," *Daily Capital Journal* (Salem, February 14, 1898), 1.

14   *Morning Oregonian* (Portland, April 11, 1900), 1.

15   Hobart Mitchell oral history, May 4, 1977, Oregon Historical Society, 4. Mitchell never mentions in this oral history the family's Jewish identity or background.

16   A search for McKinley Mitchell on the digital Historic Oregon Newspaper database, http://oregonnews.uoregon.edu, for the period from 1890–1900 yields seventy-five separate pages on which Mitchell is mentioned.

17   *Willamette Farmer* (Salem, March 24, 1882), 5. Presumably, the reference was to the Jewish cemetery in Albany, which served both the Albany and Salem Jewish communities.

18   "Dictation from McKinley Mitchell." Bancroft Collection.

19   Fred Lockley, *History of the Columbia River Valley* (online, Oregon State University Libraries, Scholar's Archive, 1928), 624.

20   On Sarah McKinley's marriage see Jean Custer and Ann Hochspeir, "Marriage Records of Marion County, vol. VI 1888–1891 and vol. VII 1891–1894," Willamette Valley Genealogical Society, Salem, Oregon, 1991.

21   "Many Societies to Get Bequests: Will of McKinley Mitchell filed for Probate," *Oregonian,* February 2, 1936. Mitchell file, Willamette Heritage Center.

22   Hasia Diner, *Jews of the United States,* (Berkeley: University of California Press, 2004), 158.

23   Ibid., 158–9. In the paragraph immediately following the quoted passage, Diner's examples include a town councilman from Iowa; a city councilman from Los Angeles; a Connecticut community's state legislator, two justices of the peace, and a secretary of state; and, from Oregon, two Portland mayors, a subsequent Portland mayoral race in which both candidates were Jewish, and a gubernatorial candidate.

24   There is a substantial literature on southern Jews and some debate over their degree of acceptance in southern society. Leonard Rogoff, one of the leading historians on this topic summarizes the situation: "Jews readily acculturated, yet they remained outsiders. The Jewish experience in the South was ambivalent. Jews were white people in a biracial society, but they were neither Christian nor Anglo-Saxon." Rogoff, "Jews in the South," *Encyclopedia of American Jewish History,* Stephen Norwood and Eunice Pollack, eds. (California: ABC-CLIO, 2008), 145.

25   That Jewish economic roles were a key factor shaping their experience of acceptance in the West has been well recognized by scholars. See Earl Pomeroy "On Becoming a Westerner" in *Jews of the American West,* 204.

26   The place of Jews in Oregon's racial landscape will be explored in Chapter Six.

27   Carl Abbott, *Portland in Three Centuries* (Corvallis: Oregon State University Press, 2011), 27. See also, MacColl, *Merchants, Money, & Power,* 2. No city government convened in Portland until 1851. See MacColl, 5.

28   Lowenstein, *The Jews of Oregon,* 43–44; "Louis Fleischner" in *Oregon Native Son,* 1 no. 6 (October 1899): 346. For a fictionalized account of the Fleischner brothers' story, see Alfred Apsler, *Northwest Pioneer: The Story of Louis Fleischner* (Philadelphia: Jewish Publication Society, 1960).

29   Lowenstein, *The Jews of Oregon,* 55.

30   Ibid., 31.

31   Ibid., 16.

32   On Rothchild, see Jack T. Sanders, *Samuel Rothchild: A Jewish Pioneer in the Days of the Old West* (Pendleton: Create Space, 2011), 36, ix. On Durkheimer, see Lowenstein, *The Jews of Oregon*, 36 and Michele Glazer, "The Durkheimers of Oregon," *Western States Jewish Historical Quarterly* 10, no. 3 (1978): 202–209.

33   Sylvan Durkheimer oral history, (March 3, 1975), Oregon Jewish Museum, 25.

34   Lowenstein's account indicates that Sigmund *commanded* the supply mission—this seems unlikely given that Sigmund had no military experience, had only arrived in the area in 1855, and had only been in the United States since 1853. Lowenstein also claims Heilner "was actively engaged in combat under Captain Driscoll." I have been unable to verify this account, and can find no reference to a Captain Driscoll fighting in the Rogue River Indian War. However, Sigmund Heilner is recognized as a veteran of the Rogue Indian War in *Morning Democrat: Eastern Oregon's Gold Fields* (Bowen & Small, May 20, 1898, Souvenir Edition), 20. Note that Baker's name was changed to Baker City in 1990.

35   Many sources refer to "Colonel Louis Fleischner," yet actual accounts of his activities during the war, or record of his position are scant. Sources do agree that Fleischner volunteered and served in the war. See Lowenstein, *The Jews of Oregon*, 44.

36   Joyce Loeb oral history, Oregon Jewish Museum (OJM 3457) and "Jews at Work" exhibit notes, courtesy of Anne LeVant Prahl, curator of collections, Oregon Jewish Museum. Cohen can be found on the Company F muster list "Early Indian Wars of Oregon," compiled by Frances Fuller Victor, accessed online, http://www.rootsweb.ancestry.com/~ormultno/military/iwars/burnetF.htm

37   Hubert Howe Bancroft, *Chronicles of the Builders of the Commonwealth*, 7 (1892): 148.

38   Rothchild invested in real estate in the expanding town of Pendleton. Some of that expansion would come at the expense of the Umatilla Indian Reservation. From the start, the reservation was smaller than planned, and, in the late 1880s, its size was further reduced as Pendleton expanded into what had been reservation land. Rothchild and his family purchased several lots from speculators in this section. Sanders, *Samuel Rothchild*, 77.

39   Ibid., 45. Rothchild's account of his experience in the Indian War, written sometime in the 1920s, was published in a volume of *Reminiscences of Oregon Pioneers* and is reprinted as appendix A of Sander's biography.

40   Lowenstein, The Jews of Oregon, 32; Robert Edward Levinson, *The Jews of Jacksonville* (master's thesis, University of Oregon, 1962), 6.

41   Lowenstein, The Jews of Oregon, 32.

42   Durkheimer oral history, 24.

43   "Hon. S. H. Friendly" in in *Pacific Jewish Annual*, vol. 2, Jacob Voorsanger, ed. (San Francisco: A. W. Voorsanger, 1898), 167.

44   Glazer, "The Durkheimers of Oregon," 202. Durkheimer oral history, 1–3. The dates of arrival cited in the oral history and in the Glazer article vary. For example, the Glazer article dates Julius's arrival in Portland to 1862; the oral history gives 1865 as the date.

45   This pattern is evident in nineteenth-century communal records for Jewish organizations in Portland, which are all in English. Portland's congregations, Jewish newspaper, and B'nai B'rith lodges all kept their records in English

from their founding. See Robert Scott Cline's *Community Structure on the Urban Frontier: The Jews of Portland Oregon, 1849–1887* (master's thesis, Portland State University, 1982), 8.

46   "Dictation from McKinley Mitchell."

47   Hobart Mitchell oral history, May 4, 1977, Oregon Historical Society, 1.

48   Sanders, *Samuel Rothchild*, part 1.

49   Morris Mensor Obituary, *Jacksonville Democratic Times*, (April 29, 1887), 3. Accessed online, http://files.usgwarchives.net/or/jackson/obits/m/mensor-morris.txt

50   Samuel Adolph obituary, *Weekly Statesman* (Salem), September 22, 1893 (Adoph file, Willamette Heritage Center Archive). See also Salem Pioneer Cemetery record http://salempioneercemetery.org. 1860 US Census, accessed via Ancestry.com. Although the *Statesman* obituary notes that he was a member of the city council, this could not be verified elsewhere.

51   Coverage in Salem's Evening Capital Journal shows that Wolf was part of a "citizens' slate" that ran against a prohibitionist slate in May 1888. Although the prohibitionists apparently won more votes, many were not counted because they were on tinted paper. The citizens' slate, including Wolf, began to serve, but the Prohibitionists successfully challenged the election, winning first in lower court and having that victory confirmed after Wolf and his comrades challenged it in the Oregon Supreme Court. See coverage in the *Evening Capital Journal* (Salem, OR), May 30, 1888; November 28, 1888; and December 5, 1888.

52   "The Merchant—History", http://silvertoninnandsuites.com/rooms/merchants-room-202-pg2.html. See also Marion County census, 1895, which lists the Wolfs as the only Jewish family in Silverton. They are listed in Independence in 1870 and 1880. For more on migration patterns, see Cline, *Community Structures*, 7–8.

53   M. Hirsch is listed as an alderman in the "First Regular Session of the Common Council for the City of Salem" minutes, September 27, 1860 (photographic print, P 1998.010.0060 Willamette Heritage Center).

54   "Solomon Hirsch" in *Portrait and Biographical Record of the Willamette Valley, Oregon* (Chicago: Chapman Publishing Company, 1903), 164–69.

55   Lowenstein, *The Jews of Oregon*, 9. Heilner had taken the name E.D. Cohen to avoid creditors, and thus the firm name was Simonsfeld and Cohen.

56   Ibid., 11–16.

57   Ibid., 31–32.

58   Margaret LaPlante "The Story of Jacksonville's Early Jewish Settlers," *Jacksonville Review*, no. 1918, March, 2010, 25. Accessed online http://www.scribd.com/doc/43445117/Jacksonville-Review-March-2010 (June 20, 2012). The "Temple of Fashion" name does not appear consistently in advertisements, suggesting that the business went under other names, including "Sachs Brothers."

59   Morris Mensor Obituary, *Jacksonville Democratic Times*, (April 29, 1887), 3. Accessed online, http://files.usgwarchives.net/or/jackson/obits/m/mensor-morris.txt; Levinson, *The Jews of Jacksonville*, 8.

60   Lowenstein, *The Jews of Oregon*, 7. These businesses are mentioned in a number of pioneer histories.

61   Ibid. Goldsmith & May is recognized as the first Jewish store in a number of pioneer histories, including an article titled "Shematic Emmigration to the

Pacific Northwest" [sic] in *Oregon Native Son*, vol. 2 (December, 1900), 374. This article will be examined in more detail later in this chapter.

62   Mitchell's partnership with Dusenberry is mentioned in Lockley, *History of the Columbia River Valley*, 624. On Dusenberry's relationship with Burgunder, see Benjamin Burgunder papers, "Biographical Note" Eastern US State Historical Society, Northwest Digital Archives, http://nwda-db.orbiscascade.org/ark:/80444/xv61474.

63   Julia Niebuhr Eulenberg, "Joseph Brown: The Deadly Errand of a Pacific Northwest Pioneer, 1862" *Western States Jewish History* 55, no. 1 (Fall 2012): 27.

64   Eisenberg, Kahn and Toll, *Jews of the Pacific Coast*, 9.

65   Ben Selling letter to Julius Wertheimer (1885), quoted in Cline, *Community Structure*, 77.

66   "I.N. Fleischner" in *Portrait and Biographical Record of the Willamette Valley*, 44.

67   A Jewish family named Schlussel lived in Albany in 1860. Presumably, the Fleischner-Schlussel connection originated there. US Census, 1860, Linn County. An A. Schlussel, a merchant, age thirty, is listed on the census, living in an extended household.

68   See, for example, *Portrait and Biographical Record of the Willamette Valley, Oregon,* 44 (Fleischner); 54 (Mayer); 164 (Hirsch).

69   Lowenstein, *The Jews of Oregon*, 32.

70   *Oregon Sentinel*, Jacksonville Oregon (November 26, 1862), 3.

71   The actual office was president of the Jacksonville trustees—trustee was the equivalent of city councilor. Muller also served repeated terms as city treasurer, country treasurer, county clerk, and postmaster. See Levinson, *The Jews of Jacksonville*, 31.

72   "S. Blumauer, Barnass [sic] of Congregation Beth Israel" in *Pacific Jewish Annual*, vol. 2, Jacob Voorsanger, ed. (San Francisco: A. W. Voorsanger, 1898), 165. "Simon Blumauer" *Oregon Native Son* 1, no. 6 (October 1899): 348. The latter biography also credits him with the third brick building in Portland (rather than the second) in 1854 (rather than 1855).

73   *Morning Democrat: Eastern Oregon's Gold Fields* (Bowen & Small, May 20, 1898, Souvenir Edition), 11, 20, 45.

74   "A Splendid Building," *Oregon Daily Statesman* (Salem), December 31, 1880 (Willamette Heritage Center, Adolph file).

75   Cline, *Community Structure*, 9–10.

76   Levinson, *The Jews of Jacksonville*, 22.

77   Cline, *Community Structure*, 14.

78   Lowenstein, *The Jews of Oregon*, 16.

79   Ibid., 36. See also Sylvan Durkheimer oral history, 4–7.

80   Leo Adler oral history (July 13, 1977), Oregon Jewish Museum, 2.

81   Sanders, *Samuel Rothchild*, 64.

82   "I.N. Fleischner" in *Portrait and Biographical Record of the Willamette Valley, Oregon,* 45.

83   "Simon Blumauer," *Oregon Native Son* vol. 1, no. 6 (October 1899), 348.

84   Lowenstein, *The Jews of Oregon*, 22.

85   Ibid., 8.

86   1860 US Census, accessed on Ancestry.com. Of the 880 people residing in Jacksonville in 1860, 76 were born in one of the German provinces, an additional 4 in Poland and 1 in Russia, which were the most common places of origin of Jews in the United States at the time. Because religious identity cannot be discerned solely by name, only those who are identified in another source as Jewish are counted here. The Mensors would eventually have 17 children.

87   1870 US Census, Jacksonville, Oregon. For example, brothers Louie and Joseph Solomon occupy house #630, one of the Caro brothers lived in house #631 (along with several others), houses 632 and 633 were occupied by brothers Newman and Abraham Fisher, and their families, as well as a clerk. House #634 was that of Gustof Karewski. The Mensor family resided in house #641. Addresses are not given in the census, but the census taker numbered houses in the order that he visited them. Consecutive houses on the census might be next door to one another, around the corner, or across the street—in any event, in close proximity to one another.

88   Morris Mensor Obituary, *Jacksonville Democratic Times*, (April 29, 1887), 3. Accessed online, http://files.usgwarchives.net/or/jackson/obits/m/mensor-morris.txt>; Max Muller obituary, *Medford Mail*, (October 3, 1902), accessed online http://files.usgwarchives.net/or/jackson/obits/m/muller2017gob.txt.

89   Gervais, Oregon. 1880 US Census, accessed on Ancestry.com. Newman Goodman is buried at the Temple Beth Israel cemetery in Portland, http://www.rootsweb.ancestry.com/~orjgs/Shalshelet/Shal_1994_Spring.pdf.

90   Lowenstein, *The Jews of Oregon*, 15–16.

91   Cline, *Community Structure*, 12.

92   The histories of the Portland congregations will be explored in more detail in chap. 2.

93   Julius J. Nodel *The Ties Between: A Century of Judaism on America's Last Frontier* (Portland: Congregation Beth Israel, 1959), 18–20.

94   Lowenstein, *The Jews of Oregon*, 38. Eisenberg, Kahn, and Toll, *Jews of the Pacific Coast*, 63.

95   Sanders, *Samuel Rothchild*, 60–62. After the 1879 mention of the congregation, there is no further record of it.

96   Lowenstein, *The Jews of Oregon*, 33.

97   Ibid., 38.

98   Ibid., 36–37.

99   Nodel, *The Ties Between*, 12.

100   Cline has shown that married families dominated in the early years of Congregation Beth Israel, although single men were still the majority among Jews in Portland. Cline, *Community Structure*, 14. The role of women in spurring the establishment of churches and synagogues on the frontier has been widely recognized. See Jeanne E. Abrams *Jewish Women Pioneering the Frontier Trail* (New York: New York University Press, 2006), chap. 2.

101   Sanders, *Samuel Rothchild*, 62–63, 64.

102   Levinson, *The Jews of Jacksonville*, 37, 39–40.

103   Leo Adler oral history, (July 13, 1977), Oregon Jewish Museum, 4–5, 21.

104   Sanders, *Samuel Rothchild*, 62.

105   "Observed," *Daily Astorian* (Astoria: September 11, 1877), 1. See also, *Oregon Sentinel* (Jacksonville), October 5, 1872), 3.

106   Sanders, *Samuel Rothchild*, 62.

107   *Oregon Sentinel* (Jacksonville), October 5, 1872, 3.

108   Sanders, *Samuel Rothchild*, 62.

109   Robert Levinson, "The Jews of Eugene, Oregon" Western States Jewish History 30, no. 1 (October 1997). Accessed online http://www.wsjhistory.com/jew_eugene_oregon.htm (July 10, 2012).

110   Salem Pioneer Cemetery burial records, http://salempioneercemetery.org. The *Capital Journal* reported that the burial would take place in Salem "and not at Portland as was at first decided." *Capital Journal* (Salem, September 20, 1893), 4.

111   Durkheimer oral history, 23, 26.

112   Nodel, *The Ties Between*, 77.

113   Sanders, *Samuel Rothchild*, 61.

114   United States Census, 1880 and 1900.

115   Lee Shai Weissbach, "The Jewish Communities of the United States on the Eve of Mass Migration." *American Jewish History* 78, no. 1 (1988): 83–85.

116   Oregon State Census, Marion County, 1895. Transcript, Willamette Valley Genealogical Society, Salem, 1993. The 1895 state census asked respondents to report their religion, giving the choices Catholic, Protestant, or F.T.—Free Thinker. Jewish families were designated as well.

117   Oregon State Census, Marion County, 1895, vol. 2: 97, 66.

118   Oregon State Census, Marion County, 1895, vol. 2: 27

119   Cline, *Community Structure*, 97.

120   *Daily Astorian* (Astoria, OR: April 19, 1881), 3.

121   *Oregon Sentinel* (Jacksonville, OR: April 23, 1881 and April 24, 1886), 3.

122   *Oregon Sentinel* (Jacksonville, OR: October 5, 1872), 3.

123   *Daily Astorian* (Astoria, OR: September 11, 1877), 1.

124   An exception was the 1866 Jacksonville *Democratic Times* article about Yom Kippur, which listed the stores closing by name. See Levinson, *Jews of Jacksonville*, 36.

125   *Oregon Sentinel* (Jacksonville, OR: September 26, 1868), 3.

126   *Oregon Sentinel* (Jacksonville, OR: March 10, 1880), 2.

127   *Daily Morning Astorian* (Astoria, March 31, 1885), 3. The article is signed with the initials H.W. Herman Wise was the owner of Uncle Sam's Cheap Cash Store. See Lowenstein, *The Jews of Oregon*, 41.

128   *Democratic Times* (Jacksonville, September 17, 1880), quoted in Levinson, *The Jews of Jacksonville*, 36.

129   *Daily Capital Journal*, (Salem: February 14, 1898), 1. Eva Adolph was the daughter of Samuel and Mary Adolph.

130   "Love Under Difficulties" *Oregon Sentinel* (Jacksonville: July 13, 1867), 2.

131   For Durkheimer and the other individuals discussed below, a search on the Historic Oregon Newspaper digital index was conducted for the family name, and all instances of the name's appearance were reviewed. The database does not include all the newspapers in the state for their runs, but it does provide extensive coverage. There were 150 page hits for the name Durkheimer, the overwhelming majority for ads placed in the *Grant County*

News in the late 1880s and early 1890s. Similar searches for Mitchell and Heilner retrieved eighty and forty-two page hits respectively.

132   The following mayors' names were searched, along with keywords "Jew," "Jewish," and "Hebrew": Max Muller (Jacksonville, 1864), Bernard Goldsmith (Portland, 1869–71), Philip Wasserman (Portland (1871–73), Newman Fisher (Jacksonville, 1872 and 1876), Henry Blackman (Heppner, 1887–90), Samson Friendly (Eugene, 1893–95), Julius Durkheimer (Burns, 1895–96), William Wurzweiler (Prineville, 1904–06), and Isaac Bergman (Astoria, 1898–1902).

133   *Morning Oregonian* (April 22, 1901), 5; (November 11, 1905), 1.

134   For Wasserman's obituary, see *Morning Oregonian* (February 27, 1895); for Goldsmith, see *Morning Oregonian* (July 23, 1901), 1.

135   *Morning Oregonian*, (December 18, 1902), 10.

136   William Toll, *The Making of an Ethnic Middle Class* (Albany: SUNY Press, 1982), 62.

137   Simon's political career is examined in more detail in chap. 4.

138   Using the Chronicling America newspaper data base, a search was conducted for "Joseph Simon" with either the term "Hebrew" or "Jew" during the month of October 1898. *Omaha Daily Bee* (October 9, 1898), 1; *The Times* (US, DC, October 11, 1898), 4; *Semi-Weekly Interior Journal* (Stanford, Kentucky, October 14, 1898); *Vermont Phoenix* (October 14, 1898), 10; *Salt Lake Herald* (October 8, 1898), 1; *The Herald* (Los Angeles, October 8, 1898), 5, (October 9, 1898), 2; *Kansas City Journal* (October 9, 1898), 1; *The Record-Union* (Sacramento, October 9, 1898) 7; *The Star* (Reynoldsville, PA, October 12, 1898), 2; *Salt Lake Herald* (October 17, 1898), 4; *The National Tribune* (US, DC, October 20, 1898), 4; *The Globe-Republican* (Dodge City, Kansas, October 13, 1898), 6: headline: "A Hebrew Senator".

139   Simon served in the Oregon Senate in the 1880, 1882, 1885, 1887, 1889, 1891, 1895, 1897, and 1898 sessions, and as president of that body in the last five of these. Overlapping with him at the state capitol were Henry Blackman (Senate 1891 and 1893), Solomon Hirsch (Senate, 1874, 1878, 1880, 1882, 1885), Ben Selling (Senate, 1897, 1898, 1899, 1909, 1912), and Edward Hirsch (State Treasurer 1878–1886, Senate 1891, 1893).

140   *Daily Capital Journal* (Salem, October 24, 1898), 2.

141   Toll, *Making of an Ethnic Middle Class*, 86. Simon was sufficiently engaged in the congregation that, when Rabbi Stephen Wise resigned in 1906, Simon was involved in amending the congregational constitution to exclude the rabbi from the board of trustees—a change that Rabbi Wise vociferously opposed. Nodel, *The Ties Between*, 97. Even in the case of Ben Selling, the politician most closely identified with the Jewish community, papers tended not to tag him as a Jew unless the story was about the Jewish community. In a search for "Ben Selling" and "Hebrew," hits were only found in articles discussing Selling's activities within the community, such as his involvement in a campaign to raise funds for Russian Jewish refugees or his election to the board of the Hebrew Benevolent Association. *Morning Oregonian* (Portland). Example of Benevolent Association article (April 22, 1901), 5; of involvement in Russian Jewish aid, (November 11, 1905), 1. For more on Simon, see chap. 4.

142   The analysis that follows is based on a search for the terms "Jew" and "Hebrew" in the Oregon digital newspaper database, 1846–80.

143   *The New Northwest* (Portland, May 25, 1877), 1.

144   *East Oregonian* (Pendleton, Nov. 9, 1878), 2

145   Benjamin I. Cohen, "The Jew in Modern History," published in *East Oregonian* (Pendleton, December 11, 1880), 4.

146   "Intelligence of the Jews" *Willamette Farmer* (Salem: September 7, 1872), 2.

147   *Grant County News* (Canyon City: October 23, 1880), 6.

148   Quoted in Lowenstein, *The Jews of Oregon*, 66–67.

149   Ibid., 67.

150   Ibid.

151   Quoted in Lowenstein, *Jews of Oregon*, 47.

152   *Oregon Native Son*, I no.1 (May 1899), 7.

153   Ibid., 8.

154   *Oregon Native Son* 1, no.3, (July 1899): 138; no. 6 (October 1899): 348.

155   *Morning Democrat: Eastern Oregon's Gold Fields* (Bowen & Small, May 20, 1898, Souvenir Edition), 45.

156   Ibid., 20.

157   Sol Blumauer: *Oregon Native Son* 1, no. 3 (July 1899): 138; Simon Blumauer & Mollie Blumauer (separate profiles): *Oregon Native Son* I, no. 6 (October 1899): 348.

158   *Portrait and Biographical Record of the Willamette Valley, Oregon*, 44–45.

159   Ibid., 495–96.

160   Ibid., 54–56.

161   *Oregon Native Son* 1, no. 1 (May 1899): 52–3.

162   *Portrait and Biographical Record of the Willamette Valley, Oregon*, 169.

163   Ibid., 348.

164   *Oregon Native Son* 2, (December 1900): 345.

165   Ibid., 374.

166   For additional analysis of the treatment of these groups, see Eisenberg, First to Cry Down Injustice, 4–5. The issue of Jewish whiteness and where Jews fit into the Oregon racial landscape will be explored further in chap. 6.

167   Lowenstein, *The Jews of Oregon*, 6.

168   *Portrait and Biographical Record of the Willamette Valley, Oregon*, 55, 165.

169   Obituary, Max Muller, July 20, 1902. Jackson County, Oregon, Archives Obituary, online http://files.usgwarchives.net/or/jackson/obits/m/muller2017gob.text (accessed May 18, 2012).

CHAPTER 2

1   Adelaide Lowenson Selling oral history, (December 7, 1973), OJM, 1–2.

2   Fannie Kenin Friedman oral history, (May 4, 1974), OJM, 4.

3   Miriam Boskowitz Aiken oral history, (January 22, 1974), OJM, 13, 28.

4   Ernie Bonyhadi oral history, (December 4, 2007), OJM 6.

5   Lowenstein, *The Jews of Oregon*, 79.

6   Diner, *The Jews of the United States*, chap. 3.

7   Eisenberg, Kahn, and Toll, *Jews of the Pacific Coast*, chap. 1.

8   Livingston, "Introduction," *Jews of the American West*, 19–21. Marc Lee Raphael, "Beyond New York: The Challenge to Local History," *Jews of the American West*, 62.

9   Lowenstein, *The Jews of Oregon*, 79.

10   On Johnstown see Ewa Morawska, *Insecure Prosperity: Small Town Jews in Industrial America, 1890–1940* (Princeton University Press, 1999). On the communities of the Ohio River Valley, see Amy Hill Shevitz, *Jewish Communities on the Ohio River* (Lexington: The University Press of Kentucky, 2007). Weissbach, "The Jewish Communities of the United States on the Eve of Mass Migration," table 2, 84–87. See also Eisenberg, Kahn, and Toll, *Jews of the Pacific Coast*, 79–80.

11   For this analysis, forty oral histories conducted through the Oregon Jewish Museum oral history project, directed by Shirley Tanzer in the 1970s with women who came of age in the 1910s, 1920s and 1930s, were used.

12   Adelaide Lowenson Selling oral history, 3. Adelaide was Laurence's wife and Ben Selling's daughter-in-law.

13   Gladys Trachtenberg oral history (1), (January 19, 1977), OJM, 8.

14   Ibid., 24–5.

15   Hannah Mihlstin Bodner oral history (February 23, 1976) OJM, 2.

16   Adelaide Lowenson Selling oral history, 6.

17   Gladys Trachtenberg oral history, (1), 31.

18   Gladys Trachtenberg oral history (2), (August 29, 1977), OJM, 16.

19   Felice Lauterstein Dreisen oral history (May 9, 1975) OJM, 17–18. The Octagonal Club was the temple youth group.

20   Gladys Trachtenberg (2), 20.

21   Lowenstein *The Jews of Oregon, 1850–1950*, 194.

22   For detail on Wise's activities in Portland see Lowenstein, *The Jews of Oregon*, chap. 9; and Nodel, *The Ties Between*, chap. 5. For a detailed discussion of Neighborhood House, see chap. 3.

23   Gladys Trachtenberg (1), 37.

24   Gladys Trachtenberg (1), 13.

25   It was not uncommon in Portland for families to be affiliated with more than one congregation.

26   Lowenstein, *The Jews of Oregon*, 106.

27   Sadie Decklebaum Horenstein oral history (December 9, 1975), OJM, 16.

28   Frances Schnitzer Bricker oral history (May 18, 1977), OJM, 10

29   Frieda Gass Cohn oral history (September 8, 1975), OJM, 2.

30   Gertrude Bachman oral history (November 28, 1973), OJM, 4.

31   Fanny Kenin Friedman oral history, (May 4, 1974), OJM, 4.

32   Estelle Director Sholkoff oral history (May 21, 1975), OJM, 4. "Chartorysk" is transcribed as "Shatrisk" in some community accounts.

33   Ibid., 5–28.

34   Kathryn Kahn Blumenfeld oral history (November 26, 1976), OJM, 9. Blumenfeld's mother was from the Friendly family of Eugene.

35   Diner, *The Jews of the United States*, 2.

36   Ibid., chaps. 1 and 2. For a comparative discussion of Poseners in San Francisco and Portland see Kahn and Eisenberg "Western Reality," 455–80.

37   Norton Stern and William Kramer, "The Major Role of Polish Jews in the Pioneer West," *Western States Jewish Historical Quarterly (WSJHQ)* 8, no. 4 (1976): 326–44. See also Stern and Kramer "The Polish Jew in Posen and the Early West," *WSJHQ* 10, no. 4 (1978): 327–29; Stern and Kramer "The Turnverein: A German Experience for Western Jewry," *WSJHQ* 16, no. 3 (1984): 227–29; Stern and Kramer "What's the Matter with Warsaw?" *WSJHQ* 17, no. 4 (1985): 305–07; and Stern and Kramer "Polish Preeminence in Nineteenth Century Jewish Immigration: A Review Essay," *Western States Jewish History* 17, no. 2 (1985): 151–55.

38   Rudolf Glanz, "Vanguard to the Russians: The Poseners of America," *YIVO* 18 (1983): 17.

39   Stern and Kramer, "The Major Role": 343–44.

40   Scott Cline, "The Jews of Portland, Oregon: A Statistical Dimension, 1860–1880," *Oregon Historical Quarterly* 88, no. 1 (1987): 7. Fully 54.5 percent of these Jews were from Bavaria in 1860, and only 13 percent from Prussia.

41   There is broad agreement among historians that Poseners made up a disproportionate number of the Jewish emigrants from Prussia. See Glanz, "Vanguard to the Russians," 1. In Portland, community histories refer repeatedly to Poseners as a substantial group; so here, "Prussian" refers to a group comprised largely of Prussian Poseners.

42   Cline, "The Jews of Portland": 7–8. Cline demonstrates that 28.5 percent (88) of Portland's foreign Jews were South German; with 18.4 percent (57) from Bavaria alone; 34 percent (104) were Prussian. In 1880, no regional origin could be determined for the 21 (or 6.6 percent) of the foreign-born Jews who were listed as born in "Germany" on the census. Thirty-one, or 10 percent, were listed as Poles. Using the same census records, and counting only male heads of household, Toll puts the percentage of Prussians in 1880 at 24.8 percent and the South Germans just slightly lower at 23.4 percent. See Toll, *Making*, 20.

43   Avraham Barkai, *Branching Out: German-Jewish Immigration to the United States, 1820–1914* (New York: Holmes and Meier, 1994), 131–33.

44   Alan Levenson, "The Posen Factor," *Shofar* 17, no. 1 (1998).

45   Glanz, "Vanguard," 6.

46   Barkai, *Branching Out*, 96–97.

47   Stern and Kramer, "The Major Role . . .": 329–30; "What's the Matter with Warsaw?": 306–07.

48   Glanz, "Vanguard," 6.

49   Kahn and Eisenberg, "Western Reality," 458.

50   An excellent example is documented by Morawska in *Insecure Prosperity*, 39, 50, 146–52. Morawska indicates that the nineteenth-century Posener immigrants were, for all intents and purposes, a part of the "German" community centered at Temple Beth Zion, although she argues that the conservative tendencies of the temple may be traceable to the influence of the "poylishe" among its leaders.

51   For immigrants from Germany see Cline "Community Structure on the Urban Frontier: The Jews of Portland, Oregon, 1849–1887," (master's thesis, Portland State University, 1982), 35. On Russian immigrants arriving after 1880, see Eisenberg, "Transplanted to the Rose City," 86–87.

52   See chap. 1 for discussion of migration patterns that fostered the use of English among pioneers.

53   By the end of the 1860s, the South Germans numbered 116 (54 percent), the Prussians 48 (22.3 percent), and the Poles 20 (9.3 percent). Cline, "The Jews of Portland," 8.

54   Gary Miranda, *Following a River: Portland's Congregation Neveh Shalom, 1869–1989* (Portland, Congregation Neveh Shalom, 1989), 10.

55   Ibid.,11.

56   Lowenstein, *The Jews of Oregon,* 53–54. See also Nodel, *The Ties Between,* 29–31.

57   Toll, *Making,* 24. See also Miranda, *Following a River,* chap. 1.

58   Miranda, *Following a River,* 15.

59   Ibid., 33.

60   Joshua Stampfer, *Pioneer Rabbi of the West: The Life and Times of Julius Eckman* (Portland, 1988), chap. 5.

61   Ibid., chaps. 2, 3, and 6.

62   Miranda, *Following a River,* 29–31.

63   Ibid., 23.

64   Ibid., 24.

65   *American Hebrew News* notices from September 28, 1894; October 12, 1894; October 19, 1894; August 30, 1895; October 4, 1895; October 28, 1898.

66   Miranda, *Following a River,* 58.

67   Ibid., 48–50, 60.

68   Scott Cline, "Community Structure": 25, 45. Since membership lists for Ahavai Sholom do not survive from this period, we cannot determine the regional origin of its membership with any accuracy.

69   On Julius Loewenberg, see Lowenstein, *The Jews of Oregon,* 65, 83.

70   Examples include Bavarian Ludwig Levy, a Turnverein officer who was a member of Ahavai Sholom. Cline's analysis of Beth Israel's membership in 1880 shows that in addition to 15 Prussians (15 percent of Beth Israel members, some, but not all, of whom may have been Poseners), 6 Poles (6 percent) belonged to the Temple. Cline, "Community Structure": 29, 45.

71   Toll, *Making,* 26.

72   Lowenstein, *The Jews of Oregon,* 68.

73   Toll, *Making,* 31.

74   Lowenstein, *The Jews of Oregon,* 74.

75   For example, Lowenstein does not mention them as a distinct group, although he mentions Posen as the place of origin of several individuals. Many of the oral histories conducted in the 1970s mention Germans, Russians/East Europeans/Poles, and Sephardim as distinct groups within the community, but few mention Posen except as the place of origin of an individual.

76   1860, 1870, 1880, 1900, 1910, 1920 US Federal Censuses, accessed on Ancestry.com.

77   Both fires were the result of arson.

78   Miranda, *Following a River,* 70–71.

79   Attendance at Ahavai Sholom Sunday school is mentioned in a number of the oral histories from Sephardic Jewish Portlanders. See, for example, Victor Menashe oral history (February 23, 2007), OJM, 4.

80   *American Hebrew News*, August 18, 1899.

81   Gerald Sorin, *A Time for Building* (Baltimore: Johns Hopkins University Press, 1992), 182.

82   Miranda, *Following a River*, 43–47.

83   This argument is developed more fully in Eisenberg, "Transplanted to the Rose City."

84   Toll, "Jewish Families," 8. In his book length study of the Portland Jewish community, Toll's analysis of the occupation of members of the "Russian" B'nai B'rith lodge shows a similar concentration in trade and white-collar work. See Toll, *Making*, 39.

85   Vera Brownstein and Manly Labby oral histories, OJM. Brownstein's father had a furniture business in Russia and found work at Director Furniture Company in Portland; Labby's father learned hat making in Woodbine, New Jersey, and found work using this skill on arrival in Portland.

86   Toll, *Making*, chap. 4. Toll demonstrates the opportunities available to immigrants in this chapter, and charts the rapid mobility of immigrant Jews and their children in Portland.

87   Portland City Directory, 1890, 1900, 1910.

88   Portland City Directory, 1910,1920. For more detail on Schnitzer's story, see Lowenstein, *The Jews of Oregon*, 128–29.

89   Eugene Nudelman, "The Family of Joseph Nudelman," unpublished manuscript, Oregon Jewish Museum: 19.

90   On the origins of Jewish colonists, see Ellen Eisenberg, *Jewish Agricultural Colonies in New Jersey, 1880–1920* (Syracuse University Press, 1995), chaps. 1, 2, and 4; "Argentine and American Jewry: A Case for Contrasting Immigrant Origins," *American Jewish Archives* 47, (Spring-Summer, 1995). On the origins of Jewish migrants to eastern cities, see George Price, "The Russian Jews in America," (1893). Reprint. *Publications of the American Jewish Historical Society* 48, part I (1958): 33; Isaac Rubinow, *Economic Conditions of the Jews in Russia* (1907 Reprint. Arno Press, 1975), 492. Of a sample of 83 East European Jewish families arriving in Portland between 1882 and World War I, the majority (55 percent) hailed from the South or Southwest Pale, and an additional 13 to 14 percent each from Romania and Poland. Only 16 percent originated in the northern Pale provinces. Data on the origins of individual families was derived from a number of sources including naturalization documents for the 1906–14 period, oral histories conducted in the 1970s by Shirley Tanzer and held in the Oregon Jewish Museum collection, unpublished memoirs from the Oregon Jewish Museum collection, and published sources such as Lowenstein. The region of towns named in these sources was determined using Chester Cohn, *Shtetl Finder* (Los Angeles: Periday, 1980) and the online "ShtetlSeeker" available through the Jewish Gen internet site. Regional definitions for the terms used in this paper (south, southwest, etc.) are based on Yoav Peled, *Class and Ethnicity in the Pale* (New York: St. Martin's Press, 1987), 23.

91   The Directors, Schnitzers, and Rosenfelds were part of a group from the Chartorysk area. Lowenstein, *The Jews of Oregon*, 76.

92   Estelle Director Sholkoff oral history, 2.

93   These include twenty-five families living in Portland during the 1900 census who had children born in midwestern or western states, and an additional six families identified as North Dakota colonists by Nudelman, "The Family of Joseph Nudelman." Because a family's time in another state is only detectable

in the census if a child was born during residence in that state, the number of sojourning families is a minimum figure.

94   Rubinow, *Economic Conditions, 555*. Those from the North and Northwest were more likely to work in the garment industry.

95   In general, these communities of the South Pale were less insular and less densely Jewish. Jews in the south were far more likely to go to Russian schools and speak the vernacular, particularly in the relatively cosmopolitan and multi-ethnic city of Odessa. See Patricia Herlihy, *Odessa: A History* (Boston: Harvard, 1986) and Steven Zipperstein, *The Jews of Odessa* (Stanford: Stanford University Press, 1985).

96   This includes eleven families listed in the 1900 census who had children born in the Dakotas, and seven additional families who are mentioned as North Dakota families in Nudelman's history. Each surname is counted only once, even in cases where several brothers and their families participated in the colony.

97   Painted Woods colonists have been identified in several ways. First, nine families are named by Eugene Nudelman in his memoir. The names of several of these, as well as of several additional families who had children who were born in the Dakotas, can be found on a list of settlers appearing in an illustration of colony life, published in W. Gunther Plaut, "Jewish Colonies at Painted Woods and Devils Lake" *North Dakota History* 32, (January 1965): 62. These families include Bromberg, Cartman, Cohen, Dellar, Gale, Goldstein, Katz, Levdansky, Lauterstein, Nudelman, and Schenk. The Dellar Family Tree, compiled by Dorothy Kohanski, places the Dellar, Cartman, and Ruvensky families, all related by marriage, at Painted Woods. Dellar Family Tree courtesy of David Bernstein, Congregation Neveh Shalom Archive. In addition, the Calof family spent time at Devil's Lake, another North Dakota colony. The experiences of some of the Calofs who did not come to Portland are vividly recorded in *Rachel Calof's Story*, J. Sanford Rikoon, ed. (Indiana University Press, 1995).

98   Lowenstein, *The Jews of Oregon*, 77.

99   Manly Labby oral history (February 23, 1976), OJM.

100   Ibid.

101   In addition to the Swetts, the Marcus Gale and Louis Dellar families briefly farmed in Oregon. Information courtesy of David Bernstein, Congregation Neveh Shalom Archives. On New Odessa, see Helen Blumenthal, "The New Odessa Colony of Oregon, 1882–1886," *Western States Jewish Historical Quarterly* 14, no. 4 (July 1983): 321–32.

102   Mary Ann Barnes Williams, *Pioneer Days of Washburn, North Dakota and Vicinity* (Washburn: 1936, reprint by the McLean County Historical Society, 1995), 18–21, 71.

103   Plaut, "Jewish Colonies," 61; Williams, *Pioneer Days*, 21. For more on the impact of such experiences on Portland settlers, see Eisenberg, "From Cooperative Farming to Urban Leadership," in *Jewish Life in the American West*, ed. Ava Kahn, 113–32.

104   Portland's Jewish population was 6,000 in 1911, 8,000 in 1917, and 9,000 in 1923. *American Jewish Yearbook*, 1901–41. The figure of 6,000 living in South Portland comes from Lowenstein, *The Jews of Oregon*, 92.

105   1920 US Census figures, Inter-University Consortium for Political and Social Research: Historical, Demographic, Economic and Social Data, United States. 1790–1970, Anne Arbor http://fisher.lib.virginia.edu/cgi-local/censusbin/. See also Toll, "Black Families and Migration to a Multiracial

Society: Portland,   Oregon,   1900–1924," *Journal of American Ethnic History* 17, no. 3 (Spring 1998): 42.

106   Lowenstein, *The Jews of Oregon*, 102. Beth Israel and Ahavai Sholom, the two synagogues that predated in East European influx, while located in South Portland, stood outside the immigrant district.

107   Lowenstein, *The Jews of Oregon*, 100. Also see account of life in South Portland in Kenneth Libo and Irving Howe, *We Lived There Too* (New York: St. Martin's Press, 1984), chap. 12.

108   Zachary Swett and Carrie Bromberg Hervin oral histories.

109   Lowenstein, *The Jews of Oregon*, 103.

110   *American Hebrew News*, Portland, Oregon (September 28, 1894).

111   *American Hebrew News* (October 4, 1895).

112   *American Hebrew News* (March 15, 1895).

113   *American Hebrew News* (April 13, 1900).

114   *American Hebrew News* (August 25, 1899 and September 23, 1898).

115   *American Hebrew News* (September 1, 1899).

116   *American Hebrew News* (November 10, 1899).

117   *American Hebrew News* (August 18, 1899).

118   Sorin, *A Time for Building*, 175.

119   Lowenstein, *The Jews of Oregon*, 104.

120   Congregation Neveh Zedek Talmud Torah, *Anniversary Book* (1936), Oregon Historical Society Archive, vertical file.

121   Lois Fields Schwartz , "Early Jewish Agricultural Colonies in North Dakota," *North Dakota History* 32, no. 4, (October 1965): 223.

122   Isadore Papermaster, "A History of North Dakota Jewry and their Pioneer Rabbi," *Western States Jewish Historical Quarterly* 10, no. 1 (October 1977): 81.

123   Eisenberg, *Jewish Agricultural Colonies*, 26–30. Sidney Baily, "Memoir" in *Jewish Agricultural Utopias in America, 1880–1910* by Uri Herscher (Detroit: Wayne State University Pres, 1981), 134–35; 146–49.

124   Papermaster, "A History of North Dakota Jewry," 81.

125   *Rachel Calof's Story,* 72.

126   Lowenstein, *The Jews of Oregon*, 123.

127   Author's interview with Felice Lauterstein Driesen, November 11, 1997. Mrs. Driesen's grandfather was Rabbi Heller.

128   Toll, *Making,* 103.

129   Nudelman, 6–13.

130   The Nudelman family was related to the Bromberg family by marriage. One of the Nudelman sons was in business in 1910 with the son of Neveh Zedek Talmud Torah rabbi, Nehemiah Mosessohn. See Portland City Directory, 1910.

131   Lowenstein, *The Jews of Oregon*, 118.

132   Toll, *Making,* 105.

133   Lowenstein, *The Jews of Oregon*, 118. Bromberg was also Jacob Lauterstein's stepfather.

134   Carrie Bromberg Hervin oral history, 4.

135   Toll, *Making,* 104.

136 Hansa Brill Shapiro oral history (February 12, 1974), OJM, 1.

137 Ahavath Achim would meet for several decades in other community buildings, first the Newsboys Club, then Neighborhood House, and finally the B'nai B'rith Building, before it finally built its own building in 1930. In 1910, when the congregation was established, it had only twelve members. The Sephardic community in Portland, unlike its much larger sister community in Seattle, remained quite small.

138 Augusta Kirshner Reinhardt oral history, (December 7, 1973), OJM, 4; Lowenstein, *The Jews of Oregon*, 109.

139 Lowenstein, *The Jews of Oregon*, 105.

140 Frances Schnitzer Bricker oral history, 24–25.

141 Mollie Blumenthal oral history, 4.

142 Rachel Fain Schneider oral history (January 4, 1978), OJM, 7.

143 Ibid., 10.

144 Toll, *Making*, 126, 108, 130.

145 The Portland Jewish community was served by the weeklies *American Hebrew News* from 1893–1900, the *Jewish Tribune* from 1902–19 and the *Scribe* from 1919–51.

146 On the important leadership role of colony veterans in this regard see Toll, *Making*, 101. On the role of immigrants and their children in Portland Zionist organizations and in the modern Hebrew school see Deborah Goldberg, "Jewish Spirit on the Urban Frontier: Zionism in Portland, 1901–1941" (unpublished senior thesis, Reed College, 1982), 81.

147 Lowenstein, *The Jews of Oregon*, chap. 9; Sorin, *A Time for Building*, 100–01. Both authors mention Ben Selling as a key figure in this regard.

148 Eisenberg, Kahn, and Toll, *Jews of the Pacific Coast*, 97. This is mentioned in several interviews, including Beulah Menashe Schauffer (July 19, 2011), OJM, 8.

149 Molly Cone, Howard Droker, and Jacqueline Williams, *Family of Strangers: Building a Jewish Community in Washington State* (Seattle: University of Washington Press, 2003), chap. 3.

150 Jonathan Singer, "History of the Sephardic Community," (Ahavath Achim history, www.ahavathachim.com).

151 Joy Babani Russell oral history (June 8, 2009), OJM, 1–2.

152 Albert Menashe oral history (August 10, 2010), OJM, 2.

153 Russell oral history, 3.

154 Schauffer oral history, 8.

155 Joanna Menashe oral history (September 29, 1975), OJM, 11.

156 Ibid., 12.

157 Harry Policar oral history (September 25, 1975), OJM, 4.

158 Ibid., 7–8.

159 Toinette Menashe oral history (November 10, 2004), OJM.

CHAPTER 3

1 Opening quotes: Lowenstein, *The Jews of Oregon*, 138. Mary Friedman Rosenberg oral history (June 5, 1975), OJM, 18. Michele Glazer, *Focus of a Community: Neighborhood House 1897–1929* (unpublished manuscript,

1982), Neighborhood House, Settlement Era, Box 3 "Historical Chronologies," OJM, 23.

2   Weissbach, "The Jewish Communities of the United States on the Eve of Mass Migration," 84.

3   Faith Rogow, *Gone to Another Meeting: The National Council of Jewish Women, 1893–1993* (Tuscaloosa: University of Alabama Press, 1993), 19.

4   Ibid., 24. See also, Melissa Klapper, *Ballots, Babies and Banners of Peace: American Jewish Women's Activism, 1890–1940* (New York: NYU Press, 2013), 8–10.

5   Rogow, *Gone to Another Meeting*, 134.

6   Ibid., 132. For a discussion of the Sisterhoods of Personal Service in New York see Felicia Herman, "From Priestess to Hostess" in *Women and American Judaism*, Pam Nadell and Jonathan Sarna, eds. (Waltham: Brandeis University Press, 2001), 150ff. On San Francisco's Sisterhood, see Eisenberg, Kahn, and Toll, *Jews of the Pacific Coast*, 140–1.

7   William Toll, "From Domestic Judaism to Public Ritual," in Nadel and Sarna, *Women and American Judaism*, 139. Notably, Diner and Benderly profile Denver's Frances Wisebart Jacobs as pioneering "a new style of female philanthropy capable of coping with the East European immigration." Although Diner and Benderly do not paint this as a regional pattern, Jacobs' prominence in the Jewish and non-Jewish social service network of Denver closely parallels patterns in other western cities, including Portland. Hasia Diner and Beryl Benderly, *Her Works Praise Her: A History of Jewish Women in America from Colonial Times to the Present* (New York: Basic Books, 2002), 224.

8   Lowenstein, *The Jews of Oregon*, 144.

9   Glazer, *Focus of a Community*, 27.

10   Toll, *Making*, 57.

11   Ibid., 54–56. Over 40 percent of married women over 30 and 25 percent of those under 30 had live-in servants.

12   For biographical information on the Loewenberg sisters, see Lowenstein, *The Jews of Oregon*, 82–85. See also Gladys ("Laddie") Trachtenberg oral history, OJM. Trachtenberg was the daughter of Ida and Zerlina's sister, Rose Loewenberg Goodman.

13   Gladys Trachtenberg oral history, 20.

14   Toll, "From Domestic Judaism to Public Ritual," 128.

15   Ibid., 128. See also Abrams, *Jewish Women Pioneering the Frontier Trail*, chap. 3.

16   Toll, *Making*, 58.

17   Some of this activity will be explored in chap. 6.

18   Rogow, *Gone to Another Meeting*, 19. Glazer notes that girls were a particular focus of the Portland section as well.

19   Miriam Rosenfeld oral history, (April 15, 1975), OJM, 15.

20   Emily Zeien-Stuckman, "Creating New Citizens: The National Council of Jewish Women's Work at Neighborhood House in Portland, 1896–1912," *Oregon Historical Quarterly* 113, no. 3 (Fall, 2012): 324.

21   Rogow, *Gone to Another Meeting*, 130. See also Diner and Benderly, *Her Works Praise Her*, 225. A Portland Section NCJW yearbook from 1931–32 noted, "The policy of the Neighborhood House has always been to relinquish

such parts of the work as have been assumed by public agencies. Pioneers in English classes for foreign born, Manual Training, Domestic Science, Kindergarten, it has changed its program to meet present need." "Yearbook," NCJW, Portland Section, 1931–32, NCJW, Box 1, Administration, OJM.

22 Glazer, *Focus of a Community*, 69–72

23 Sadie Cohen Geller oral history (January 22, 1976), OJM, 9–10

24 Miriam Rosenfeld oral history, 15.

25 The word "chairman" is consistently used in Neighborhood House records from the period under discussion, despite the fact that a woman held the position. I have retained that language.

26 See, for example, Report of the President, April 30, 1912. National Council of Jewish Women, Box 1, Administration, "Administration." Another, later example is Neighborhood House Board minutes, September 10, 1929. Neighborhood House, Settlement Era, Box 3, "Minutes, 1928–1945," OJM.

27 Trachtenberg oral history, 16.

28 Letter Deputy District Attorney's Office to Ida Loewenberg, November 1, 1917, Neighborhood House, Settlement Era, Box 2, "Correspondence, general," OJM.

29 City of Portland, Department of Public Safety, Women's Protective Division to Ida Loewenberg, April 27, 1917, Neighborhood House, Settlement Era, Box 2, "Correspondence, general," OJM.

30 Mary Adams, assistant secretary of the Native Sons and Native Daughters Central Committee on Homeless Children in San Francisco, to Ida Loewenberg, July 6, 1933. Neighborhood House, Settlement Era, Box 1, "Adoption," OJM.

31 Ida Loewenberg to Oregon State Hospital, various dates. Neighborhood House, Settlement Period, Box 2, "Medical," OJM.

32 Trachtenberg oral history, 16.

33 Cited in Glazer, *Focus of a Community*, 26.

34 Miriam Boskovitz Aiken oral history (July 22, 1974), OJM, 15.

35 Sadie Bloch, "Headworkers Annual Report" (1912–1913), *Year Book*, Council of Jewish Women, Portland Section, Box 1, Administration, "Chronology," OJM.

36 Glazer, *Focus of a Community*, 109–10.

37 Blumenthal oral history, 8.

38 Marguerite Swett Dilsheimer oral history (June 11, 1975), OJM, 5.

39 Glazer, *Focus of a Community*, 157.

40 Ibid., 157–58.

41 Program "Under the Stars and Stripes," Neighborhood House, Settlement Era, Box 1, "Classes and Clubs," OJM.

42 Victor Greene, "Old-time Folk Dancing and Music among the Second Generation, 1920–50," in *American Immigration and Ethnicity*, David Gerber and Alan Kraut, eds. (New York: Palgrave Macmillan, 2005): 111–19.

43 Quoted in Glazer, *Focus of a Community*, 87.

44 See, for example, Loewenberg's editorial, "The Sacrifice of the First Generation," *The Neighborhood* 2, no. 5 (October 1920): 2. National Council of Jewish Women, Box 9, OJM.

45 Neighborhood House, Board Minutes, April 16, 1919. Neighborhood House, Settlement Era, Box 3, "Minutes, 1928–1945," OJM.

46 Sadie Bloch, Headworker's Annual Report, (1912–13).

47 Glazer, *Focus of a Community*, 109.

48 Zionism made greater inroads at Temple Beth Israel than at some of its sister synagogues up and down the West Coast, largely through the influence of Rabbi Stephen Wise, an ardent Zionist. Still, there was an anti-Zionist contingent at Temple Beth Israel. These anti-Zionists objected to the idea of Judaism as a national identity and felt that Zionists were liable to accusations of dual loyalty. Zionism and anti-Zionism are discussed in more detail in Chapter Five.

49 Quoted in Glazer, *Focus of a Community*, 87.

50 Lowenstein, *The Jews of Oregon*, 118.

51 Ibid., 105.

52 Lowenstein, *The Jews of Oregon*, 118.

53 Ibid., 119.

54 As discussed in chap. 2, the selective migration pattern that brought East uropeans to Portland likely reinforced this attitude.

55 Lowenstein, *The Jews of Oregon*, 118.

56 Trachtenberg oral history, (August 29, 1977), 37.

57 Ibid., 19.

58 Neighborhood House, *Annual Report*, 1928. Neighborhood House, Settlement Era, Box 4, "Reports, Annual and Monthly," OJM.

59 Special Committee Report, Portland Section, National Council of Jewish Women, 1954. Neighborhood House, Community Center Era, Box 5, "Building Use and Program Changes," OJM.

60 Gertrude Feves oral history (May 27, 1975), OJM, 2.

61 Frieda Gass Cohn oral history, 2.

62 Diane Holzman Nemer oral history (May 27, 1975), OJM, 2–3.

63 Frances Schnitzer Bricker oral history (May 18, 1977), OJM, 23–4.

64 Nettie Enkilis Olman oral history (n.d., circa 1976), OJM, 7.

65 Augusta ("Gussie") Kirshner Reinhardt oral history (December 7, 1975), OJM, 4. Those oral histories that do note the diversity of the area consistently paint a picture of harmonious relations. For example, Diane Holzman Nemer recounted that Failing School "was made up of the Italian and the Jewish, so they had quite a large neighborhood of Italian people around us. . . . They knew all of our customs and we knew all of their customs, it was a nice relationship, always one which we felt was good." Nemer oral history, 16.

66 Glazer, *Focus of a Community*, 61.

67 Ibid., 22.

68 Ibid., 61.

69 Ibid., 62.

70 Blanche Blumauer, "Report of the Chairman of the Neighborhood House Committee," April 30, 1912. NCJW, Box 1 "Administration," OJM.

71 Toll, *Making*, 120.

72   Glazer, *Focus of a Community*, 62–63. The Manley Center was operated by the Women's Division of Board of Missions and Church Extension of the Methodist Church.

73   Ida Loewenberg, undated memo (approximately 1925–1928). Neighborhood House, Settlement Era, Box 1, "B'nai B'rith Relations," OJM.

74   "The Neighborhood House" (editorial), *The Scribe* (April 16, 1926): 3.

75   Neighborhood House, Annual Report, 1928. Neighborhood House, Settlement Era, Box 4, "Reports, Annual and Monthly," OJM.

76   Survey of gym classes, 1932–33. Neighborhood House, Settlement Era, Box 4, "Survey Questionnaires and Results, 1932–33," OJM.

77   Report, undated (approximately 1933–38). Neighborhood House, Settlement Era, Box 1, "Classes and Clubs, General Information," OJM.

78   Gertrude Feves, cited above, for example, was born in 1912 and moved to Portland from Colorado when she was eight. Her memories of the house and growing up in the neighborhood would date to the 1920s and early 1930s (she married in 1932).

79   Ida Loewenberg, editorial, *The Neighborhood* 3, no. 2 (July, 1921): 2. NCJW, Box 9, OJM.

80   Toll, *Making*, 121.

81   Toll, *Making,* 120–1. Toll's analysis of residential patterns demonstrates that there was a general pattern in the 1920s of "communal stability."

82   *The Neighborhood House Bulletin* (November, 1924). National Council of Jewish Women, Box 7, Publications, OJM.

83   Neighborhood House (author unknown) to *B'nai B'rith Messenger* (Los Angeles), March 26, 1928. Neighborhood House, Settlement Era, Box 2, "Correspondence, general," OJM.

84   Lowenstein, *The Jews of Oregon*,189–90.The Portland Jewish population declined from approximately 10,000 in the 1920s to 7,000 in 1946.

85   Toll, *Making*, 169.

86   Glazer, *Focus of a Community*, 37.

87   Ibid., 98.

88   "Portland Neighborhood Councils: A Community Clearing House" and Southwest Neighborhood Council agenda, November, 1940. Neighborhood House, Settlement Era, Box 4, Folder "Southwest Neighborhood Council," OJM.

89   Correspondence, Mrs. C.H. Van Meter, Helen Kelly Manley Community Center to Neighborhood House and Neighborhood House response to Mrs. Van Meter, signed by Mrs. Arthur (Henriette) Senders, May, 1946. Neighborhood House, Community Center Era, Box 5, Folder "NCJW Neighborhood House Board, 1945–1947," OJM.

90   List of Recommendations, 1946. Neighborhood House, Community Center Era, Box 5, Folder "NCJW Neighborhood House Board, 1945–1947." Several additional documents indicating Neighborhood House discussions of the recommendations appear in Neighborhood House, Community Center Era, Box 5, folder "Council of Social Agencies," OJM.

91   Mrs. Berkowitz (Flora Fleischner Berkowitz), Neighborhood House Board Chairman to various recipients, November 26, 1947. Neighborhood House, Community Center Era, Box 5, "Goldman, Arthur," OJM.

92   Neighborhood House, Camp Advertisement, 1940. Settlement Era, Box 1, "Camp," OJM.

93   Neighborhood House, Community Center Era, Box 5, "Americanization, 1946–7," OJM.

94   Neighborhood House, Community Center Era, box 5, "Classes and Clubs, 1945–8," OJM.

95   US Bureau of the Census, 1930, 1940, 1950.

96   The causes and impact of the embrace of liberalism in the Jewish community will be explored in detail in chap. 6.

97   Neighborhood House report, undated (war years). Neighborhood House, Community Center Era, Box 6, "NH Monthly and Annual Reports," OJM.

98   Neighborhood House Board Minutes, November 14, 1944. Neighborhood House, Settlement Era, Box 3, "Minutes, 1928–1945," OJM.

99   Portland Council of Social Agencies, Report, June 22, 1945. Neighborhood House, Settlement Era, Box 1, "Annual Reports," OJM.

100   Neighborhood House Board Minutes, September 11, 1945 and October 9, 1945. Neighborhood House, Settlement Era, Box 3, "Minutes, 1928–1945," OJM.

101   Quoted in letter from Mrs. Aubrey Davis, Portland CJW section secretary to Harry Kenin, March 5, 1947, Neighborhood House, Community Center Era, Box 5, "NCJW Neighborhood House Board," OJM.

102   Job announcements, March 14, 1947 and April 9, 1947. Neighborhood House, Community Center Era, Box 6, "Personnel," OJM.

103   Arthur Goldman, Letter to the Editor of the *Oregonian*, November 23, 1947. Neighborhood House, Community Center Era, Box 5, "Goldman, Arthur, Exec. Dir. 1947–1948," OJM. Goldman received several letters in response, one of which supported the restaurant's refusal of service, decrying the increasing diversity in Portland, and suggesting that Goldman "go to Jerusalem."

104   Program Committee, Council of Social Agencies, March 1, 1948. Neighborhood House, Community Center Era Box 5, "Council of Social Agencies," OJM.

105   Correspondence between John McDowell, executive secretary, National Federation of Settlements, New York, and Arthur Goldman, executive director, Neighborhood House, February 9, 1948. Neighborhood House, Community Center Era, box 5, "Correspondence, 1945–1964," OJM.

106   Goldman to Gertrude Wilson, School of Social Work, Cathedral of Learning, University of Pittsburgh, June 10, 1948. Neighborhood House, Community Center Era, Box 5, "Correspondence, 1945–1964," OJM.

107   Herman, "From Priestess to Hostess," 149.

108   Ibid., 158–60. In Herman's discussion of the history of the Sisterhoods in New York, there is no mention of service provision to clients who were not Jewish. Interestingly, Faith Rogow's book-length study of the NCJW discusses the creation of settlement houses in some detail, but also does not indicate that these houses generally worked with diverse populations.

109   Elizabeth Rose, "From Sponge Cake to Hamentashen: Jewish Identity in a Jewish Settlement House, 1885–1952," *Journal of American Ethnic History* 13, no. 3 (Spring 1994): 23.

110   Arthur Goldberg, Neighborhood House, to Samuel Kohs, Western States Section, National Jewish Welfare Board (San Francisco), March 1948.

Neighborhood House, Community Center Era, Box 6, "Jewish Welfare Board," OJM.

111 Arthur Goldberg, NH, to John McDowell, National Federation of Settlements, November 11, 1948. Neighborhood House, Community Center Era, Box 6, "Jewish Welfare Board," OJM.

112 Special Committee Report, Portland Section, National Council of Jewish Women, (1954), 2–3. Neighborhood House, Community Center Era, Box 5, "Building Use and Program Changes," OJM.

113 *The Bulletin*, a publication of the Portland Section of NCJW, demonstrates support for such causes. See, for example, support for state level civil rights legislations (March 1953), school integration (December 1955), and, on a national level, support for the Civil Rights Act of 1964 (October, 1963). NCJW, Box 7, Publications, OJM. See discussion in chap. 6.

CHAPTER 4

1   *Voters' Pamphlet*, "Measures," State of Oregon, general election, (1916) 32. Accessed online via Oregon Voters' Pamphlet Project, Oregon State Archive http://library.state.or.us/repository/2010/201003011350161/ORVPGenMari1916m.pdf

2   Eisenberg, Kahn, and Toll, *Jews of the Pacific Coast*, 18. On Jews and office holding in the West more broadly, see Earl Pomeroy, "On Becoming a Westerner" in *Jews of the American West*, 196.

3   During the span between Goldsmith's election as Portland mayor and Meier's as governor, Jews never made up even 4 percent of the population of Portland—and were a far smaller percentage of the statewide population. For 1880, see Eisenberg, Kahn, and Toll, *Jews of the Pacific Coast*, 59. The 1927 population of Jews in Portland was approximately 12,000, of a total population of just over 301,000. 1927 figure, *American Jewish Year Book*, volume 31, 1929–30, General Table A, pp. 228. For the 1930 Portland population see http://www.portland.com/portland/articles/population-of-portland/.

4   The idea of a Jewish vote was criticized on a number of occasions in the *Scribe*. See, for example, the editorial by David E. Cohen, September 28, 1928, 3. Historians tend to agree that there was little evidence of ethnic politics among Jewish westerners in the nineteenth and early twentieth centuries. Ready acceptance and integration is a dominant theme in discussions of Jewish settlement in the West, as discussed in chap. 1.

5   Toll, *Making*, 88

6   Quoted in Toll, *Making*, 88

7   Julius Meier, quoted in the *American Hebrew News and Jewish Tribune*, (March 23, 1934), 379, reprinted in *Western States Jewish History* 30, no. 1 (1997): 40. This attitude toward ethnic politics was characteristic of the native-born, Reform community. See Henry Feingold, *A Time for Searching: Entering the Mainstream, 1920–1945* (Baltimore: American Jewish Historical Society/Johns Hopkins University Press, 1992), 189.

8   For South Portland, such analysis is not possible until the 1910s, as it was not until that time that a neighborhood of sufficient concentration for such a study existed. It is not possible to analyze Jewish voting behavior in the rest of the state, as there were no precincts outside of South Portland that had a concentrated Jewish population. The lack of data on actual voting patterns

for the earlier period and for any area outside of South Portland means that assessments of Jewish political participation and views for those eras and areas must rely on press accounts and individual stories. This reinforces the emphasis of the dominant narrative on individual politicians.

9   There is an extensive literature on the gap between native-born elites and East European immigrant Jews in this period. Although there are disagreements about the extent of conflict, many historians, such as Henry Feingold, characterize the inter-war period as one in which the American Jewish community was torn by conflict, and that this conflict was in part around the question of ethnic politics. See Feingold, *A Time for Searching*, chap. 7.

10 Examination of the 1910 census shows that about one-fourth of households in Precinct 37 in South Portland were Jewish (148 of 627 households). Only 28 percent (42) of those households were headed by a citizen. However, another 41 percent (61 heads of household) had filed their first papers, putting them on the path toward citizenship. By 1920, new precinct boundaries had been drawn, but in one of those in the same area, Precinct 89, 41 percent of the households were Jewish (89 of 217 households) and 37 percent were headed by a citizen, with another 25 percent on the way to citizenship. These numbers suggest that it is reasonable to assume that Jewish voters comprised an increasing portion of the voters in these precincts over this time period. Identification of Jewish households was made based on a combination of name, origin, and language (sometimes identified as Yiddish or Hebrew). Because ambiguous cases were not counted as Jewish, these numbers represent a conservative estimate of the population.

11 *Voters' Pamphlet*, "Measures" (1916), 32.

12 For a discussion of Sunday closing laws, see Jonathan Sarna and David Dalin, *Religion and State in the American Jewish Experience* (Notre Dame: University of Notre Dame Press, 1997), chap. 6.

13 *Jewish Tribune* (Portland, October 20, 1916), 4.

14 *Jewish Tribune* (October 27, 1916), 7.

15 *Jewish Tribune* (November 3, 1916), 4.

16 Precinct level voting records, 1916. Abstract of Votes, Multnomah County, Oregon State Archives. I have used two groups of precincts to analyze the South Portland vote. For the elections from 1907–16, precincts 32, 33, 34, 37, 38, and 40 cover the area generally considered to be South Portland. However, they extend well beyond the core Jewish area. Within this area, precincts 33, 37, and 38 can be considered the "core Jewish precincts," which correspond to the most heavily Jewish areas, identified by Toll and others. Still, these should be considered approximations since precinct boundaries do not correspond to neighborhood boundaries and since, even in the most heavily Jewish areas, there were various non-Jews, including Italians, living in the neighborhood. See Toll, *Making*, 118–20. For the elections after 1917, the broader South Portland area includes precincts 79, 80, 81, 82, 83, 89, 90, 91 and 93. Precincts 89, 90, 91 are considered the "core Jewish precincts." It is important to note that, because they lived in a less concentrated area, it is not possible to measure the vote of the wealthier, established segment of the Jewish community in the same way.

17 Ben Olcott, "Proclamation Against the Ku Klux Klan, 1922" (May 13, 1922), Oregon Historical Society, accessed online.

18   Lawrence Saalfeld, *Forces of Prejudice in Oregon, 1920–1925* (Portland: Archdiocesan Historical Commission, 1984), 30.

19   *Scribe*, (May 19, 1922).

20   *Scribe*, (May 12, 1922), 7.

21   *Scribe*, (July 21, 1922), 3 (editorial), 4 (KKK story).

22   *Scribe*, (August 4, 1922), 3. Such coverage continued throughout the late summer and fall, including warnings on the dangers of the School Bill and Klan backed candidates, reprints of anti-Klan editorials from other outlets, and reports on Klan and other anti-Semitic activity elsewhere in the country.

23   *Scribe*, (November 3, 1922), 3. An anti-School Bill piece was also the lead editorial the week before, on October 27, 1922.

24   *Scribe*, (November 3, 1922), 13.

25   Saalfeld, *Forces of Prejudice in Oregon*, 73.

26   *Oregon Voter*, (October 22, 1922), 13.

27   *Portland Telegram*, (November 3, 1922); *Oregonian*, (October 21, 1922), 15; cited in Benjamin Morris "True American: The Media Battle on Private Schools and the Oregon Compulsory Education Bill, 1922–1925" (unpublished senior thesis, University of Portland, December 2005), 14.

28   Robert Johnston, *The Radical Middle Class: Populist Democracy and the Question of Capitalism in Progressive Era Portland, Oregon* (Princeton: Princeton University Press, 2003).

29   Robert McCoy, "The Paradox of Oregon's Progressive Politics: The Political Career of Walter Marcus Pierce," *Oregon Historical Quarterly* 110, no. 3 (2009): 392–99.

30   Precinct level voting records, Abstract of Votes 1922, Oregon State Archives. The School Bill was struck down by the US Supreme Court in *Pierce v. Society of Sisters*, 1925.

31   Editorial, *The Neighborhood*, Neighborhood House, 4(6), (November 1922), 2. National Council of Jewish Women Collection, OJM.

32   "Public Forum" *The Neighborhood*, Neighborhood House, 4(6), (November 1922), 7.

33   Johnston, *The Radical Middle Class*, 233. He does note that his analysis may neglect "other hidden ethnocultural variables." Johnston is very hesitant to place the Klan and its agenda within the radical middle-class tradition. Certainly, the Klan agenda was strongly at odds with the racial equality that Johnston says was a tenuous part of the radical middle class ideology. That said, the correspondence between areas of support for the pro-Klan vote (for Pierce and for the school bill) and for other radical middle class initiatives is strong. Johnston explains this in part by emphasizing the "egalitarian argument" about the role of public schools and antipathy toward "elitist" private schools, and de-emphasizing nativism as a primary motive. Johnston, *The Radical Middle Class*, chap. 18.

34   McCoy, "Paradox of Oregon's Progressive Politics," 392.

35   Ibid., 393.

36   Eisenberg, Kahn, and Toll, *Jews of the Pacific Coast*, 58–59.

37   MacColl, *Merchants*, 244.

38   Toll, *Making*, 85–86.

39   MacColl, *Merchants*, 246, 320–22, 340–42.

40   Ibid., 326.

41   bid., 417. On Simon's mayoral term and promotion of business interests, see Jewel Lansing, *Portland: People, Politics and Power; 1851–2001* (Corvallis: Oregon State University Press, 2003), 273–79.

42   MacColl, *Merchants*, 431–33. See also Carl Abbott, *Portland: Gateway to the Northwest* (Northridge: Windsor *Publications*, 1985), 91.

43   Because Simon's final election, the 1909 Portland mayoral election, occurred at an early stage in the emergence of the Jewish neighborhood in South Portland, precinct-level analysis is a questionable tool for gauging a Jewish vote, as the concentration of eligible Jewish voters in the area at that time was low. Simon's victory has been attributed more to the split in the Democratic Party than to his own popularity. Voter turnout for this election was notably low. See MacColl, *Merchants*, 418. It should also be noted that Simon's earlier election to the US Senate preceded the shift to direct election of senators, so there is no popular vote to measure.

44   For example, Simon appointed merchant Julius Lowenberg to the water committee (dubbed the "Oligarchy of 15"), and during his term as mayor, he appointed Sig Sichel to the Board of Public Commissioners. See MacColl, *Merchants*, 246; Nodel, *The Ties Between*, 77.

45   MacColl, *Merchants*, 244. Hirsch and Simon were both members of Beth Israel congregation, yet they seem to have been at odds on congregational politics. Hirsch was president of the congregation when Rabbi Stephen Wise was hired, and Wise regarded Hirsch as a key supporter. Simon, who clashed with Wise over the vice issue, was critical of the rabbi's outspoken involvement in public affairs, and, at the time of Wise's departure, tried to amend the congregation's constitution so as to limit the power of future rabbis. Wise saw this as a "slap in the face." Nodel, *The Ties Between*, 97.

46   MacColl, *Merchants*, 324–25. The Board of Police Commissioners, which, through Simon's efforts had been removed from city control and placed in the hands of this governor-appointed body, was a major source of political strength for Simon. See Lansing, *Portland*, 185, 206.

47   "Cohen for Senator," *Morning Oregonian* (Portland, April 8, 1902), 8.

48   For biographical information on Solis-Cohen, see *Scribe* obituary, (November 16, 1928), and "Biography" by Rabbi Elliot Burstein, February 28, 1929, 5. See also Lowenstein, *The Jews of Oregon*, 63–64; Nodel, *The Ties Between*, 53–54; Miranda, *Following a River*, 57–61; and Toll, *Making*, 90–92.

49   MacColl, *Merchants*, 325. See also Lansing, *Portland*, 273–79.

50   MacColl, *Merchants*, 328, 341–42. The Police Commission was one of the most contentious bodies in Oregon politics in this era. It had been created in 1870, and existed on and off until 1903, with the city and state vying for control. The body was sometimes elected (Solis-Cohen had been elected police commissioner in the early 1890s), but generally, it was an appointment, sometimes in the hands of the governor and at others in the hands of the mayor.See Lansing, *Portland*, 137–38,

51   MacColl, *Merchants*, 342.

52   Ibid., 348.

53   Lowenstein, *The Jews of Oregon*, 63.

54   Toll, *Making*, 90.

55   Ibid., 94–95.

56   Ibid., 90; Miranda's profile of Solis-Cohen is similar in tone. Miranda, *Following a River*, 58.

57   Lowenstein, *The Jews of Oregon*, 80.

58   Ibid., 80–82.

59   Ben Selling, Charitable giving ledger, 1927–28, Selling Collection, OJM.

60   MacColl, *Merchants*, 346; Oregon Voters Pamphlet, 1912, 47.

61   Johnston, *The Radical Middle Class*, 29. For more on Harry Lane, see Johnston, chap. 3.

62   *Oregon Voters Pamphlet*, (1912), 46–49.

63   *New York Times*, (March 10, 1912).

64   Walter Pierce, quoted in MacColl, *Merchants*, 346.

65   For example, as Oregon Senate president he played a key role in the enactment of Governor Oswald West's reform legislation, including the creation of the Oregon Public Utilities Commission, the State Tax Commission, and the State Corporations Commission. MacColl, *Merchants*, 444–45.

66   Ibid.

67   *Jewish Tribune*, (November 1, 1912). Advertisements for Selling appear on pp. 8, 10, 11, and 12.

68   The increasing Jewish presence in the neighborhood over the course of the 1910s is clearly visible in community histories and census records. In 1910, East European Jews made up approximately a quarter of the households in Precinct 37, and a quarter of those were headed by a citizen (native born or naturalized). By 1920, in (newly renumbered) Precinct 89, just over 40 percent of households were East European Jews, and of them, nearly 40 percent were citizens. US Census (manuscript), 1910 and 1920.

69   As noted earlier, Solis-Cohen held dual membership in Beth Israel and Ahavai Sholom.

70   Lowenstein, *The Jews of Oregon*, 86. See also Johnston, *The Radical Middle Class*, 32–33. Rabbi Stephen Wise left the city several years before the US Senate campaign in which Lane defeated Ben Selling.

71   "Oregon at War: World War I and the Oregon Experience" State of Oregon Archives, web exhibit, http://arcweb.sos.state.or.us/pages/exhibits/war/

72   In its inaugural issue, the *Scribe* invited all views: "Every form of Jewish life is herewith offered a fair means of publicity. Zionist and non-Zionist, orthodox and reform, race, national and religious adherents will find in these columns news of their leaders and their thots [sic], We shall welcome and give publicity, equal to that given our own, the opinions of any man or woman on the subjects connected with Jewish life." *Scribe*, (September 26, 1919), 1.

73   Ibid.

74   *Scribe* (April 16, 1920), 3.

75   *Scribe* (May 20, 1921), 3.

76   See editorial *Scribe*, (June 45, 1920), 3.

77   See editorials endorsing "Educational Bill" and funding for state institutions, *Scribe*, (May 14, 1920, April 16, 1920), 3

78   For a discussion of western Jews' attitudes toward Asian immigrant communities, see chap. 6 of this volume. See also Eisenberg, *The First to Cry Down Injustice*, chap. 1.

79   *Scribe*, (April 6, 1923), 3. The following month, Wise endorsed the CCAR Social Justice Committee report, which included positions opening

immigration to all people "fleeing persecution and misery" and advocated that "all aliens be unequivocally equal in their legal right with citizens." *Scribe*, (July 16, 1920), 5.

80   The program was published in full in the August 6, 1920 edition, 4, and again on September 28, 1923, 4.

81   *Scribe* (July 16, 1920), 5.

82   *Scribe* (June 22, 1923), 3.

83   Toll, *Making,* chap. 4.

84   Ibid., 110.

85   Ibid., 115. See also Johnston, *The Radical Middle Class,* 74–75.

86   Johnston, *The Radical Middle Class,* 16.

87   Ibid., xi and chap. 1.

88   It must be noted that these precincts included not only the immigrant Jewish community but also diverse others, many of them also immigrants. In the analysis that follows, I provide election results for all the South Portland districts, noting particularly the core Jewish areas. Although none of the precincts can be taken as a perfect representation of the Jewish vote, the heavy Jewish presence in these largely immigrant areas, combined with the fact that Jewish immigrants tended to naturalize relatively quickly, means that these returns were strongly influenced by Jewish constituencies.

89   Lawrence M. Lipin and William Lunch, "Moralistic Direct Democracy: Political Insurgents, Religion and the State in Twentieth Century Oregon" *Oregon Historical Quarterly* 110, no. 4 (2009): 517–28. For the analysis of the vote, see Johnston, *The Radical Middle Class,* 170.

90   Johnston, *The Radical Middle Class,* chap. 7. According to Johnston's analysis, Daly was overwhelmingly opposed on the West Side "except for immigrant South Portland," 110.

91   Ibid., 109.

92   Ibid., 147–48. Despite mutual support between the two causes, Johnston notes a puzzling distance between the two movements.

93   Ibid., 149.

94   Ibid., 150.

95   Precinct level voting records, 1908. Note that, because of the early date, this election is a less reliable approximation of the Jewish vote than are the later elections.

96   Joyce Antler, *The Journey Home: Jewish Women and the American Century* (New York: The Free Press, 1997), 58. Susan Glenn demonstrates that Jewish women on the Lower East Side of New York in 1915 overwhelmingly favored suffrage, and that Jewish immigrant precincts "provided the strongest and most consistent support for suffrage of all Manhattan voters" in the 1915 and 1917 referenda. Susan Glenn, *Daughters of the Shtetl: Life and Labor in the Immigrant Generation* (Ithaca: Cornell University Press, 1990), 215. See also Elinor Lerner, "Jewish Involvement in the New York City Woman Suffrage Movement," *American Jewish History* 70, no. 4 (1981): 442–61 and Klapper, *Ballots, Babies,* chap. 1.

97   Klapper, *Ballots, Babies,* 44.

98   "Boys Like 'Suffrage'" *Oregonian* (April 24, 1919), 15, accessed on *Century of Action: Oregon Women Vote 1912–2012,* centuryofaction.org.

99   Glazer, *Focus of a Community*, 13–14. On the Wise-Duniway friendship, see Klapper, *Ballots, Babies*, 56.

100   Solomon Hirsch served two terms as party chairman. He was elected three times to the state senate and served a term as senate president. He was also nearly elected to the US Senate. Lowenstein, *The Jews of Oregon*, 44.

101   Kimberly Jensen, "Neither Head nor Tail to the Campaign: Esther Pohl Lovejoy and the Oregon Woman Suffrage Victory of 1912," *Oregon Historical Quarterly* 108, no. 3 (2007), 360.

102   Mrs. Selling is listed as one of the attendees at a pro-suffrage lunch in April of 1912. *Oregonian* (April 12, 1912), 16, Centuryofaction.org.

103   *Oregonian* (April 24, 1919), 15, Centuryofaction.org.

104   *Jewish Tribune*, (October 18, 1912), 3.

105   *Jewish Tribune*, (November 1, 1912), 4, 5, 11.

106   Glazer, *Focus of a Community*, 78ff. Nationally, many leaders of the NCJW were strong supporters of suffrage, yet the national convention in 1917 (much to the surprise of the leadership) voted a pro-suffrage resolution down. See Rogow, *Gone to Another Meeting*, 78–80. It is notable that none of this division was evident six years later, when women's suffrage was passed nationally. In 1920, the Portland *Scribe* hailed the passage of the "Susan B. Anthony amendment," commenting that "it is not untimely to regret the slowness with which democracies have recognized the right of women to a full share in the responsibilities as well as the privileges of government." "Events of the Week," *Scribe* (April 2, 1920), 5.

107   *The Bulletin* (newsletter of the Portland Section, NCJW), November, 1924. NCJW Box 7 (publications).

108   Klapper, *Ballots, Babies*, 51

109   Ibid., 52.

110   Ibid., 55

111   Ibid., 36–37.

112   Dave Reid, "City of Brews and Roses: A History of the Social Power of Alcohol in Portland, Oregon from Prohibition to the Present," (Senior Thesis, Willamette University, December 2010), 11–18. Reid emphasizes that Oregon suffrage leader Abigail Scott Duniway worked hard to distance suffrage from prohibition in the 1912 campaign to win votes for suffrage. Indeed, prohibition failed several votes before passing, just after women were enfranchised.

113   Johnston, *The Radical Middle Class*, 170.

114   *Jewish Tribune* (October 30, 1914), 4–5.

115   Ibid., 4.

116   In the October 30, 1914 edition, advertisements appeared for Star Brewery and for Weinhard's Beer.

117   Precinct level voting returns, 1914.

118   Johnston, *The Radical Middle Class*, 169–70. Several different single-tax measures appeared on Oregon ballots in these years. The 1914 measure discussed here proposed a single tax on individuals (not corporations) and exempted the first $1500 of personal property. See also Lipin and Lunch, "Moralistic Direct Democracy," 516–22.

119   Johnston, *The Radical Middle Class*, 169.

120   Lipin and Lunch, "Moralistic Direct Democracy," 522.

121   Johnston, *The Radical Middle Class*, 170. Fifteen West Side precincts voted
       in favor of the single tax, including the precincts of Jewish South Portland.
       None of these fifteen voted in favor of prohibition.

122   Ibid., 178.

123   Ibid.,, 207–08.

124   Ibid., 208.

125   Precinct level voting records, 1916. In his analysis Johnston notes that a run
       of "64 consecutive precincts, beginning in immigrant South Portland" and
       continuing on to the East Side voted in favor of the measure. In this, he
       overlooks the quite mixed response in South Portland. Johnston, *The Radical
       Middle Class*, 209.

126   Glazer, *Focus of a Community*, 75.

127   In this period, these causes included social hygiene and food and drug
       regulation. Glazer, *Focus of a Community*, 137.

128   *The Neighborhood* (Neighborhood House Newsletter) 1, no. 9 (February
       1920), 1. NCJW-Portland Section papers, Oregon Jewish Museum, box 9.
       Regarding the association with the Visiting Nurses Association, see Glazer,
       Focus of a Community, 76.

129   *Scribe*, (October 22, 1920 and October 29, 1920), 3.

130   Toll, *Making*, 146–47.

131   A shift toward more liberal politics, including greater support for labor and
       minorities rights, was beginning to take place during this period in response
       to both the shifting demographics of the Jewish community and growing
       anti-Semitism. These shifts will be discussed in more detail in Chap. 6.

132   For a discussion of the B'nai B'rith lodges, and a broader discussion of the
       emergence of this "ethnic middle class," see Toll, *Making*, chap. 4–5.

133   This was the case in several western communities, including both Portland
       and Seattle. See Eisenberg, Kahn and Toll, *Jews of the Pacific West*, chap. 5.

134   Toll, *Making*, 136.

135   MacColl, *Growth of a City*, 406–09.

136   Ibid.

137   *Oregon Voter's Pamphlet* (1930), 15.

138   Lowenstein, *The Jews of Oregon*, 186.

139   "Julius Meier," *Oregon History Project*, biographies, http://www.
       oregonhistoryproject.org/articles/biographies/julius-meier-biography/.

140   *Oregon Voter* 63, no. 5 (November 1, 1930): 16. See also, numbers 2 and 3,
       October 11 and 18, 1930.

141   MacColl, *Growth*, 389.

142   *Scribe* (August 8, 1930), 1. Interestingly, during the election season, the
       Scribe also published a series of full-page advertisements arguing against
       public power—the central plank in Meier's platform. Such advertisements
       appeared on page two of the paper at least twice a month during this period.

143   Robert Stone, "The Election Jew," *Scribe* (September 26, 1930), 3.

144   *Scribe*, (October 31, 1930), 1.

145   Multnomah County, Abstract of Votes, 1930. Multnomah County Archives.

146   The 96th Precinct was bounded by Sherman, Woods, Second, and the
       Willamette River.

147   In early 1932, the paper noted that the governor and his wife had returned
       from a month in California, running a full-page photo of the couple on the

cover *Scribe* (January 8, 1932), 1. Likewise, the paper noted when Meier left several weeks later for business in Washington, DC, *Scribe* (January 29, 1932), 3.

148   *Scribe* (July 7, 1933), 2, 7.

149   *Scribe* (June 17, 1932), 3, 4.

150   *Scribe* (January 19, 1934), 3; (September 7, 1934), 3.

151   *Scribe* (December 21, 1934), 3.

152   Neveh Zedek's new Torah was dedicated as part of its anniversary celebration in December, 1931. See *Scribe*, (December 18, 1931), 9. Ahavai Sholom's was dedicated in honor of Meier's election. See Gary Miranda, *Following a River*, 80.

153   *Scribe*, (November 7, 1930), 9.

CHAPTER 5

1   Livingston, "Introduction" and Moses Rischin "The Jewish Experience in America: A View from the West," in *Jews of the American West*, 15–25, 26–47.

2   Livingston, *Jews of the American West*, 21.

3   Leonard Dinnerstein, "Desert Oasis to Desert Caucus," in *Jews of the American West*, 147; Thomas Kolsky, *Jews Against Zionism: The American Council for Judaism, 1942–1948* (Philadelphia, 1990), chap. 4.

4   The Pittsburgh Platform, 1885. Jewish Virtual Library (accessed June 5, 2013). For a discussion of the relationship between the emerging nineteenth-century American Reform Movement and Zionism, see Melvin Urofsky, *American Zionism: From Herzl to the Holocaust* (Lincoln: University of Nebraska Press, 1975), 63–64.

5   CCAR Montreal Statement, 1897. Quoted in Evyatar Friesel, "The Meaning of Zionism and Its Influence among the American Jewish Religious Movements" in *Zionism and Religion*, Shmuel Almog, Jehuda Reinharz, and Anita Shapira, eds. (Hanover: Brandeis University Press, 1998), 180.

6   Michael A. Meyer, "American Reform Judaism and Zionism: Early Efforts at Ideological Rapprochement," in *Studies in Zionism* 4, no. 1 (1983): 49–64; Jonathan Sarna, "Converts to Zionism in the American Reform Movement," *Zionism and Religion*, 188–203.

7   Sarna, "Converts to Zionism," 189.

8   Melvin Urofsky, "Zionism in America," in *Encyclopedia of American Jewish History*, Stephen H. Norwood and Eunice G. Pollack, eds. (Santa Barbara: ABC/CLIO, 2008), 1:203.

9   Evyatar Friesel, "The Meaning of Zionism and its Influence among the American Jewish Religious Movements," *Zionism and Religion*, 181.

10   Meyer, "American Reform Judaism and Zionism," 50.

11   Urofsky, "Zionism in America," 204.

12   Ibid., 205.

13   Ibid., 206.

14   Sarna, *American Judaism*, 250.

15   Ibid., 251.

16   See Kolsky, *Jews Against Zionism* (1990), chap. 1; Howard R. Greenstein, *Turning Point: Zionism and Reform Judaism* (Chico: Scholars Press, 1981), chaps. 1–2.

17   Jason Lustig, *Resigning to Change: The Foundation and Transformation of the American Council for Judaism* (master's thesis, Brandeis University, 2009), 15.

18   For a book-length account of the development of the ACJ, see Kolsky, *Jews Against Zionism* (1990).

19   Ibid., chap. 2; Greenstein, *Turning Point*, 45.

20   Lessing J. Rosenwald, "Reply to Zionism" *Life* (June 28, 1943), 11. For a fuller discussion of the ACJ position, see Kolsky, *Jews Against Zionism* (1990), and Robert Silverberg, *If I Forget Thee O Jerusalem* (New York: Pyramid Books, 1970), 197–98.

21   Kolsky, *Jews Against Zionism* (1990), 82.

22   Ibid., 77.

23   Ibid., 82.

24   Thomas Kolsky, *Jews Against Zionism: The American Council for Judaism, 1942–1948* (PhD diss., George Washington University, 1986), 241.

25   Ibid., 241–3, Table 3. San Francisco, with Jews comprising 6.7 percent of the population, had a higher than expected participation rate in the ACJ. Nearly three percent of San Francisco's Jews were council members, in contrast to less than one percent for cities with comparably sized Jewish population.

26   Fred Rosenbaum, "Zionism versus Anti-Zionism," in *Jews of the American West*, 120, 123–24.

27   For Portland figures see Goldberg, "Jewish Spirit on the Urban Frontier," Appendices 2 and 3. For San Francisco figures see Kolsky, "Jews Against Zionism" (1986), 241–43, Table 3.

28   Toll, *Making*, 92.

29   Ibid., 132.

30   Nodel, *The Ties Between*, 107–8.

31   Kolsky, *Jews Against Zionism* (1990), 47, 49, 50, 52. Rabbi Jonah Wise served at Beth Israel until 1926.

32   Kolsky, "Jews Against Zionism" (1986), Appendix D, 507.

33   Lena Kleinberg Holzman and Arthur Markewitz note an ACJ presence at Beth Israel. Holzman and Markewitz oral histories, OJM. Felice Lauterstein Driesen, interview with the author, November 11, 1997.

34   Harold Hirsch oral history (March 14, 1978), OJM, 4.

35   Berkowitz to J. Wise, February 14, 1934, Berkowitz correspondence, colleagues. Congregation Beth Israel Collection, Oregon Jewish Museum. Here, the specific disagreement was over intermarriage ceremonies which Wise was willing to perform but Berkowitz was not. Interestingly, Berkowitz names Max Hirsch as part of this "old crowd" — Hirsch would go on to be a key Portland ACJ activist.

36   Nodel, *The Ties Between*, 135. Sidney Teiser oral history, (January 12, 1977) OJM, 3. In this interview, Teiser notes his involvement in ACJ at the time, and indicates that his position was "mistaken."

37   Oregon Émigré Committee records, Oregon Jewish Museum. Five ACJ activists are listed as members in the OEC records. Mrs. Julius Meier, named as an ACJ activist by Kolsky, while apparently not an OEC member, was affiliated with the group and on at least one occasion wrote an affidavit for a refugee at the request of the committee. An additional two ACJ activists, Aaron Frank and Herbert Sichel, are listed as members of the OEC in community histories, although their names do not appear in the organizational records, which are

incomplete for the 1940s. See Toll, *Making*, 188; and Lowenstein, *Jews of Oregon*, 199.

38   Oregon Émigré Committee minutes, October 7, 1948.

39   Berkowitz to Dr. and Mrs. S. Oppenheimer, April 7, 1942. Berkowitz correspondence, personal, Beth Israel Collection, OJM.

40   John Christgau, *Enemies: World War II Alien Internment* (Ames, Iowa: Bison Books, 1985), 51–85. Christgau documents the cases of several German Jewish internees from the West Coast. See also Harvey Strum, "Jewish Internees in the American South, 1942–1942," *American Jewish Archive* 42, no. 1 (Spring 1990), 27–48.

41   Eisenberg, *The First to Cry Down Injustice*, 83–85. No comparable group opposing the wartime measures against West Coast Nikkei existed in Portland.

42   Rabbi Henry Berkowitz, "Courage and Faith in the Crisis," (sermon, December 12, 1941), Beth Israel Collection, OJM. Unlike his counterparts, Rabbi Irving Reichert at San Francisco's Emanu-El and Rabbi Samuel Koch at Seattle's Temple de Hirsch, Rabbi Berkowitz did not specifically extend his concerns to Japanese Americans. Eisenberg, *The First to Cry Down Injustice*, xi.

43   Jewish Service Association minutes, January 14, 1942 and March 11, 1942, OJM.

44   *Scribe*, January 9, 1942.

45   Kolsky, *Jews Against Zionism* (1990), 49, 64.

46   Lustig, *Resigning to Change*, 31–32, 78, 83.

47   See, for example, oral histories of Lena Kleinberg Holzman (April, 22, 1975) and Arthur Markewitz (September 29, 1977), OJM.

48   Mollie Blumenthal, interview with the author, November 11, 1997. See also Mollie Blumenthal oral history (March 17, 1976), OJM.

49   Toll, *Making*, chap. 4.

50   Lustig, *Resigning to Change*, 15–16.

51   Rabbi Henry Berkowitz to Mrs. Isaac Gilbert (October 3, 1941). Berkowitz, personal correspondence, Beth Israel Collection, OJM. See also Nodel, *The Ties Between*, 132–3.

52   Lowenstein, *The Jews of Oregon*, 77; Nodel, *The Ties Between*, 114.

53   Felice Lauterstein Driesen (daughter of Paula Heller Lauterstein) interview. For further discussion of the role of former colonists as community leaders in Portland, see Eisenberg "From Cooperative Farming to Urban Leadership," 113–132.

54   For an excellent account of Zionism in Portland, and of Wise's role, see Deborah Goldberg, "Jewish Spirit." See also Lowenstein, *The Jews of Oregon*, 152.

55   Sarna, "Converts to Zion," 190. Mark A. Raider, "Stephen S. Wise and the Urban Frontier: American Jewish Life in New York and the Pacific Northwest at the Dawn of the 20th Century" in *Quest Issues in Contemporary Jewish History. Journal of Fondazione CDEC*, 2 (October 2011): 240.

56   Nodel, *The Ties Between*, 83.

57   Lowenstein, *The Jews of Oregon*, 87.

58   Ibid. Goldberg, "Jewish Spirit," 47.

59   Nodel, *The Ties Between*, chap. 5; Lowenstein, *The Jews of Oregon*, chap. 9.

60   Nodel, *The Ties Between*, 98.

61   Toll, *Making*, 93–4.

62   Goldberg, "Jewish Spirit," 31.

63   Toll, *Making*, 93.

64   Nodel, *The Ties Between*, 179. Interestingly, Mrs. Julius Meier was one of the anti-Zionist listed by Kolsky. Kolsky, *Jews Against Zionism* (1986), 507.

65   Goldberg, "Jewish Spirit," 59–60.

66   Rabbi J. Wise to Rabbi H. Berkowitz, February 14, 1934. Henry Berkowitz "Personal Correspondence--Colleagues," Beth Israel Collection, OJM.

67   Rabbi J. Wise to Rabbi H. Berkowitz, January 31, 1934. Berkowitz personal correspondence. Beth Israel Collection, OJM.

68   Berkowitz to Rabbi Edward Israel, January 19, 1940, Berkowitz correspondence. Beth Israel Collection, OJM.

69   Berkowitz to Rabbi Edward Sandrow, July 5, 1935. Berkowitz correspondence. Beth Israel Collection, OJM.

70   Berkowitz to Dr. Felix A. Levy, July 3, 1935. Berkowitz correspondence. Beth Israel Collection, OJM.

71   Kolsky, *Jews Against Zionism*, (1990), 34.

72   Berkowitz to Adolph Oko (former librarian of HUC), August 5, 1937. Berkowitz correspondence. Beth Israel Collection, OJM.

73   Berkowitz to Rabbi James Heller, May 4, 1942. Berkowitz wrote in response to a plea that Heller, as president of the CCAR, sent to the entire membership, appealing for the cancellation of the Atlantic City meeting. Berkowitz correspondence. Beth Israel Collection, OJM. See also Kolsky, *Jews Against Zionism*, (1990), 47. For an example of such a letter see Berkowitz to Rabbi Samuel Goldenson, May 6, 1942.

74   Berkowitz to Heller, June 8, 1942. Berkowitz correspondence. Beth Israel Collection, OJM.

75   Nodel, *The Ties Between*, 139.

76   Berkowitz to Rabbi Edward Israel, January 19, 1940, Berkowitz correspondence. Beth Israel Collection, OJM.

77   Berkowitz to Dr. B. Mossinson, June 9, 1937. Berkowitz correspondence. Beth Israel Collection, OJM.

78   Berkowitz to "Dave and Jeanette," October 24, 1935. Berkowitz correspondence. Beth Israel Collection, OJM.

79   Berkowitz, "Louis D. Brandeis—A Great American," October 10, 1941. Berkowitz sermons.

80   Berkowitz, "Why A Palestine Army?" March 13, 1942. Berkowitz sermons. Beth Israel Collection, OJM.

81   Nodel, *The Ties Between*, 139. An example of a friendship that crossed this line was that between Milton Kahn, the most prominent anti-Zionist in Portland, and Dr. Isadore Brill, another Temple Beth Israel trustee, who gave a speech in March 1944 to the B'nai B'rith lodge, supporting Zionism and attacking the ACJ. Reported in *The New Horizon*, April 1944.

82   Goldberg, "Jewish Spirit," 82.

83   Ibid., 52.

84   Ibid., 48.

85   Interestingly, Newman had served as rabbi of San Francisco's Emanu-El in the late 1920s, where his ardent Zionism antagonized the congregation. He was succeeded by Rabbi Reichert. Fred Rosenbaum, *Visions of Reform: Congregation Emanu-El and the Jews of San Francisco, 1849–1999,* (Berkeley: Judah L. Magnes Museum, 2000), 155–57.

86   *Scribe*, May 15, 1942, June 1942 (in June, the paper began publishing as a monthly).

87   *Scribe*, March 13, 1942.

88   For example, see Lena Kleinberg Holzman oral history (April 22, 1975), OJM, 14.

89   Goldberg, "Jewish Spirit," 52–55.

90   Ibid., chap. 3. Goldberg does an excellent job of reviewing this activity.

91   Friesel, "Meaning of Zionism," 179.

92   Goldberg, "Jewish Spirit," 61–62.

93   Ibid., 59.

94   Ibid., 60; Lowenstein, *The Jews of Oregon,*155.

95   Goldberg, "Jewish Spirit, 64.

CHAPTER 6

1   Eric Goldstein, *The Price of Whiteness: Jews, Race and American Identity* (Princeton: Princeton University Press, 2006), chap. 3. See also Hasia Diner, *In the Almost Promised Land: American Jews and Blacks, 1915–1935* (Baltimore: Johns Hopkins University Press, 1995).

2   There is a growing literature on Jews and whiteness, or, in some of the more popularized versions, of how Jews "became white." Key works include Goldstein, *The Price of Whiteness,* Michael Alexander *Jazz Age Jews* (Princeton: Princeton University Press, 2001), David Roediger *Working Toward Whiteness: How America's Immigrants became White* (New York: Basic Books, 2006), and Matthew Frye Jacobson *Whiteness of a Different Color: European Immigrants and the Alchemy of Race* (Cambridge: Harvard University Press, 1998).

3   This chapter expands a discussion of these themes developed in Eisenberg, *The First to Cry Down Injustice,* chap. 1.

4   Cline, *Community Structure,* 98–105. The parallel structure of Jewish and Christian gentlemen's clubs was common in American cities in this period. Jenna Weissman Joselit, "Fun and Games: The American Jewish Social Club" in *The Columbia History of Jews and Judaism in America*, Marc Lee Raphael, ed. (New York: Columbia University Press, 2008), 248.

5   For example, Lowenstein frames an 1858 anti-Semitic outburst by *Oregonian* editor Thomas Dryer as one of several "occasional expressions of anti-Semitism," exceptions to the general pattern. Lowenstein, *The Jews of Oregon,* 66.

6   See Goldstein, *The Price of Whiteness;* Roediger, *Working Toward Whiteness;* and Jacobson, *Whiteness of a Different Color.*

7   Patricia Limerick, *Legacy of Conflict: The Unbroken Past of the American West* (New York Norton, 1987), 27.

8   Alexander Saxton, *Indispensable Enemy: Labor and the Anti-Chinese Movement in California* (Berkeley and Los Angeles: University of California Press, 1971).

9   Linda Gordon, *The Great Arizona Orphan Abduction* (Cambridge: Harvard University Press, 2001).

10   Tomas Almaguer, *Racial Fault Lines: The Historical Origins of White Supremacy in California* (Berkeley: University of California Press, 1994), 7.

11   Frank Van Nuys, *Americanizing the West: Race, Immigrants, and Citizenship, 1890–1930* (Lawrence: University Press of Kansas, 2002), 15.

12   Hubert Howe Bancroft, *Chronicles of the Builders of the Commonwealth*, vol. 7, (1892), 148.

13   Lowenstein, *The Jews of Oregon*, 32.

14   Sylvan Durkheimer oral history, (March 3, 1975), OJM, 15. Durkheimer was Moses Fried's grandson.

15   Durkheimer oral history, 24.

16   Samuel Rothchild, "The Indian War of 1878" originally published in *Reminiscences of Oregon Pioneers*, compiled by the Pioneer Ladies Club, Pendleton, Oregon, 1937. The piece appears as Appendix A in Sanders, *Samuel Rothchild*.

17   Raider, "Stephen S. Wise and the Urban Frontier," 244–45.

18   By 1880, 5.4 percent of the total Oregon population was born in China. Since the overwhelming majority of Chinese immigrants were adult men, they represented a far larger portion of the adult male population. US Census, 1880.

19   MacColl, *Merchants, Money, Power*, 167.

20   Toll, *Making*, 82–83. MacColl, *Merchants, Money, Power*, 167.

21   MacColl, *Merchants, Money, Power*, 239–40. See also William Toll, "The Chinese Community," in *Commerce, Climate, & Community: A History of Portland & Its People*, Oregon History Project, http://www. oregonhistoryproject.org/narratives/commerce-climate-and-community-a-history-of-portland-and-its-people/ accessed August, 2012. Although several sources list Selling and Goldsmith as part of this force, Wasserman is included in some sources, including Cline, *Community Structure*, 86.

22   Toll, *Making*, 82.

23   Elaine S. Friedman, "Ben Selling" *Oregon Encyclopedia*, http:// oregonencyclopedia.org/articles/selling_ben_1852_1931_/.

24   Cline, *Community Structure*, 85.

25   See Toll, *Commerce, Climate, & Community*.

26   Carl Abbott, *Portland in Three Centuries* (Corvallis: Oregon State University Press, 2011), 57.

27   Cline, *Community Structure*, 85–86.

28   The efforts were led by Simon's Oregon rival, Sen. John Mitchell, and Rep. Julius Kahn, a member of the San Francisco Jewish community. See Martin B. Gold, *Forbidden Citizens: Chinese Exclusion and the US Congress: A Legislative History* (Alexandria, VA: The Capitol.Net, 2012), 327. Although Simon had won Mitchell's seat in 1898, Mitchell was subsequently elected to Oregon's other seat, in 1900.

29   MacColl, *Merchants, Money, Power*, 239.

30   Ibid., 167–68; Cline, *Community Structure*, 85.

31   MacColl, *Merchants, Money, Power*, 239. Scott is considered a key shaper of conservative opinion during his forty years as editor. See "Harvey W. Scott," Oregon History Project, http://www.ohs.org/education/oregonhistory/Oregon-Biographies-Harvey-Scott.cfm

32   MacColl, *Merchants, Money, Power,* 238.

33   Toll, *Making,* 83.

34   Ibid. Toll goes on to explore the attitudes of a younger, emerging Jewish leader, David Solis-Cohen, who expressed rather mixed responses to the Chinese, criticizing their living conditions and failure to adopt American standards, while expressing respect for Chinese culture and connection to their heritage.

35   A good example is the difference in the two communities' responses to Zionism and anti-Zionism. See Chap. 5.

36   Reva Clar and William M. Kramer, "Chinese-Jewish Relations in the Far West: 1850–1950," *Western States Jewish History* 21, no. 1 (1988): part I, 22–25.

37   Ibid., 30–34.

38   Ibid., 24. See also Rudolph Glanz, "Jews and Chinese in America," *Jewish Social Studies* 16, no. 3 (1954): 219–34. Glanz's assessment of early California Jewish attitudes is somewhat more mixed, although he, too, documents the clash between the eastern and western Jewish press on this issue in the 1870s and 1880s.

39   Clar and Kramer, "Chinese-Jewish Relations," part 1, 24–25.

40   Ibid., 25–26.

41   Clar and Kramer, "Chinese-Jewish Relations in the Far West" *Western States Jewish History,* 20, no. 2 (1989): part 2, 134.

42   These emerging sensibilities have been explored by a number of historians. See Marc Dollinger, *Quest for Inclusion: Jews and Liberalism in Modern America* (Princeton University Press, 2000) and Goldstein, *The Price of Whiteness.*

43   See Tony Michels, *A Fire in Their Hearts: Yiddish Socialists in New York* (Cambridge: Harvard University Press, 2009) and Diner, *In the Almost Promised Land.*

44   There are several schools of thought about the reasons for the increasing liberalism/Progressivism of the Jewish community in this period. Mervis emphasizes the broader embrace of Progressivism among religious leaders in America. See Leonard Mervis, "The Social Justice Movement and the American Reform Rabbi," *American Jewish Archives* 7, no. 2 (July 1955): 175–76. On "outsider status," see Michael Rogin, *Black Face, White Noise: Jewish Immigrants in the Hollywood Melting Pot.* (Berkeley: University of California Press, 1998); on rising anti-Semitism, see Gulie Ne'eman Arad, *America, Its Jews and the Rise of Nazism* (Bloomington: Indiana University Press, 2000); Henry Feingold *A Time for Searching* (Baltimore: Johns Hopkins University Press, 1995); Dollinger's *Quest for Inclusion* focuses instead on liberal politics as a mechanism for acculturation.

45   Sarna, *American Judaism,* 195–96.

46   Jeff LaLande, "Oregon's Last Conservative US Senator: Some Light Upon the Little Known Career of Guy Cordon," *Oregon Historical Quarterly* 110, no. 2 (Summer 2009): 230. See also Abbott, *Portland in Three Centuries,* 113.

47   Jonah Wise, "The Rabbinical Convention," *Scribe* (July 16, 1920), 5.

48   "Social Justice Program: Adopted by the Central Conference of American Rabbis at Rochester, NY, July, 1920," *Scribe* (August 6, 1920), 4.

49   Editorial, "A Social Program" *Scribe* (August 6, 1920), 3.

50   *Scribe.* The article on the CCAR position appeared on June 8, 1923; with editorials endorsing this view on June 22 and June 29, 1923.

51   See "The Twelve Hour Day" editorial, *Scribe* (June 22, 1923), 3.

52   "My Problem and Your Responsibility," (May 4, 1928), Rabbi Henry Berkowitz sermons, Beth Israel Collection, OJM.

53   Berkowitz often cited the committee in sermons. For example, in a 1941 sermon, titled "American Labor in Crisis," Berkowitz referenced the CCAR platform. (April 25, 1941), Congregation Beth Israel records, OJM.

54   Berkowitz, "The White Feather in the Blue Eagle," Yom Kippur sermon, September 30, 1933 Beth Israel Collection. OJM.

55   "A Race Problem," *The Neighborhood* (newsletter) 2, no. 6 (November 1920), Neighborhood House, Council of Jewish Women Collection, Box 9, OJM.

56   *Scribe,* March 23, 1923.

57   *Scribe,* July 3, 1925, 5.

58   *Scribe,* May 12, 1922, 7; May 19, 1922, 3.

59   The *Scribe* provided much positive coverage of Meier during the campaign but said little about the anti-Semitic tone of some of the attacks on him. See Chap. 4.

60   For example, in the *Scribe* ran a detailed piece on the dangers of international anti-Semitism in the August 6, 1920 issue. "Israel Zangwill and the Jewish Peril" (August 6, 1920), 4.

61   These included stories on German opposition to Hitler, Austrian Nazis, Romanian opposition to Nazism, a local relief drive for German refugees in Palestine, a plea to Roosevelt to help German Jews, a Congressional investigation of Nazi propaganda in the United States, an American charged with sponsoring pro-Nazi propaganda, and the establishment of a Palestine campaign to assist German refugees. *Scribe* (January 19, 1934), 1.

62   *Scribe* (July 31, 1936), 3.

63   *Scribe* (February 18, 1938), 1.

64   Toll, *Making,* chap. 4.

65   Elaine Cohen oral history, OJM, (April 21, 2009), 2.

66   Quoted in Harry Stein, *Gus J. Solomon: Liberal Politics, Jews, and the Federal Courts* (Portland: Oregon Historical Society Press, 2006), 8.

67   Quoted in Lowenstein, *The Jews of Oregon,* 178.

68   Stein, *Gus J. Solomon,* 18; Lowenstein, *The Jews of Oregon,* 170.

69   Lowenstein, *The Jews of Oregon,* 162.

70   Leo Levinson oral history, OJM (August 13, 1976), 49, 7.

71   It is notable that Dolph, Simon, and Mitchell from this firm all served in the US Senate. Mitchell and Simon—by then no longer law partners— made rival claims to the Senate seat in the disputed 1896 election. Future Oregon governor, Julius Meier, was a lawyer at Dolph, Mallory and Simon early in his career as well.

72   Solomon, quoted in Stein, *Gus J. Solomon,* 22–4

73   Stein, *Gus J. Solomon,* 28.

74   Michael Munk, "Oregon's Scottsboro Case" *The Portland Alliance* (February, 2001). Accessed online at http://college.lclark.edu/programs/

political_economy/student_resources/past/ (October 12, 2012). See also Stein, *Gus J. Solomon*, 28.

75   Goldstein, *Price of Whiteness*, 159.

76   Diner, *In the Almost Promised Land*, 42.

77   *Scribe*, April 21, 1933, 1, 4.

78   *Scribe*, May 5, 1933, 4.

79   Theodore Jordan Case. Folders: "International Labor Defense: Jordan Case, Petitions" [AF 160957] and "International Labor Defense: Jordan Case Resolution/Unconditional Release" [AF 160958], Portland City Archives.

80   Theodore Jordan Case. Folder: "ILD: Jordan Case, Leaflets and Flyers." Portland City Archives.

81   "Mob Violence," (December 22, 1933), Rabbi H. Berkowitz sermons, Beth Israel Collection, OJM. Berkowitz spoke from an outline, so it is impossible to know with certainty whether the rabbi mentioned the Oregon case. The collection of sermons for this period is incomplete. Jordan's conviction and death sentence were frequently referred to as a "legal lynching" in the campaign materials. See, for example, *Oregon Defender* (Oregon Section, International Labor Defense) 1, no. 3 (August 1933): 1.

82   *The Neighborhood*, 2, no. 12 (May 1921): 2–3.

83   For a more detailed discussion of Jewish responses to anti-Japanese measures through the World War II era, see Eisenberg, *The First to Cry Down Injustice*.

84   *Scribe* (April 6, 1923), 3.

85   *Scribe* (February 20, 1942), 4. For further analysis of this coverage, see Eisenberg, *The First to Cry Down Injustice*, 64–66.

86   Rabbi Henry Berkowitz, "Liberty and Justice for all—Except Negroes," (March 20, 1942) Berkowitz sermons, Beth Israel Collection, OJM.

87   I have analyzed the Jewish silence on this issue at length in *The First to Cry Down Injustice*. On the national response, see also Cheryl Greenberg, "Black and Jewish Responses to Japanese Internment" *Journal of American Ethnic History* 14, no. 2 (Winter 1995): 3–37.

88   Gus Solomon, oral history, (February 16, 1976) OJM.

89   Peter Irons credits Solomon with bringing the Yasui case to the attention of the national ACLU, but they chose not to get involved. Irons, *Justice at War: The Story of the Japanese American Internment Cases,* (Oxford: Oxford University Press, 1983), 114.

90   Stein, *Gus J. Solomon*, 76.

91   Ibid, 80.

92   Ibid., 38.

93   Ibid., 43.

94   Ibid., 79.

95   Gus Solomon oral history, (OJM), 9.

96   Goldstein, *Whiteness of a Different Color*, 57.

97   Dollinger, *Quest for Inclusion*, 5.

98   Goldstein, *Whiteness of a Different Color*, 57.

99   Ibid., 195.

100 Diner, *Jews of the United States*, 260. On postwar "racial liberalism," see Goldstein, *Whiteness of a Different Color*, 194–201. See also Cheryl

Greenberg, *Troubling the Waters: Black-Jewish Relations in the American Century* (Princeton: Princeton University Press, 2006), chap. 4.

101   Diner, *Jews of the United States*, 265–66.

102   Ibid., 271. See also Goldstein, *Whiteness of a Different Color*, 199; Greenberg, *Troubling the Waters*, 163–65

103   Gus Solomon oral history (OJM), 14.

104   Meeting program, Council of Jewish Women, Portland Section, February 6, 1946 (NCJW Records, Box 7, Publications), OJM.

105   Gus Solomon oral history (OJM), 14.

106   For details on the committee's efforts, see Stein, *Gus J. Solomon*, 80–82.

107   "Oregon Nikkei History: A Brief Summary" (part 3), Oregon Nikkei Endowment. Accessed online http://www.discovernikkei.org/en/journal/2010/6/4/oregon-nikkei-history/

108   Both McWilliams and Berry are quoted in Stuart McElderry, *The Problem of the Color Line: Civil Rights and Racial Ideology in Portland Oregon, 1944–1965* (PhD Dissertation, University of Oregon 1996), 112–13.

109   "Judaism and the Dignity of Man," October 9, 1942, 5–6. Rabbi H. Berkowitz sermons, Beth Israel Collection, OJM.

110   *Bulletin*, October 20, 1950. Beth Israel Collection, OJM.

111   *Bulletin*, November 3, 1950. Though reported in the November 3 newsletter, in the "Rabbi in the Community" column, the date of the event was on October 4. Likewise, the YWCA event took place on March 18, 1952, but was reported in the April 6 *Bulletin*.

112   *Bulletin*, April 30, 1954. Beth Israel Collection, OJM.

113   *Bulletin*, February 14, 1958. Beth Israel Collection, OJM.

114   Goldstein, *Price of Whiteness*, 148.

115   Ibid., 147–48.

116   William Gordon oral history, OJM (January 28, 1975), 4.

117   See the detailed discussion of this shift in chap. 3.

118   Archie Goldman to John Whitelaw, Executive Secretary of the Council of Social Agencies, December 27, 1948. Neighborhood House, Community Era Box 5 folder: Council of Social Agencies, OJM. The state bill passed in 1949.

119   Mrs. Seymour Coblens, "State Legislation," *The Bulletin* (March, 1953), NCJW collection, box 7, OJM. Note that the phrase "under God" would be added to the Pledge of Allegiance in 1954.

120   "Juvenile Justice" (folder), NCJW collection, box 3, OJM.

121   *The Bulletin* (December 1955), NCJW collection, box 7, OJM.

122   *The Bulletin* (October, 1963), NCJW collection, box 7, OJM.

123   McElderry, *Problem of the Color Line*, 119.

124   Ibid., 123. As McElderry notes, this was met by some resistance within the African American community and preexisting civil rights groups, including the NAACP.

125   Lowenstein, *The Jews of Oregon*, 170.

126   Greenberg, *Troubling the Waters*, 122.

127   "Portland 1952: One Ethnic Group Supporting Another" (1962), David Robinson to Hyman Balk (October 3, 1952), Congregation Tifereth Israel collection, OJM. This folder also contains a number of undated newspaper clippings about the incident.

128   Irvin Goodman is listed as the "Author of Ordinance to End Jim Crow, submitted to City Council on Jan. 27, 1949," on a poster for a public meeting at the YWCA. Poster published in Lowenstein, *The Jews of Oregon,* 182.

129   Lowenstein, *The Jews of Oregon,* 182–83.

130   McElderry, *Problem of the Color Line,* 155.

131   Ibid., 144, 149–51.

132   Ibid., 158. Maurine, who was not Jewish, was the wife of Richard Neuberger. Both Maurine and Richard would serve in the Oregon legislature, and Richard would go on to serve as one of Oregon's US Senators, elected in 1954. Maurine also served as an elected US Senator after her husband's death in March 1960.

133   Ibid., 190–92.

134   Ibid., 183.

135   Susannah Malarkey oral history (OHS), quoted in McElderry, *Problem of the Color Line,* 179–80.

136   Harry Gevurtz oral history, (April 3, 1974), OJM, 16–17. Gevurtz would become president of Congregation Beth Israel in 1958.

137   McElderry, *Problem of the Color Line,* 182.

138   Stein, *Gus J. Solomon,* 203.

139   Meyer Eisenberg, recounted to the author via e-mail, June 7, 2013. (Eisenberg is the author's father).

140   Donna Sinclair, "Arlington Club", *Oregon Encyclopedia,* http://oregonencyclopedia.org/articles/arlington_club/#.VTmFqiFVhHw.

141   Stein, *Gus J. Solomon,* 203.

142   *The Jewish Review* 3, no. 10 (June 1962): 8.

143   Stein, *Gus J. Solomon,* 203–06.

144   Ibid., 204.

145   Nodel, *The Ties Between,* 129.

146   *The Jewish Review* 1, no. 6 (July-August 1959): 3.

147   Rabbi Emanuel Rose oral history, (March 10, 1981), OJM, 6.

AFTERWORD

1   There is a vast literature on the dissolution of this coalition in the mid-1960s and its complex causes. For a strong summary see Greenberg, *Troubling the Waters,* chap. 6. Tellingly, she titles this chapter "Things Fall Apart."

2   For example, reports from groups such as the Community Relations Council and the Anti-Defamation League appear periodically and mention civil rights as a continuing key priority and action area. See, for example, *Jewish Review,* 9, no. 6 (June 1968): 2.

3   Growing only from 7,128 in 1950 to 8,000 in 1980, the Portland Jewish community shot up to 8,735 in 1980 and then nearly tripled in the final decades of the century, to 25,000 in 1999. Eisenberg, Toll, and Kahn, *Jews of the Pacific Coast,* Table 3, 207.

Bibliography

PERIODICALS
American Hebrew News (Portland, 1893-1900)
The Bulletin (Portland Section, Council of Jewish Women newsletter)
Chronicling America newspaper database. http://chroniclingamerica.loc.gov/
Historic Oregon Newspaper database, University of Oregon. http://oregonnews.
   uoregon.edu
The Jewish Review (Portland, 1959-2012)
The Jewish Scribe (Portland, 1919-53)
The Jewish Tribune (Portland, 1902-19)
The Neighborhood (Portland, Neighborhood House newsletter)
Oregon Native Son
Oregon Voter

MANUSCRIPT COLLECTIONS
Oregon Historical Society
   Congregation Neveh Zedek Talmud Torah. *Anniversary Book*. 1936.
   Olcott, Ben. "Proclamation Against the Ku Klux Klan, 1922." (May 13, 1922),
      accessed http://www.ohs.org/education/oregonhistory/historical_records
Oregon Jewish Museum
   Congregation Beth Israel Collection
   Congregation Tifereth Israel Collection
   Jewish Service Association Collection
   Neighborhood House Collection
   Nudelman, Eugene. "The Family of Joseph Nudelman"
   Oregon Émigré Committee Collection
   Portland Section, Council of Jewish Women Collection
   Ben Selling Collection
   Shaarie Torah Collection
   Shirley Tanzer Oral History Collection
Oregon State Archives
   Oregon, Precinct Level Voting Records, 1916, 1922, 1930. Abstract of Votes,
   Multnomah County
   Oregon *Voters' Pamphlets*, 1912, 1914, 1916, 1930. Oregon Voters' Pamphlet
      Project, State of Oregon Archives, accessed online: http://library.state.or.us/
      databases/subjects/Voters_Pamphlet.php.
Portland City Archives
   Theodore Jordan Case Files

Willamette Heritage Center, Salem, Oregon
  Samuel Adolph file
  City of Gervais Centennial Commemorative Book, 1878-1978, written & compiled by Mrs. Carl Prantl (1978)
  City of Salem collection
  Salem and Marion County Directories, 1893, 1905, 1909, 1911
  McKinley Mitchell file

PRIMARY SOURCES
Benjamin Burgunder papers, "Biographical Note." Eastern Washington State Historical Society, Northwest Digital Archives, http://nwda-db.orbiscascade. org/ark:/80444/xv61474

"Dictation from McKinley Mitchell," Gervais. Notes by J.A. Moore, 1885. Bancroft Collection.

The Jewish Immigration Bulletin, March 1915, "Sixth Annual Report of the Hebrew Sheltering and Immigrant Aid Society of America" 5, no. 3 (March 1915).

Kohanski, Dorothy. "The Dellar Family Tree." Congregation Neveh Shalom Archive.

Oregon State Census, 1895.

Portland City Directories, 1890, 1900, 1910, 1920.

Portrait and Biographical Record of the Willamette Valley, Oregon. Chicago: Chapman Publishing Company, 1903.

Salem Pioneer Cemetery. Burial Records. www.salempioneercemetery.org

United States Federal Census, 1850, 1860, 1870, 1880, 1900, 1910, 1920, 1930. www.ancestry.com

ORAL HISTORIES
Oregon Jewish Museum:
  Leo Adler (July 13, 1977)
  Miriam Boskowitz Aiken (July 22, 1974)
  Gertrude Bachman (November 28, 1973)
  Kathryn Kahn Blumenfield (November 26, 1976)
  Mollie Blumenthal (March 17, 1976)
  Hannah Mihlstin Bodner (February, 23, 1976)
  Ernie Bonyhadi (December 4, 2007)
  Frances Schnitzer Bricker (May 18, 1977)
  Vera Slifman Brownstein (February 21, 1978)
  Ilaine Cohen (April 21, 2009).
  Frieda Cohn (April 25, 1975)
  Marguerite Swett Dilsheimer (June 11, 1975)
  Felice Lauterstein Driesen (May 9, 1975)
  Sylvan Durkheimer (March 3, 1975)
  Gertrude Feves (May 27, 1975)
  Fannie Kenin Friedman (May 4, 1974)
  Sadie Cohen Geller (January 22, 1976)

Harry Gevurtz (April 3, 1974)

William Gordon (January 28, 1975)

Carrie Bromberg Hervin (May 3, 1974)

Harold Hirsch (July 7 and 26, August 10, 11, 13, 1977; December 14, 1977; March 14, 1978)

Lena Kleinberg Holzman (April 22, 1975)

Sadie Decklebaum Horenstein (December 9, 1975)

Manly Labby (January 27, 1975; February 3, 1976)

Joyce Loeb (September 3, 2008; May 27, 2010)

Arthur Markewitz (September 29, 1977)

Albert Menashe (August 10, 2010).

Joanna Menashe (September 29, 1975).

Toinette Menashe (November 10, 2004)

Victor Menashe (February 23, 2007)

Leo Levinson (August 13, 1976)

Adelaide Lowenson Selling (December 7, 1973)

Diane Holzman Nemer (May 27, 1975)

Nettie Enkilis Olman (n.d., circa 1976)

Harry Policar (September 25, 1975 and January 29, 1976).

Augusta ("Gussie") Kirshner Reinhardt (December 7, 1975)

Rabbi Emanuel Rose (March 10, 1981)

Mary Friedman Rosenberg (June 5, 1975)

Miriam Rosenfeld (April 15, 1975)

Joy Babani Russell (June 8, 2009).

Rachel Fain Schneider (January 24, 1978)

Beulah Menashe Schauffer (July 19, 2011).

Hansa Brill Shapiro (February 12, 1974).

Estelle Director Sholkoff (May 21, 1975)

Gus Solomon (February 16, 1976)

Theodore Swett (February 15, 1982)

William Swett (February 24, 1977)

Sidney Teiser (January 12, 1977)

Gladys Trachtenberg (December 11, 1973; August 29, 1977)

Oregon Historical Society:

Hobart Mitchell (May 4, 1977)

Interviews with the Author:

Mollie Blumenthal (November 11, 1997).

Felice Lauterstein Dreisen (November 11, 1997).

SECONDARY SOURCES

Abbott, Carl. *Portland: Gateway to the Northwest*. Northridge: Windsor Publications, 1985.

———. *Portland in Three Centuries*. Corvallis, OR: Oregon State University Press, 2011.

Abrams, Jeanne E. *Jewish Women Pioneering the Frontier Trail*. New York: New York University Press, 2006.

Alexander, Michael. *Jazz Age Jews*. Princeton: Princeton University Press, 2001.

Almaguer, Tomas. *Racial Fault Lines: The Historical Origins of White Supremacy in California*. Berkeley: University of California Press, 1994.

Almog, Shmuel, Jehuda Reinharz and Anita Shapira, eds. *Zionism and Religion*. Hanover, NH: Brandeis University Press, 1998.

Antler, Joyce. *The Journey Home: Jewish Women and the American Century*. New York: The Free Press, 1997.

Apsler, Alfred. *Northwest Pioneer: The Story of Louis Fleischner*. Philadelphia: Jewish Publication Society, 1960.

Arad, Gulie Ne'eman. *America, Its Jews and the Rise of Nazism*. Bloomington: Indiana University Press, 2000.

Bancroft, Hubert Howe. *Chronicles of the Builders of the Commonwealth*, vol. 7, 1892.

Bauman, Mark K. *The Southerner as American: Jewish Style*. Cincinnati: American Jewish Archives, 1996.

Barkai, Avraham. *Branching Out: German-Jewish Immigration to the United States, 1820-1914*. New York: Holmes and Meier, 1994.

Barkan, Elliot. *From All Points: America's Immigrant West, 1870s–1952*. Bloomington: Indiana University Press, 2007.

Blumenthal, Helen. "The New Odessa Colony of Oregon, 1882–1886." *Western States Jewish Historical Quarterly* 14, no. 4 (July 1983): 321–332.

Century of Action: Oregon Women Vote 1912-2012, www.centuryofaction.org.

Christgau, John. *Enemies: World War II Alien Internment*. Ames, Iowa: Bison Books, 1985.

Clar, Reva and William M. Kramer. "Chinese-Jewish Relations in the Far West: 1850-1950," pt. 1, *Western States Jewish History* 21, no. 1 (1988): 12–35.

Clar, Reva and William M. Kramer. "Chinese-Jewish Relations in the Far West: 1850-1950," pt. 2. *Western States Jewish History* 21, no. 2 (1989): 243–253.

Cline, Robert Scott. *Community Structure on the Urban Frontier: The Jews of Portland Oregon, 1849–1887*. Master's thesis, Portland State University, 1982.

_____. "The Jews of Portland, Oregon: A Statistical Dimension, 1860–1880." *Oregon Historical Quarterly* 88, no. 1 (1987): 4–25.

Cone, Molly, Howard Droker, and Jacqueline Williams. *Family of Strangers: Building a Jewish Community in Washington State*. Seattle: University of Washington Press, 2003.

Diner, Hasia. "American West, New York Jewish." In *Jewish Life in the American West*, edited by Ava F. Kahn, 33–52. Seattle and Los Angeles: University of Washington Press and Autry Museum of Western Heritage, 2002.

_____. *In the Almost Promised Land: American Jews and Blacks, 1915–1935*. Baltimore: Johns Hopkins University Press, 1995.

_____. *Jews of the United States*. Berkeley: University of California Press, 2004.

Diner, Hasia and Beryl Benderly. *Her Works Praise Her: A History of Jewish Women in America from Colonial Times to the Present*. New York: Basic Books, 2002.

Dinnerstein, Leonard. "Desert Oasis to Desert Caucus." In *Jews of the American West*, edited by Rischin and Livingston, 136–163.

Dollinger, Marc. *Quest for Inclusion: Jews and Liberalism in Modern America.* Princeton: Princeton University Press, 2000.

Eisenberg, Ellen. "Argentine and American Jewry: A Case for Contrasting Immigrant Origins," *American Jewish Archives* 47, (Spring-Summer 1995): 1–16.

_____. "Beyond San Francisco: The Failure of Anti-Zionism in Portland, Oregon," *American Jewish History* 86, no. 3 (September 1998): 309–321.

_____. *The First to Cry Down Injustice? Western Jews and Japanese Removal during WWII.* Lanham, MD: Lexington Books/Rowman & Littlefield, 2008.

_____. "From Cooperative Farming to Urban Leadership." In *Jewish Life in the American West*, edited by Ava F. Kahn, 113–131.

_____. "Immigrants, Ethnics, and Natives: Jewish Women in Portland, 1910–1940," unpublished paper, Western Jewish Studies Association annual meeting, March 1999.

_____. *Jewish Agricultural Colonies in New Jersey, 1880-1920.* Syracuse: Syracuse University Press, 1995.

_____. "Transplanted to the Rose City: The Creation of East European Jewish Communities in Portland," *Journal of American Ethnic History* 19, no. 3 (Spring 2000): 82–97.

Eisenberg, Ellen, Ava F. Kahn, William Toll. *Jews of the Pacific Coast: Reinventing Community on America's Edge.* Seattle: University of Washington Press, 2009.

Eulenberg, Julia Nieburhr. "Joseph Brown: The Deadly Errand of a Pacific Northwest Pioneer, 1862." *Western States Jewish History* 45, no. 1 (Fall 2012): 27–37.

Feingold, Henry. *A Time for Searching: Entering the Mainstream, 1920–1945.* Baltimore: American Jewish Historical Society/Johns Hopkins University Press, 1995.

Ferris, Marci Cohen and Mark I. Greenberg, editors. *Jewish Roots in Southern Soil: A New History.* Hanover, NH: University Press of New England/Brandeis University Press, 2006.

Friedman, Elaine S. "Ben Selling" *Oregon Encyclopedia*, http://oregonencyclopedia. org/articles/selling_ben_1852_1931_/

Friesel, Evyatar. "The Meaning of Zionism and Its Influence among the American Jewish Religious Movements." In *Zionism and Religion*, edited by Almog, Reinharz and Shapira, 175–187.

Glanz, Rudolph. "Vanguard to the Russians: The Poseners of America" *YIVO* 18 (1983): 1–37.

Glazer, Michele. "The Durkheimers of Oregon," *Western States Jewish Historical Quarterly* 10, no. 3 (1978): 202–209.

_____. *Focus of a Community: Neighborhood House 1897–1929.* Unpublished manuscript, 1982. Oregon Jewish Museum.

Glenn, Susan. *Daughters of the Shtetl: Life and Labor in the Immigrant Generation.* Ithaca: Cornell University Press, 1990.

Gold, Martin B. *Forbidden Citizens: Chinese Exclusion and the US Congress: A Legislative History.* Alexandria, VA: The Capitol.Net, 2012.

Goldberg, Deborah. "Jewish Spirit on the Urban Frontier: Zionism in Portland, 1901–1941." Unpublished senior thesis, Reed College, 1982.

Goldstein, Eric. *The Price of Whiteness: Jews, Race and American Identity.* Princeton: Princeton University Press, 2006.

Gordon, Linda. *The Great Arizona Orphan Abduction.* Cambridge: Harvard University Press, 2001.

Greenberg, Cheryl. "Black and Jewish Responses to Japanese Internment," *Journal of American Ethnic History* 14, no. 2 (Winter 1995): 3–37.

_____. *Troubling the Waters: Black-Jewish Relations in the American Century.* Princeton: Princeton University Press, 2006.

Greene, Victor. "Old-time Folk Dancing and Music among the Second Generation, 1920–50." In *American Immigration and Ethnicity*, edited by David Gerber and Alan Kraut, New York: Palgrave Macmillan, 2005.

Greenstein, Howard R. *Turning Point: Zionism and Reform Judaism.* Chico, CA: Scholars Press, 1981.

Herlihy, Patricia. *Odessa: A History.* Boston: Harvard University Press, 1986.

Herman, Felicia. "From Priestess to Hostess." In *Women and American Judaism*, edited by Jonathan Sarna and Pam Nadell, 148–181. Hanover, NH: Brandeis University Press, 2001.

Irons, Peter. *Justice at War: The Story of the Japanese American Internment Cases.* Oxford: Oxford University Press, 1983.

Jacobson, Matthew Frye. *Whiteness of a Different Color: European Immigrants and the Alchemy of Race.* Cambridge: Harvard University Press, 1998.

Jensen, Kimberly. "Neither Head nor Tail to the Campaign: Esther Pohl Lovejoy and the Oregon Woman Suffrage Victory of 1912" *Oregon Historical Quarterly* 108, no. 3 (Fall 2007): 350–383.

Johnston, Robert. *The Radical Middle Class: Populist Democracy and the Question of Capitalism in Progressive Era Portland, Oregon.* Princeton: Princeton University Press, 2003.

Joselit, Jenna Weissman. "Fun and Games: The American Jewish Social Club." In *The Columbia History of Jews and Judaism in America*, edited by Marc Lee Raphael, 246–262. New York: Columbia University Press, 2008.

Kahn, Ava F., ed. *Jewish Life in the American West.* Los Angeles: Autry Museum of Western Heritage/University of Washington Press, 2002. Reprint, Berkeley: Heyday Books, 2004.

Kahn, Ava F. and Ellen Eisenberg. "Western Reality: Jewish Diversity during the 'German' Period." *American Jewish History* 92, no. 4 (December 2004): 455–479.

Klapper, Melissa. *Ballots, Babies, and Banners of Peace: American Jewish Women's Activism 1890–1940.* New York: New York University Press, 2013.

Kolsky, Thomas. *Jews Against Zionism: The American Council for Judaism, 1942–1948.* Philadelphia: Temple University Press, 1990.

_____. *Jews Against Zionism: The American Council for Judaism, 1942–1948.* Ph.D. diss., George Washington University, 1986.

LaLande, Jeff. "Oregon's Last Conservative US Senator: Some Light Upon the Little Known Career of Guy Cordon." *Oregon Historical Quarterly* 110, no. 2 (Summer 2009): 228–261.

Lansing, Jewel. *Portland: People, Politics and Power; 1851–2001.* Corvallis: Oregon State University Press, 2003.

LaPlante, Margaret. "The Story of Jacksonville's Early Jewish Settlers," *Jacksonville Review*. Number 1918, (March 2010), 25.

Lerner, Elinor. "Jewish Involvement in the New York City Woman Suffrage Movement." *American Jewish History* 70, no. 4 (June 1981): 442–461.

Levenson, Alan. "The Posen Factor." *Shofar* 17, no. 1 (1998): 72–80.

Levinson, Robert. "The Jews of Eugene, Oregon." *Western States Jewish History* 30, no. 1 (October 1997), pages. http://www.wsjhistory.com/jew_eugene_oregon.htm, accessed on July 10, 2012.

_____. *The Jews of Jacksonville*. Master's thesis, University of Oregon, 1962.

Libo, Kenneth and Irving Howe. *We Lived There Too*. New York: St. Martin's Press, 1984.

Limerick, Patricia. *Legacy of Conflict: The Unbroken Past of the American West*. New York: Norton, 1987.

Lipin, Lawrence M. and William Lunch. "Moralistic Direct Democracy: Political Insurgents, Religion and the State in Twentieth Century Oregon," *Oregon Historical Quarterly* 110, no. 4 (Winter 2009): 517–528.

Lockley, Fred. *History of the Columbia River Valley*. Oregon State University Libraries, Scholar's Archive, 1928.

Lowenstein, Steven. *The Jews of Oregon, 1850–1950*. Portland: Jewish Historical Society of Oregon, 1987.

Lustig, Jason. *Resigning to Change: The Foundation and Transformation of the American Council for Judaism*. Master's thesis, Brandeis University, 2009.

MacColl, E. Kimbark . *Merchants, Money, & Power: The Portland Establishment, 1843–1913*. Portland: Georgian Press, 1988.

McCoy, Robert. "The Paradox of Oregon's Progressive Politics: The Political Career of Walter Marcus Pierce." *Oregon Historical Quarterly* 110, no. 3 (Fall 2009): 392–399.

McElderry, Stuart. *The Problem of the Color Line: Civil Rights and Racial Ideology in Portland Oregon, 1944–1965*. PhD Dissertation, University of Oregon, 1996.

Mervis, Leonard. "The Social Justice Movement and the American Reform Rabbi." *American Jewish Archives* 7, no. 2 (July 1955): 171–230.

Meyer, Michael A. "American Reform Judaism and Zionism: Early Efforts at Ideological Rapprochement." *Studies in Zionism* 4, no. 1 (1983): 49–64.

Michels, Tony. *A Fire in Their Hearts: Yiddish Socialists in New York*. Cambridge: Harvard University Press, 2009.

Miranda, Gary. *Following a River: Portland's Congregation Neveh Shalom, 1869-1989*. Portland: Congregation Neveh Shalom, 1989.

Morawska, Ewa. *Insecure Prosperity: Small Town Jews in Industrial America, 1890–1940*. Princeton: Princeton University Press, 1999.

Morris, Benjamin. "True American: The Media Battle on Private Schools and the Oregon Compulsory Education Bill, 1922–1925." Senior thesis, University of Portland, 2005.

Munk, Michael. "Oregon's Scottsboro Case." *The Portland Alliance* (February, 2001). http://college.lclark.edu/programs/political_economy/student_resources/past/, accessed on October 12, 2012.

Nadell, Pamela and Jonathan Sarna, editors. *Women and American Judaism*. Hanover, N.H.: Brandeis University Press, 2001.

Nodel, Julius J. *The Ties Between: A Century of Judaism on America's Last Frontier.* Portland: Congregation Beth Israel, 1959.

"Oregon at War: World War I and the Oregon Experience" State of Oregon Archives, web exhibit, http://arcweb.sos.state.or.us/pages/exhibits/war/.

Oregon Nikkei Endowment. "Oregon Nikkei History: A Brief Summary" (part 3). http://www.discovernikkei.org/en/journal/2010/6/4/oregon-nikkei-history.

Papermaster, Isadore. "A History of North Dakota Jewry and their Pioneer Rabbi." *Western States Jewish Historical Quarterly* 10, no. 1 (October 1977): 74–89.

Peled, Yoav. *Class and Ethnicity in the Pale.* New York: St. Martin's Press, 1987.

Plaut, W. Gunther. "Jewish Colonies at Painted Woods and Devils Lake." *North Dakota History* 32 (January 1965): 61–64.

Pomeroy, Earl. "On Becoming a Westerner." In *Jews of the American West,* edited by Rischin and Livingston, 190–212.

Price, George. "The Russian Jews in America" (1893). Reprint. *Publications of the American Jewish Historical Society* 48, part 1 (1958), 28–133.

Raider, Mark A. "Stephen S. Wise and the Urban Frontier: American Jewish Life in New York and the Pacific Northwest at the Dawn of the 20th Century." *Quest Issues in Contemporary Jewish History. Journal of Fondazione CDEC* (Centro Di Documentazione Ebraica Contemporanea) 2, (October 2011), http://www.quest-cdecjournal.it/focus.php?id=225.

Raphael, Marc Lee. "Beyond New York: The Challenge to Local History." In *Jews of the American West,* edited by Rischin and Livingston, 48–65.

Reid, David. "City of Brews and Roses: A History of the Social Power of Alcohol in Portland, Oregon from Prohibition to the Present." Unpublished Senior thesis, Willamette University, December 2010.

Rikoon, J. Sanford, ed. *Rachel Calof's Story.* Bloomington: Indiana University Press, 1995.

Rischin, Moses and John Livingston, editors. *Jews of the American West.* Detroit: Wayne State University Press, 1991.

Roediger, David. *Working Toward Whiteness: How America's Immigrants became White.* New York: Basic Books, 2006.

Rogin, Michael. *Black Face, White Noise: Jewish Immigrants in the Hollywood Melting Pot.* Berkeley: University of California Press, 1998.

Rogoff, Leonard. "Jews in the South," *Encyclopedia of American Jewish History,* edited by Stephen Norwood and Eunice Pollack, 1:145–48. California: ABC-CLIO, 2008

Rogow, Faith. *Gone to Another Meeting: The National Council of Jewish Women, 1893–1993.* Tuscaloosa: University of Alabama Press, 1993.

Rose, Elizabeth. "From Sponge Cake to Hamentashen: Jewish Identity in a Jewish Settlement House, 1885–1952." *Journal of American Ethnic History* 13, no. 3 (Spring 1994): 3–23.

Rosenbaum, Fred. *Visions of Reform: Congregation Emanu-El and the Jews of San Francisco, 1849–1999.* Berkeley: Judah L. Magnes Museum, 2000.

_____. "Zionism versus Anti-Zionism." In *Jews of the American West,* edited by Rischin and Livingston, 116–135.

Rubinow, Isaac. *Economic Conditions of the Jews in Russia.* 1907. Reprint: New York: Arno Press, 1975.

Saalfeld, Lawrence. *Forces of Prejudice in Oregon, 1920–1925.* Portland: Archdiocesan Historical Commission, 1984.

Sanders, Jack T. *Samuel Rothchild: A Jewish Pioneer in the Days of the Old West.* Pendleton, OR: Jack T. Sanders, 2011.

Sarna, Jonathan. *American Judaism: A History.* New Haven: Yale University Press, 2004.

———. "Converts to Zionism in the American Reform Movement." In *Zionism and Religion,* edited by Almog, Reinharz, and Shapira, 188-203.

Sarna, Jonathan and David Dalin. *Religion and State in the American Jewish Experience.* Notre Dame: University of Notre Dame Press, 1997.

Saxton, Alexander. *Indispensable Enemy: Labor and the Anti-Chinese Movement in California.* Berkeley and Los Angeles: University of California Press, 1971.

Schwartz, Lois Fields. "Early Jewish Agricultural Colonies in North Dakota." *North Dakota History* 32, no. 4 (October 1965): 217–232.

Shevitz, Amy Hill. *Jewish Communities on the Ohio River.* Lexington, KY: The University Press of Kentucky, 2007.

Silverberg, Robert. *If I Forget Thee O Jerusalem: American Jews and the State of Israel.* New York: Pyramid Books, 1970.

Singer, Jonathan. "History of the Sephardic Community," Ahavath Achim history, www.ahavathachim.com.

Sorin, Gerald. *A Time for Building.* Baltimore: Johns Hopkins University Press, 1992.

Stampfer, Joshua. *Pioneer Rabbi of the West: The Life and Times of Julius Eckman.* Portland: 1988.

Stein, Harry. *Gus J. Solomon: Liberal Politics, Jews, and the Federal Courts.* Portland: Oregon Historical Society Press, 2006.

Stern, Norton and William Kramer. "The Major Role of Polish Jews in the Pioneer West." *Western States Jewish Historical Quarterly (WSJHQ)* 8, no. 4 (1976): 326–344.

———. "The Polish Jew in Posen and the Early West." *WSJHQ* 10, no. 4 (1978): 327–329.

———. "Polish Preeminence in 19th Century Jewish Immigration: A Review Essay." *Western States Jewish History* 17, no. 2 (1985): 151–155.

———. "The Turnverein: A German Experience for Western Jewry." *WSJHQ* 16, no. 3 (1984): 227–229.

———. "What's the Matter with Warsaw?" *WSJHQ* 17, no. 4 (1985): 305–307.

Strum, Harvey. "Jewish Internees in the American South, 1942-1942." *American Jewish Archive* 42, no. 1 (Spring 1990): 27–48.

Toll, William. "Black Families and Migration to a Multiracial Society: Portland, Oregon, 1900-1924" *Journal of American Ethnic History* 17, no. 3 (Spring 1998): 38–70.

———."Commerce, Climate, & Community: A History of Portland & Its People," Oregon History Project, www.ohs.org. accessed August 2012.

———. "From Domestic Judaism to Public Ritual." In *Women and American Judaism,* edited by Nadell and Sarna, 128–147.

———. "Jewish Families and the Intergenerational Transition in the American Hinterland" *Journal of American Ethnic History* 12, no. 2 (Winter 1993): 3–34.

———. *The Making of an Ethnic Middle Class.* Albany: SUNY Press, 1982.

Urofsky, Melvin. *American Zionism: From Herzl to the Holocaust*. Lincoln: University of Nebraska Press, 1975.

_____. "Zionism in America." In *Encyclopedia of American Jewish History*, edited by Stephen H. Norwood and Eunice G. Pollack, 1:203-8. Santa Barbara: ABC/CLIO, 2008.

Van Nuys, Frank. *Americanizing the West: Race, Immigrants, and Citizenship, 1890–1930*. Lawrence: University Press of Kansas, 2002.

Voorsanger, Jacob, editor. *Pacific Jewish Annual*. San Francisco: A.W. Voorsanger, 1898.

Weissbach, Lee Shai. "The Jewish Communities of the United States on the Eve of Mass Migration." *American Jewish History* 787, no. 1 (1988): 79–108.

_____. *Jewish Life in Small-Town America: A History*. New Haven: Yale University Press, 2005.

Williams, Mary Ann Barnes. *Pioneer Days of Washburn, North Dakota and Vicinity*. 1936. Reprint, McLean County Historical Society, 1995.

Zeien-Stuckman, Emily. "Creating New Citizens: The National Council of Jewish Women's Work at Neighborhood House in Portland, 1896–1912." *Oregon Historical Quarterly* 113, no. 3 (Fall 2012): 312–333.

Zipperstein, Steven. *The Jews of Odessa*. Stanford: Stanford University Press, 1985.

Index